FOUNDATIONS OF

# MULTIMETHOD
# RESEARCH

*To Ettie and Renée*

---

*Numbers and Faces*

The Kingdom of Number is all boundaries
Which may be beautiful and must be true;
To ask if it is big or small proclaims one
The sort of lover who should stick to faces.

Lovers of small numbers go benignly potty,
Believe all tales are thirteen chapters long,
Have animal doubles, carry pentagrams,
Are Millerites, Baconians, Flat-Earth-Men.

Lovers of big numbers go horribly mad,
Would have the Swiss abolished, all of us
Well purged, somatotyped, baptized, taught baseball,
They empty bars, spoil parties, run for Congress.

True, between faces almost any number
Might come in handy, and One is always real;
But which could any face call good, for calling
Infinity a number does not make it one.

—W. H. Auden

SOURCE: "Numbers and Faces," copyright © 1951 by W. H. Auden, from *Collected Poems* by W. H. Auden. Used by permission of Random House, Inc.

# FOUNDATIONS OF
# MULTIMETHOD RESEARCH

## SYNTHESIZING STYLES

## JOHN BREWER
TRINITY COLLEGE

## ALBERT HUNTER
NORTHWESTERN UNIVERSITY

**SAGE Publications**
Thousand Oaks ■ London ■ New Delhi

*For information:*

 Sage Publications, Inc.
2455 Teller Road
Thousand Oaks, California 91320
E-mail: order@sagepub.com

Sage Publications Ltd.
1 Oliver's Yard
55 City Road
London EC1Y 1SP
United Kingdom

Sage Publications India Pvt. Ltd.
B-42, Panchsheel Enclave
Post Box 4109
New Delhi 110 017 India

Printed in the United States of America

*Library of Congress Cataloging-in-Publication Data*

Brewer, John, 1936-
Foundations of multimethod research: synthesizing styles / John Brewer, Albert Hunter.
        p. cm.
Includes bibliographical references and index.
ISBN 0-7619-8861-0 (pbk.)
    1. Social sciences—Research—Methodology. I. Hunter, Albert. II. Title.
H62.B658 2006
300.72—dc22                                    2005008156

This book is printed on acid-free paper.

05   06   07   08   09   10   9   8   7   6   5   4   3   2   1

| Acquisitions Editor: | Lisa Cuevas Shaw |
| Editorial Assistant: | Karen Gia Wong |
| Production Editor: | Melanie Birdsall |
| Copy Editor: | Nancy Sixsmith, Freelance Editorial Services |
| Typesetter: | C&M Digitals (P) Ltd. |
| Proofreader: | Mary Meagher |
| Cover Designer: | Glenn Vogel |

# Contents

# Preface

This book is about multimethod research—what it is, where it came from, and where it is going. Our previous book, *Multimethod Research: A Synthesis of Styles* (Brewer & Hunter, 1989), was a call for social scientists to more consciously and systematically develop strategies for combining different styles or methods in the same research project. This call for heightened consciousness has been answered.

Multimethod research is no longer just a rarely realized dream; its widespread use in practice means that it is now an established reality. The social science research community has come to adopt multimethod research as a style in its own right; a style that provides increased power of persuasion and strengthened claims to validity. This book grows out of our previous book—it continues to define the evolving nature of multimethod research and also explores its historical and espisetmological foundations.

The social sciences are well-known for disputes between proponents of different methods, or styles, of research. In a sense, these methodological debates are a healthy sign. Skepticism is an essential part of scientific inquiry, and different types of methods represent important critical perspectives. Equally important, however, is the increasing recognition of the fact that different research methods offer possible solutions for one another's problems. This is the central premise of this book.

Many social scientists will, of course, recognize multimethod research as an approach that they have followed all along, and many more are consciously coming to incorporate a multimethod strategy as they design their research projects. Multimethod measurement, or *triangulation*, is perhaps the multimethod strategy's most familiar application. However, as many researchers have also discovered, the multimethod approach has far wider uses and implications. Theorizing and theory testing, problem formulation and data collection, sampling and generalization, hypothesis testing and causal analysis, social problem and policy analysis, and even the writing and publication of results may benefit from bringing a multi-method perspective to bear upon social research.

We have written this new book to address these broad uses and implications of multimethod research and also to provide a broader foundation and evolutionary context for the method as to its historical origins, its grounding in and addressing of positivist assumptions and concerns, and its implications for a postpositivist perspective. It begins with a historical introduction that traces some of the early developments and exemplars of multimethod research, though it was unlabelled as such at the time. Chapter 1 presents the basic multimethod strategy. Chapter 2 examines the relationship of multimethod research to theory. The succeeding chapters essentially follow the sequence of stages in the research process. Chapter 3 deals with the formulation of research problems from a multimethod viewpoint; Chapter 4, with data collection; Chapter 5, with sampling and generalization; Chapter 6, with measurement and measurement validation; and Chapter 7, with causal hypothesis testing and the analysis of multimethod test results. Chapter 8 explores the multimethod implications of recent postpositivist developments in the social sciences by looking at newer analytical styles emphasizing rhetoric, social constructivism, and narrative. We conclude with a discussion of the place of multimethod research within the social sciences and the relevance of multimethod research to wider social issues and concerns.

# Historical Introduction

Multimethod research takes its name from Campbell and Fiske's famous 1959 article on measurement validation. Campbell later wrote that with this piece "Fiske and I struck one of the first public blows in psychology against logical positivism as epitomized in the 'operational definition' of theoretical terms. . . . In contrast, in the multitrait-multimethod paper, we announced that all psychological measures had to be validated against other imperfect measures, also of unknown validity. There were no foundational measures to start with" (Fiske & Shweder, 1986, p. 130). The term "multimethod" soon came to imply for many social scientists, including ourselves, both a critique of much social research and a possible strategy for improvement. The critique warned of overreliance upon, and overconfidence in, any single type of research method. And the strategy was to systematically employ different types of methods in concert with one another.

Max Weber (1949), in his writings on the methodology of the social sciences, stated emphatically that: "Only by laying bare and solving *substantive problems* can sciences be established and methods developed. . . . purely epistemological and methodological reflections have never played the crucial role in such developments." But Weber admitted one exception: "Such discussions can become important for the enterprise of science only when, as a result of considerable shifts of 'viewpoint' from which a datum becomes the object of analysis. The idea emerges that the new 'viewpoint' also requires a revision of the logical forms in which the 'enterprise' has heretofore operated and, when accordingly, uncertainty about the 'nature' of one's own work arises" (p. 116).

Campbell and Fiske's (1959) work appeared at just such a moment. Fiske and Shweder (1986) have described the intellectual climate of the era well:

> There was a time, not so very long ago, when the very idea of rationality was equated with the results and findings of positive (i.e., objective) science. The results of positive science were considered worthy of respect because scientists had possession of a unitary method for discovering truths, and they knew how to employ that method to discover useful knowledge. . . . The drift in contemporary thinking has been to raise serious doubts about whether there are any standards, canons, or methods definitive of scientific or rational thinking. The idea of objectivity has been under attack from many quarters, and it has been variously defended, clarified, revised and abandoned. (pp. 16–17)

By the 1980s many social scientists were beginning to adopt a postpositivist viewpoint on their work and were looking for models to implement that viewpoint. Developing the idea of multimethod research more fully seemed to us a very promising place to carry on the search, offering as it does a pragmatic rather than a dogmatic path of inquiry.

We wrote the first edition of this book in the late 1980s to introduce multimethod research as a distinctive research strategy with applications throughout the research process. To the best of our knowledge, it was the first book-length attempt to treat the approach in such a defining and comprehensive fashion. Although less familiar than now, the idea of multimethod research and its practice were neither totally new nor untried. Indeed, a major premise of the book was that the promise of multimethod research was not its novelty but rather in doing more fully, systematically, and consciously what many had done before. We had each personally published research that we regarded as multimethod studies and knew from both the literature and from our smaller immediate circle of professional colleagues that many others had as well. We had no trouble finding research examples and indeed chose as a central example the study of crime, an area in which the need for a multimethod approach had by then become widely recognized and its practice virtually institutionalized in the public policy arena with the establishment in 1973 of the U.S. Department of Justice's Criminal Victimization Surveys to supplement the FBI's Uniform Crime Reports.

Perhaps because of the relative ease with which the ideas and examples came to mind, we felt no need to provide a history of the approach beyond the appropriate citation and discussion of earlier works.

However, in rereading the book 15 years later we realize that the historical context that we took for granted at the time may no longer be so familiar to readers. Also we have discovered some material that was either unknown or unavailable to us at the time of the first writing. We have decided therefore to add this brief historical introduction, which we hope will provide useful background for current readers as well as some new information for readers of the earlier edition.

## Toward a History of Multimethod Research

Although Campbell and Fiske's (1959) work is of central importance, the underlying logic of multimethod inquiry certainly has a far wider and older base than this single article on psychological method. For example, the French historian Marc Bloch (1953) writes: "The variety of historical evidence is nearly infinite. . . . Everything that man says or writes, everything that he makes, everything he touches can and ought to teach us about him. It would be sheer fantasy to imagine that for each historical problem there is a unique type of document with a specific sort of use. On the contrary, the deeper the research, the more light of the evidence must converge from sources of many different kinds. What religious historian would be satisfied by examining a few theological tracts or hymnals? He knows full well that the painting and sculpture of sanctuary walls and the arrangement and furnishing of tombs have at least as much to tell him about dead beliefs and feelings as a thousand contemporary manuscripts" (pp. 66–67). And of another sort of history, paleontology, Stephen Jay Gould (1989) has written that "We work with our strength of rich and diverse data recording the consequences of past events; we do not bewail our inability to see the past directly. We search for repeated pattern, shown by evidence so abundant and so diverse that no other coordinating interpretation could stand, even though any item, taken separately, would not provide conclusive proof." Gould notes, for example, the variety of evidence upon which Charles Darwin's theory of evolution rested and turns to the nineteenth-century philosopher of science William Whewell to explicate Darwin's logic of inference. Whewell, Gould (1989) writes, "devised the word consilience, meaning 'jumping together,' to designate the confidence gained when many independent sources 'conspire' to indicate a particular historical pattern. He called the strategy of coordinating disparate results from multifarious sources consilience of induction" (p. 282).

Similarly, the actual practice of employing multiple research methods certainly antedates the definition of multimethod research as a distinct research style. As Platt (1996) concludes in her history of sociological methods in America from 1920 through 1960: "it need not be the case that all aspects of method actually practiced are written about, or conceptualized as distinct" (p. 32). She finds, in fact, that monographs on particular methods generally followed rather than preceded the actual use of these methods. In this, she corroborates another of Max Weber's (1949) assertions: "methodology can only bring us reflective understanding of the means which have *demonstrated* their value in practice by raising them to the level of explicit consciousness; it is no more the precondition of fruitful intellectual work than the knowledge of anatomy is the precondition for 'correct' walking" (p. 115). And this is certainly true of multimethod research. Examples of multimethod research are, we suggest, more frequently found in the social science literature than even their authors may be aware. The debriefing interview from an experiment, the pretesting of survey questions, the insightful quote from a curator of archives, the drawing upon of personal experiences—all of these exemplify ways in which a second method can, sometimes unwittingly, inform a primary piece of research. Moreover, there are many early studies employing multiple methods so clearly at "the level of explicit consciousness" (to borrow Weber's phrase) that they may be regarded as early exemplars of multimethod research.

## Four Early Exemplars

Kuhn (1970) argues that "exemplars" play a crucial role in scientific research for socializing neophytes into not just the substance but also the style of good research. We offer a brief look at four studies as exemplars of the use of multimethod strategies: Roethlisberger and Dickson's (1939) account of the famous "Hawthorne Studies"; W. Lloyd Warner and his associates' (1941) studies of "Yankee City"; Lipset, Trow, and Coleman's (1956) study of union democracy; and finally, Lazarsfeld, Jahoda, and Zeisel's (1933/1973) "sociography" of unemployment in the Austrian village of Marienthal.

### The Hawthorne Studies

In 1924, the management of the Hawthorne Works of the Western Electric Company near Chicago began a series of experiments to test the possible effects of different levels of illumination on their workers' morale and productivity. What they discovered instead, of course, is the famous "Hawthorne effect." Their experimental variations in lighting conditions apparently had far weaker effects than did the workers' awareness of being seriously studied. For example, output increased with improved illumination but failed to decline when the usual illumination was restored or even reduced below its original levels. Intrigued by these findings, so the story goes, the Hawthorne management turned to the recently founded Harvard University Department of Industrial Relations. And in 1927, five more years of research began. The research, as reported by Roethlisberger and Dickson (1939), comprised a series of three major investigations: the relay assembly test room study, the interview project, and the bank wiring observation room study. Each of the investigations was designed to help interpret and expand upon the findings of the preceding phase.

The relay test assembly room study was designed to help understand better the Hawthorne management's first experimental findings. The researchers set up a very small-scale experimental study consisting of six women whose work was typical in important ways of the factory's general work (i.e., essentially a microcosm). The women were then studied for several years under experimentally varied working conditions, and, as in the earlier experiments, their productivity generally rose. But looked at now, this study appears less like classic experimental design and more like a field study of an experiment to determine how a particular effect is produced. For example, there was a "test room observer" present in the room, and the women were interviewed and tested in various ways individually, including collection of some life-history data. As Roethlisberger and Dickson (1939) note, this probing into the experiment prompted a drastic reconceptualization of the research problem:

No longer were the investigators interested in testing for the effects of single variables. In place of a controlled experiment, they substituted the notion of a social situation which needed to be described and understood as a system of interdependent elements. . . . The situation included not only the external events but the meaning which individuals assign to them and their preoccupations about them. Rather than trying to keep these 'psychological factors' constant, the investigators had to regard them as important variables in the situation. As much attention had to be given to these psychological factors as to output in assessing the external changes which took place. (pp. 183–184)

Their rethinking of the problem led them simultaneously in two different methodological directions, both of which they followed. The emphasis on "psychological factors" led to the interviewing program, which involved some 1600 employees with whom over 10,000 interviews were conducted. The interviews at first followed a schedule of questions about working conditions, and so on. Later, however, they took a more nondirective form, and the program itself began to take on a counseling as well as a data-gathering function.

Their emphasis on "the social situation" led in another direction: to the establishment of the Bank Wiring Observation Room. This was a completely nonexperimental field site in which the researchers, using standard fieldwork techniques, could observe firsthand the work and everyday social relations of workers. Their observations, of course, provided the beginnings of our present day understanding of the interplay of formal and informal behavior and structure in organizations.

Reviewers today, in the light of our current knowledge of research techniques, have severely criticized the experimental design of the Hawthorne studies, even expressing strong doubts as to whether the data really demonstrated a Hawthorne effect (e.g., Jones, 1992). However, while it is perhaps a weak example of experimentation, the study considered as a whole is a good example of how the purposeful use of multiple methods can open new and valuable lines of inquiry.

## Yankee City

Newburyport, Massachusetts may seem an unlikely place to locate a study that would purport to represent the nature of community life in the United States. But, like the Lynds' (1927) research in "Middletown," W. Lloyd Warner, trained as an anthropologist, was most interested in capturing the full round of day-to-day life and the structure of activities of a community, whose institutions and residents could in some way represent broader issues of social life in the United States (Hunter, 1990a, 1990b). This meant that the community should have an industrial economic base, have diversity with respect to social class and ethnicity, and be of a size to permit a limited number of researchers to fully observe and document the community's varied social life. Given this broad agenda, Warner drew together a research team that employed a variety of methods that would allow him to capture more specifically the history of the community, its stratification system and class structure, the structure of its major institutions (including economic and religious life), and the cultural meanings and symbolism of the whole. To study these diverse topics and the different questions they posed would require an openness to a variety of research strategies and methods to get at the different data sets necessary to answer them.

It is worth quoting at length the diverse methods that were used and the researchers' sensitivity to the fact that different methods have different strengths and weaknesses to answer different questions:

> The fundamental and most important technique we used to gather material in the field was the interview. . . . In addition to the interview, various types of sustained observations were made; a great variety and number of printed documents were collected; case histories, biographies, autobiographies, and other intimate histories were gathered from our informants; photographs were made of houses and other objects of significance; and an aerial survey was made. Many other surveys were also pursued, and the newspapers were systematically used. The distribution of various kinds of phenomena were mapped. Each of these separate techniques will be described in detail, and the use of some of them in the Yankee City research will be evaluated according to the tests of (1) reliability; (2) time required; (3) area of social relations covered; (4) insight into the social behavior which use of the technique gives to the investigator; (5) comparative depth or superficiality; (6) value at various periods in the research and not at others; (7) special uses, such as quantification of behavior already defined and isolated and prepared for measurement; (8) availability for the isolation and definition of social behavior at that time unknown or not yet sufficiently understood to define; and (9) special uses associated with particular techniques. (Warner & Lunt, 1941, pp. 44–45)

More specifically, Warner and Lunt (1941) describe how they located a "key informant," a leader in the community who would introduce them to others and how quantitative questionnaires supplemented interviews. They detailed the archives and records that included local police crime reports, school records, and health department records and statistics, among others. It is very clear in their analysis that they gave different weight to different methods at different points, but in general they spoke to the power of combining these multimethods to achieve their primary purpose of documenting the full round of social life in this community. They clearly bridged dichotomous choices that are often falsely held up today by "methodological ideologues," such as quantitative versus qualitative, inductive versus deductive, and so on. Focused on substance, the

Yankee City researchers speak to a conscious pragmatic but systematic use of eclectic methods to achieve their objectives.

## Union Democracy

Philosophers have debated for millennia the ideal form of government, and, having settled in our day on democracy as that form that most closely adheres to the central values of our culture, the next question (an empirical one) is: How does one construct and maintain a democratic political system? This is the question that Seymour Martin Lipset, Martin Trow, and James Coleman (1956) attempted to answer in their landmark study of the International Typographical Union in North America.

The researchers quickly recognized that to explore these issues thoroughly required distinguishing between three different levels or units of analysis: the union as a whole, the intermediate units of the union locals, and finally the individual union members themselves. They quickly recognized that strategic choices and tradeoffs must be made between depth versus breadth with respect to the amount of data to be collected from the different levels. As they write about the survey sampling strategy among the three levels:

> [I]nterviewing more men in each shop would have meant interviewing each man less thoroughly or else covering fewer shops, thus gaining knowledge about shops at the expense of knowledge about either individuals or the union as a whole. (Lipset, Trow, & Coleman, 1956, p. 473)

Using three distinct levels in their analysis required that they clearly identify the different types of data appropriate to each level. In a concise chart that arrays "types of data gathered" by "types of units," Lipset et al. (1956) present a clear picture of their multimethod strategy (p. 474). For the "total system" (the union as a whole), they indicated the wide use of records and archival material: "Issues; Data on Occupation; Union Laws; Policies; Historical Data; Convention Reports." For the "intermediate units" they used "Local Histories and Voting Records; Issues on Local Level; Size of Locals." Finally, for the "individual" level they have "Interviews with Leaders; Interviews of the Sample of Men." In short, they have drawn on a variety of data sets generated by different methods—archives and records, sample surveys, and interviews. And most significantly they integrated them in an innovative analysis that allows them to explore the "structural effects" that larger units have upon their constituent units, and, in turn, the way in which constituent units aggregate to produce unique structural features of the larger, more-inclusive units.

One of the important lessons to be learned from Union Democracy is that combining different methods in the same investigation opens up whole new theoretical questions to investigation, which previously remained unexplored. In this case, it was the structural features of the union that promoted democratic participation by its members (e.g., an independent union newspaper) and certain characteristics of the members that promoted structural characteristics (e.g., the high literacy rate of members). Clearly, multimethod research has implications far beyond the methodological questions of increased validity and reliability, and can directly contribute to broader theoretical advances in the field.

## Marienthal

At the start of the great economic depression of the 1930s, Marie Jahoda, Paul F. Lazarsfeld, and Hans Zeisel—three young Austrians, who would later emigrate and become eminent social scientists abroad—set out to investigate the impact of widespread and prolonged unemployment by studying the small Austrian industrial village of Marienthal in which unemployment was nearly total. They collected data for more than a year and reported spending about 120 working days in Marienthal, during which they amassed about 66 pounds of material (Jahoda, Lazarsfeld, & Zeisel, 1971, p. 9). However, it is not the sheer weight of their data that makes this study important but rather the enduring significance of the conclusions that its authors drew and of the research strategy that they very consciously employed. Lazarsfeld, writing in 1971, notes that "One of the main theses of the Marienthal study was that prolonged unemployment leads to a state of apathy in which the victims do not utilize any longer even the few opportunities left to them. The vicious cycle between reduced opportunities and reduced level of aspiration has remained the focus of all subsequent discussions." And as he also notes: "The combination of quantification and interpretative analysis [employed in the study] is today in the forefront of the research fraternity's interest" (Jahoda, Lazarsfeld, & Zeisel, pp. vii and xi). However, neither of these contributions was to be widely recognized until many years later. The delay may be explained by their work's publication history.

Jahoda, Lazarsfeld, and Zeisel's research resulted in a book, first published in 1933 under the title *Die Arbeitslosen von Marienthal* and reissued in translation 40 years later as *Marienthal: The Sociography of an Unemployed Community*. In the interim the book became a classic of European sociology but was little known in the United States until its translation. Indeed, Jahoda (1992) wrote that the study received little attention anywhere until it was republished in Germany in the 1960s. She attributes this inattention to the fact that in 1933, with Hitler in power, the original publisher refused to place the names of three Jewish writers on the cover, thereby rendering their work virtually invisible.

The translation was delayed until 1971 by the authors because (in Lazarsfeld's words) "Certain aspects of our approach were very naive. . . . Many of the standards on which my collaborators and I would later insist in our teaching were neglected." However, as Lazarsfeld goes on to emphasize: "And yet we had a very definite methodological program" (Jahoda, Lazarsfeld, & Zeisel, 1971, p. x). "Our idea," they wrote, "was to find procedures which would combine the use of numerical data with immersion [sich einleben] into the situation" (p. 1). Their strategy was to explore "every path that could bring us close to our objective" (p. 2). This included the compilation of personal data for each member of the 478 families in the village, plus a family diary; life histories, timesheets, meal records for smaller samples; participant observation in everyday as well as specially planned activities (such as a clothing distribution project); and a variety of data from official archives.

Lazarsfeld laid out "four rules" for conducting such sociographic studies that he later summarizes as follows in his foreword to the first English translation of the study in 1971:

1. For any phenomenon one should have objective observations as well as introspective reports.

2. Case studies should be properly combined with statistical information.

3. Contemporary information should be supplemented by information on earlier phases of whatever is being studied.

4. Natural and experimental data should be combined. By experimental, I meant mainly questionnaires and solicited reports, while by natural I meant what is now called 'unobtrusive measures'—data derived from daily life without interference from the investigator. (p. xiv)

He concludes this summary: "It is unlikely that I was entirely aware of the rules underlying the Viennese research tradition as it developed. But its structure was close enough to the surface that I could articulate it fairly easily when I had leisure here in this country [the United States] to reflect on our work" (pp. xiv-xv).

In writing the history of the study in 1971, Lazarsfeld was mindful both of the inspiration for its methodology and also of how that methodology "fit into new use": "The combination of quantification and interpretative analysis of qualitative material is today in the forefront of the research fraternity's interest" (p. xii). He attributes Marienthal's varied methodology to the influence of the Viennese psychologist Karl Buhler, who stressed "the need to transcend any one approach or any one immediate body of information, to reach a broad conceptual integration" (pp. xii–xiii). But then, in summarizing the significance of the four rules, he makes the link to contemporary methodology by using the multimethod term "triangulation": "Mere description was not enough. In order to get 'behind' it, a variety of data had to be collected on any issue under investigation, just as the true position of a distant object can be found only by triangulation, by looking at it from different sides and directions" (p. xiv).

Marie Jahoda, writing in 1992, was even more explicit in linking the Marienthal study (with "its peculiarly open-ended approach") to modern multimethod research. "Because it was problem-, not method-centred [sic], triangulation, quantitative and qualitative approaches were used, economic and psychological data juxtaposed. This is all to the good, and perhaps too often missing in modern research. When a central result is supported by a variety of methods one's confidence in it is increased." She then goes on to raise one of the key questions that multimethod research must face and illustrates the need for full analysis of the strategy: "But what about instances where triangulation yields different results? Such a case actually occurred in Marienthal; . . . since at the time no way of dealing with it was seen, it was silently ignored" (p. 355).

A final note is necessary to place Marienthal in its own historical context and to call attention to the broader research tradition to which it belonged. Jahoda, Lazarsfeld, and Zeisel (1971) labeled their study a sociography, presumably because "The object of the investigation was the unemployed community, not the unemployed individual" (p. 2). "Sociography" is a term unfamiliar we suspect to many contemporary social scientists (it was unfamiliar to us, at least) but that was widely used in early European discourse. Barnes and Becker in 1938 explained it in this way: "The best American analogues of sociography are probably the Lynd's [sic] Middletown and Middletown in Transition, Blumenthal's Small Town Stuff, and the various ecological studies of Chicago" (p. 929). In an afterward to the Marienthal volume, Zeisel provided an historical overview and methodological appraisal of sociographic research from its inception, which he dated from the late seventeenth century with the appearance of Sir William Petty's "Down Surveys" and his "Political Anatomy of Ireland," through American "social surveys" and the work especially of Chicago sociologists up to 1930.

Zeisel's history is notable especially for his attention to the extent to which the various studies employed varied methods of investigation; for example, going beyond archival sources to employ questionnaires, interviewing, and direct field observation; and combining qualitative and quantitative techniques. His account of Max Weber's empirical work is of special interest for its emphasis on Weber's own consciousness of methodology. "A new epoch of sociographic work began with the extensive investigations . . . into the career decisions of workers in various branches of industry. This work, initiated by Max Weber and his brother Albert, consisted of a series of monographs on a number of different factories. . . . The core data . . . were obtained from the payrolls and personnel records of the factories in question, and from interviews with the workers and the managerial staff. The inquiry turned on an analysis of the workers' performance on their jobs in terms of their age, sex, social background, political interests and other such characteristics." Zeisel went on to stress that "The notion of selecting 'relevant data' was here a very conscious step in the development of sociography. . . . However once the problem was defined—and that was the second decisive feature of these studies—a great effort was made to reach out as far as possible to make the description complete. Every aspect of behavior conceivably affected by industrial employment was of interest . . . nothing short of the whole pattern of life and work became the object of inquiry" (pp. 117–118).

## Methodological Diversity and Synthesis in Historical Perspective

From its beginnings in the late nineteenth and the early twentieth centuries, social research in the United States has been a methodologically diverse and often contentious enterprise. The distinction between what we now refer to as qualitative and quantitative methods is one of the major and earliest defined dimensions of this diversity and contentiousness. In the period between 1890 and 1915, as Camic and Xie (1994) have shown, statistical methods imported from Europe began to supplement and challenge the more library- and archive-oriented comparative and historical approaches then prevalent in American universities. By the 1920s the diversity had increased to include qualitative field methods, such as the "case study." As the sociologist Ernest W. Burgess observed in 1927:

> With a growing realization, especially on the part of younger sociologists, that the future of their science lay more in field research rather than in "book learning" has come a keener interest in the technique of investigation. Professor Franklin H. Giddings for years has stressed the use of statistical method while Professor Charles H. Cooley has advocated the method of sympathetic introspection. Meanwhile the methods of statistics and of case study were being applied to various aspects of social life and at first almost entirely by others than sociologists. (Burgess, 1927/1974, p. 367)

Burgess (1927/1974) noted in particular the case study's prior use by journalists, social workers, and cultural anthropologists as a separate method not just as "a handmaiden to statistics" to be "thought of primarily in terms of a questionnaire . . . to secure data on points susceptible to enumeration and tabulation" and cites the psychiatrist W. Healy who, after studying 1000 cases of juvenile delinquency, concluded that "statistics will never tell the whole study" (p. 370).

Burgess went on to urge that "the methods of statistics and of case study are not in conflict with one another, they are, in fact, mutually complementary. Statistical comparisons and correlations may often suggest leads for research by the case study method, and documentary materials as they reveal social processes will inevitably point the way to more adequate social indices"(p. 373). And he predicted that "The interaction of the two methods is certain to prove fruitful" (p. 373). As the foregoing implies, social scientists have made efforts from early on to reconcile methodological differences and to exploit the advantages that a variety of methods might afford. For example, Reinharz (1992), in her study of feminist research, has called attention to the work of Margaret Hagood (1939), who in her research on fertility patterns of Southern white women decided (in Hagood's own words) "to be both more realistic and comprehensive in a sort of attempt to get away from the restricted statistical treatment and stereotyped 'case studies,' and yet to combine as far as possible some features of the statistical, case, and survey methods" (quoted by Reinharz, 1992, pp. 197–198). The deliberate, but tentative, tone of Margaret Hagood's remarks suggests the daring and the resolve that it takes to depart from recognized research styles.

Innovation is made easier by social support, however. Historians of sociological methods have suggested that the famous pre-World War II Chicago School of Sociology, of which Burgess, along with Robert E. Park (a former journalist), was a leading member, provided such support (Turner & Turner, 1990, pp. 45–53). Platt (1996) writes that "The interior Chicago department was a very meaningful unit for its members, not so much because there was a shared viewpoint or method as because research was treated as a communal activity . . . despite the statistics versus case study cleavage, data were shared and theses and monographs typically used multiple methods and data sources" (p. 203).

Cortese (1995), in his history of sociology at the University of Chicago, characterizes the variety and synthesis of different methods there during the 1920s and 1930s as follows.

> The Chicago School combined three broad types of sociological method: (1) the case study which was descriptive of the "whole"; (2) the historical method which included the use of autobiographies, diaries, and personal letters; and (3) the statistical method which provided measurement. There was a sequence in the use of methods during the process of a research project. Existing statistical data, historical narratives, and descriptive accounts were first examined. Then case studies were conducted in the form of observation, research interview, or diary. Historical methods were used to understand the traditions and past of the group. Finally, statistical analyses were run with case study results. The emphasis on complimentary [sic] research methods was characteristic of the Chicago School, reflecting an openness to different approaches and a focus on high quality research. (p. 235)

However, this characterization should perhaps be read more as an ideal type reconstruction of early Chicago School methodology than as a description of those early sociologists' methodological consciousness. For as Platt (1996) quotes from an interview with one member of the early Chicago Department: "I came along at a time when we never worried much about what was a method or wasn't. Park was a newspaperman, you went out there and got the story" (p. 52).

Among the early recognized types of research, the "social survey" was perhaps the closest to what we would now call a multimethod study. When we speak of a survey today we usually mean a questionnaire study of a population sample. However, in the early years of the twentieth century the term "survey" was often used to designate something quite different; something similar to the "sociographic" studies discussed earlier. George Lundberg, in the 1941 edition of his research methods text, writes:

> The social survey is not a special method of research. . . . The survey is rather a type of organization of field work. . . . The practice of classifying the survey as a distinct method of research, or even placing it on a coordinate basis with such methods as the historical method, the case method, and the statistical method is clearly erroneous, a survey may, and usually does, utilize all of these methods. It could, in fact, have no existence apart from these methods. The term "survey" merely indicates a certain degree of comprehensiveness and coordination with respect to the content or subject matter of an inquiry." (pp. 388–389)

Twenty years later, Everett Hughes—considering the method of fieldwork as we now understand it—would look back and write:

> Until a generation ago the phrase field work might . . . have brought to mind what was then called the "social survey." At the turn of the century the social surveyors were going to the slums of the great cities of Britain and North America to observe the "conditions" in which the urban industrial poor lived. They then reported them in simple statistical tables on consumption of food and clothing, wages, illness and crime. But they also described what they found, "fully, freely, and bitterly," as Robert E. Park used to say, in the hope that an aroused public would change things. (Junker, 1960, p. viii)

Something similar occurred with the method of experimentation. Today we clearly distinguish "true" experimental designs, not only from non-experimental work but also from "quasi" experiments. In the earlier era, social science experiments arguably included—according to Greenwood, who in 1945 examined "over one hundred statements of what a sociological experiment is, can or should be"—not only the "pure experiment" but also the "uncontrolled experiment," the "ex post facto experiment," the "trial and error experiment," "the natural experiment" and the "controlled observational study" (p. 8). And even this now disparate appearing array seems precise compared to the methodology brought to mind by Park and Burgess's statement in 1924 that "Sociology seems now in a way to become, in some fashion or other, an experimental science" (Park & Burgess, 1924, p. 45).

Viewed historically, Platt (1983) suggested, our conceptions of research methods "come in sets" in which "the same or similar practices may be conceptualized in different ways, so that even if the total field covered by two such sets is much the same boundaries drawn within it, and the aspects picked out as defining them, may differ. It is even possible for the same word to be used in different ways, although the idea to which it corresponds in each differs" (p. 379). These sets, she further suggests, emerge from historically specific discussions of methodology. This is clearly true here.

What had happened between the first and second halves of the century was that the methods of social research had become more specialized and narrowly redefined. A major catalyst for this redefinition may have been the rise and increasing hegemony in social science of modern survey research in the years following World War II (Sieber, 1973; Turner & Turner, 1990; Platt, 1996). It certainly prompted some practitioners of fieldwork, for instance, to define the method independently of the declining social survey tradition and instead as a coequal, with own special strengths, of the newer survey research. Hughes, for one, wrote that in modern survey research "Going to the field means getting out to interview the sample. Some place is given to less formal field observation, but it is called 'pilot study' or 'exploratory study,' and is conducted preparatory to the main business of getting a questionnaire on the road. . . . However . . . field research is more than a preparatory step for large statistical surveys. It is an ongoing part of social science. Most surveys . . . would be much more useful if they were followed by even more intensive field work than that which precedes them" (Junker, 1960, p. x).

The newer differentiation of research styles also led researchers to make, and sometimes to dispute, comparisons of various methods' relative strengths and weaknesses. Comparisons of this sort can often generate considerable heat, but they can also be illuminating. For example, Campbell's 1957 comparative analysis of different research designs' capacities for testing causal hypotheses, in effect, deconstructed the idea of causal validity as a unitary concept exclusively founded on experimental method.

Validity will be evaluated in terms of two major criteria. First, and as the basic minimum internal validity: did in fact the experimental stimulus make some significant difference in this specific instance? The second criterion is that of external validity, representativeness, or generalizability: to what populations, settings, and variables can this effect be generalized? Both criteria are obviously important although it turns out that they are to some extent incompatible, in that the controls required for internal validity often tend to jeopardize generalizability. (Campbell, 1957, p. 297)

Although giving the edge to experimentation by prioritizing internal validity as the "basic minimum," this established a multifaceted standard for causal research that neither purely experimental nor nonexperimental methods could fully satisfy.

Building on Campbell and Fiske's (1959) work, Webb, Campbell, Schwartz, and Sechrest (1966) advanced the multimethod idea a step further in their critique of survey research and their development of the idea of non-reactive methods. These are comprised of archival naturally occurring data and data obtained by unobtrusive observational techniques. They acknowledged the versatility of survey research and the strength of survey sampling. But they criticized the survey's vulnerability to reactive error and the restrictions on access to content and populations that interviewing, questionnaires, and typical survey sampling entail. But chiefly they emphatically objected to the fact that this very widely used method was used alone: "No research method is without bias. Interviews and questionnaires must be supplemented by methods testing the same social science variables but having different methodological weaknesses" (Webb et al., 1966, p. 1).

In the late 1950s, fieldworkers and survey researchers squared off in a now famous debate over the relative merits of their methods. Becker and Geer (1957), in a comparison of the two research styles, assert that "The most complete form of the sociological datum, after all, is the form in which the participant observer gathers it. . . . Participant observation can thus provide us with a yardstick against which to measure the completeness of data gathered in other ways" (p. 28). They were referring chiefly to data about directly observable events. Trow (1957), however, took their point more broadly and strenuously objected to the implication that "a given method of collecting data—any method—has an inherent superiority over others by virtue of its special qualities and the nature of the problem being studied. . . . Different kinds of information about main society are gathered most fully and economically in different ways. . . . The problem under investigation properly dictates the method of investigation" (p. 33). A few years later, Zelditch (1962) compared fieldwork and survey techniques with respect to their "efficiency and informational adequacy" for collecting different kinds of social science data: frequency distributions, incidents and histories, and institutionalized norms and statuses. He argued that each style of research was the "prototypical and best form" for collecting some—but not all—of these types of data.

Zelditch's comparison served to establish at least a rhetorical foundation for a division of labor in which these two competing research styles might cooperate to provide a range of social data that neither could effectively or efficiently provide on its own.

Burgess' (1927/1974) earlier quoted prediction of fruitful interaction between quantitative and qualitative research styles must often have appeared to be overly optimistic during the foregoing debate. But in the 1970s, Sam D. Sieber (1973) confirmed the fruitful interaction that Burgess had predicted. He remarked that "It is curious that so little attention has been paid to the intellectual and organizational problems and to the prospects of the integration of research methods. A few methodologists have sought to compare the results of different approaches, but these endeavors were conceived within the traditional framework of mutually exclusive techniques, inasmuch as the problem was to determine the consequences of using either one or another technique" (p. 1337). He then went on to demonstrate that the two apparently antagonistic research styles of fieldwork and survey methods could instead and often had been profitably integrated in the design, data collection, and analysis phases of single research projects.

Sieber (1973) concluded that "one could almost say that a new style of research is born of the marriage of survey and fieldwork methodologies." He argued "that the respective techniques need to be modified for their special roles in a set of interlocking methods. It is this combination of adjustments which, in our opinion, produces a distinctly new style of investigation" (p. 1337). Sieber's work is important in this way for defining multimethod research as a distinctive research style to be created by synthesizing different existing styles in planned ways rather than simply by confronting these styles results and asking which style is best. In doing this, Sieber built upon the earlier work of Campbell and Fiske and their colleagues, but extended that work in at least two important directions. He demonstrated that a multimethod approach to research could be usefully employed not only to cross-check the validity of research results (by taking advantage of different methods' areas of informational overlap) but also to improve and build upon one another by utilizing each type of method for its particular strengths at any stage of the research process.

In the first decades of the twentieth century, before American social scientists had really done much research, "statistics" versus "case studies" was a heated issue, representing in its time the quantitative versus qualitative divide that continues to this day. By the late decades of the century, the divisions had become yet more numerous, and the controversies had become more complex. Survey research versus fieldwork, experimentation versus observational and quasiexperimental work, and nonreactive versus reactive methods were by then all at issue and implied important distinctions within as well as between qualitative and quantitative work. The emergence of these four modern styles of research and the discussions and disputes surrounding them shaped the idea of multimethod research and the manner in which we have presented it in this book in many important ways, as readers will clearly see. But also in a way that may less evident: We were led to move beyond the broad longstanding contrast between qualitative and quantitative methods to newer, more nuanced methodological distinctions that recognize—and so allow us to exploit—important differences within as well as between qualitative and quantitative research styles.

# One

# The Multimethod Approach and Its Promise

Social research today is highly diverse in nearly every respect, including methodology. Researchers in different social scientific disciplines and subdisciplines now study a myriad of research problems—not only from a number of different theoretical perspectives but also with several quite different types of research methods. This diversity of methods implies rich opportunities for cross-validating and cross-fertilizing research procedures, findings, and theories. However, to exploit these opportunities, we must develop more cosmopolitan research strategies. What is needed are approaches that systematically explore the new avenues of research that methodological diversity affords. Multimethod research is one such approach.

## Four Imperfect But Useful Research Methods

The principal methods now employed by social researchers are fieldwork, survey research, experimentation, and nonreactive research. Each of these four methods, or styles, of research involves a different strategy for collecting data. Fieldworkers observe people and events firsthand in natural social settings. Survey researchers either interview or administer questionnaires to samples of respondents drawn statistically from the populations in which the phenomena of interest occur. And experimentalists study phenomena under controlled conditions deliberately established by the experimenter to test particular causal hypotheses. The strategy of nonreactive research (Webb, Campbell, Schwartz, & Sechrest, 1966) requires a bit more explanation, however. Fieldwork, surveys, and experiments all involve social contact between researchers and their subjects and often require considerable cooperation to generate data. To avoid reactive error (e.g., guinea pig effects) and the need for subjects' cooperation, nonreactive researchers either employ various unobtrusive observational techniques or study artifacts, archives, official statistics, and other natural by-products of past social life.

Each type of method, if it is well and appropriately applied, can lead to potentially valid empirical and theoretical generalizations about society and social life. But interpreting the findings of any of these methods is an uncertain task, at best. A major source of this uncertainty is that any study employing a single type of research method—and most studies still use only one method—leaves untested rival hypotheses (or alternative interpretations of data) that call the validity of the study's findings into question. Some of these rival hypotheses defy testing because they are beyond our current practical, theoretical, or methodological capabilities. But a good many others merely elude testing. They elude testing for two reasons; either because the particular method employed fails to provide the data needed to test them or because they stem from possible biases inherent in the study's single method. Each type of method, considered alone, is imperfect in this respect.

## Measuring Crime, for Example

Consider two of the methods that are now used to measure the frequency with which crimes are committed. One is an older method that employs naturally occurring data, which is one of the techniques of nonreactive research. The other is a relatively new survey method. In the past, crime rates were most often estimated with data borrowed from the police blotter, or "crimes known to the police."

These data include all offenses that come to the attention of the authorities and that are also confirmed, by official investigations, as having occurred. However, because the police usually act only after a formal complaint has been lodged (except in the cases of vice and traffic offenses, their records exclude most crimes that are unreported by either the victims or other concerned parties. The sum of these unreported criminal acts (often referred to as the "dark figure of crime") is therefore a largely unknown quantity when official statistics are the only measuring instruments employed. Consequently, when crime is measured with police data alone, it is never clear whether crime rates vary from one time, place, or group to another because more offenses have actually been committed or merely because more have been formally reported.

To improve measurement and to dispel the shadow of uncertainty that the "dark figure of crime" casts over much research in criminology and the study of deviance, a different technique—the criminal victimization survey—has been increasingly used in recent years. In these surveys, people from carefully drawn samples of the population at large are interviewed about the crimes that may have been perpetrated against them in the recent past. Crime rates are then estimated from respondents' reports. Of course, it is possible that respondents will fail to mention crimes to a survey interviewer for the same reasons they did not report the crimes to the police (fear, embarrassment, oversight, etc.). But despite this possibility, the surveys have shown that a substantial number of the crimes that respondents describe to interviewers have not been previously reported to the police. These findings have called the uncritical use of official crime data seriously into question. As Skogan (1977) cautions: "It is now always necessary to refute systematically all plausible, error-based, rival interpretations of research findings based on reported crime data" (Skogan, 1977, p. 43).

However, some people now also question the validity of the criminal victimization surveys. For example, Levine (1976) suggests that survey respondents might mistake for crime incidents that in a technical legal sense are only trivial personal annoyances, or respondents might recall *real* crimes as occurring more recently than they actually did, thereby artificially increasing current rates. Respondents might also exaggerate their experiences—or even lie outright—to make themselves appear more important, to dramatize the seriousness of crime as a social problem, or perhaps to placate a persistent interviewer by saying what they think the interviewer wants to hear. Furthermore, overly zealous survey researchers, eager to demonstrate that surveys are indeed more sensitive measuring instruments than official statistics, might be overly willing to accept respondents' reports at face value. More generally, Levine (1976) argues that "while police reports no doubt suffer from crime underreporting, surveys may be flawed by crime overreporting which leads to inflated crime rates" (Levine, 1976, pp. 309–310).

Measuring crime is an important matter in itself, but we introduce it here primarily as an illustration of a more general problem in social science research today: Two or more reasonably reliable methods are applied to a research question, and neither method produces an unambiguous answer. Instead, the characteristic weaknesses of each method are suspected of distorting social reality in a different direction.

## A Broader Multimethod View

To some critical consumers of social research, the admission that our methods are fallible might seem to "prove" the ultimate futility of empirical social science. However, a growing knowledge of the individual weaknesses of our methods has led many researchers to reach a different conclusion: Social science methods should not be treated as mutually exclusive alternatives among which we must choose and then passively pay the costs of our choices. Our individual methods might be flawed, but fortunately the flaws in each are not identical. A diversity of imperfection allows us to combine methods, not only to gain their individual strengths but also to compensate for their particular faults and limitations. The multimethod approach is largely built upon this insight. Its fundamental strategy is to *attack a research problem with an arsenal of methods that have nonoverlapping weaknesses in addition to their complementary strengths.*

This multimethod strategy is simple but powerful. For if our various methods have weaknesses that are truly different, then their convergent findings can be accepted with far greater confidence than any single method's findings would warrant. Each new set of data increases our confidence that the research results reflect reality rather than methodological error. And divergent findings are equally important, but for another reason. They signal the need to analyze a research problem further and to be cautious in interpreting the significance of any one set of data.

### Multiple Measurement (or Triangulation)

When applied to problems of measurement (such as measuring crime), the multimethod strategy suggests the tactic of *triangulation* (Campbell & Fiske, 1959; Webb et al., 1966; Denzin, 1978). Broadly speaking, *measurement* is the operation of assigning either qualitative or quantitative values (that is, either names or numbers) to social phenomena. *Triangulated measurement* tries to pinpoint the values of a phenomenon more accurately by sighting in on it from different methodological viewpoints. To be useful, a measuring instrument must give both consistent results and measure the phenomenon that it purports to measure. When two reliable instruments yield conflicting results, then the validity of each is cast into doubt. When the findings of different methods agree, we are more confident. But experience has so often revealed serious contradictions that only rarely can agreement be assumed without actual empirical investigation.

We have seen, for instance, that official statistics and criminal victimization surveys frequently are at odds about the actual rate of crime in a society. The multimethod approach to such contradictions is to accept the fact that no method measures perfectly and to exploit the fact that multiple measurement offers the chance to assess each method's validity in the light of other methods. Levine's (1976) conclusion about the measurement of crime expresses the multimethod attitude well:

> Only an omniscient deity would be capable of providing an exact tabulation of crime, and in lieu of such an authoritative accounting it is probably most sensible to develop a crime index based on various admittedly faulty measures than to pretend that any single source of data provides a perfect image of reality. (Levine, 1976, p. 326)

Crime is, of course, a subject of interest not only to scholars but also to the public and to the government. Since 1929, the U. S. Department of Justice has measured crime nationwide with data collected from local police agencies and collated by the FBI in its Uniform Crime Report (UCR). In 1972, recognizing the limitations of police data, the Justice Department initiated a new program conducted by the Bureau of Justice Statistics: the National Criminal Victimization Survey (NCVS). The Justice Department emphasizes that these two measurement programs are not interchangeable; they have "unique strengths" and are designed and conducted to complement one another. "The UCR provides a measure of the number of crimes reported to law enforcement agencies throughout the country. . . . The NCVS is the primary source of information on the characteristics of criminal victimization and on the number and types of crimes not reported to law enforcement authorities" (U. S. Department of Justice, 2003). One of the most important uses of official statistics on crime is to track trends in crime over time. The Justice Department stresses the value of these different programs for measuring such changes. Prior to the NCVS, it was impossible to determine whether nationwide changes in the rate of crime measured by the UCR were due to actual increases or decreases or instead to differences in the reporting and recording of crimes.

The Justice Department reports that since the NCVS's inception, long-term trend lines for crimes measured by both the UCR and NCVS have tended to converge, thereby increasing confidence in each measure and in the trends. However, there have been exceptions. For example, in 2000 the FBI issued the news that after several years of steady decline, the incidence of violent crime as measured by the UCR had apparently stabilized. But two weeks later, the Bureau of Justice Statistics issued the much better news that the same violent crimes, when measured by the NCVS, had declined by about 15 percent. The news media reacted with dismay over this discrepancy and expressed doubt about the validity of the methods employed. Rand and Rennison (2002) attribute the media reaction to "confusion about the purposes, advantages, and disadvantages of the UCR and the NCVS" (Rand & Rennison, 2002, p. 47). They also show how detailed comparison of the two measures' findings could explain the divergence in this case. They conclude that "The steep 1999–2000 decline measured by the NCVS largely resulted from a decline in crimes victims said they did not report to the police. Violent crimes not reported to police fell by 20%, while violent crimes reported to police fell by 6%" (Rand & Rennison, 2002, p. 50). In other words, the previously declining trend in violent crime appears to have continued in that year but did not register in UCR measurements because more victims called the police than in the earlier year. Because estimates of crime trends in the United States derived from these two programs are now routinely compared and publicized for social policy purposes, the need for improved ability to interpret the convergence and divergence of multimethod findings is clearly a matter of public as well as academic importance.

## Interpreting Convergence and Divergence

Usually, evidence from two sources is intuitively more persuasive than evidence from only one. But intuition can be misleading. Even strongly agreeing multiple measurements can be wrong if undetected sources of error affect each method equally. Convergent findings are compelling only if it can be demonstrated empirically that when the methods err, they typically err in opposite ways. Successful triangulation requires careful analysis of each method in relation to other methods and also in relation to the demands of the research problem.

For example, surveys and official data combined may give a triangulated picture of a crime, such as rape, that the victim is reluctant to report. But survey research on traffic offenses would probably not provide very enlightening results when compared to police data for the same time and place. Citizens are too often unaware of one another's (or even their own) traffic violations to be reliable informants. (For instance, how often do you note whether the driver behind you at an intersection has obeyed the stop sign, or whether you have strayed across a double yellow line?) A comparison of data on traffic arrests with the results of a field study in which a trained observer systematically recorded motorists' behavior would be more informative in this instance.

The multimethod premise that no method is perfect underscores the need to study the sources of measurement error to determine precisely what it is that's being measured. If methods measure the same phenomenon, their findings will converge as errors are corrected. But if the methods measure different phenomena, then convergence will stop well short of complete agreement, even when sources of divergent error have been identified and eliminated. For example, in one of the earliest comparisons of survey and official crime data, Ennis (1967) employs a panel of police and attorneys to judge the 3400 "crimes" that survey respondents from a nationwide sample reported. This expert panel rejected 1300 of the victimization reports. Nonetheless, the 2,100 remaining incidents suggested that the actual rate of crime during the time period studied might be nearly twice as high as the officially reported rate.

Research findings that sharply and persistently diverge lead social scientists to rethink research problems. Thus, although official data are still used by many as an admittedly imperfect measure of actual crime, many others argue that these data really measure the amount of law enforcement more nearly than they do the amount of law violation. And some researchers have come to redefine the concept of crime altogether. They suggest that it is more useful and accurate to conceive of crime as a phenomenon composed of several empirical subtypes, which might vary independently of one another and which no single method purporting to measure the simpler idea of "actual crime" can adequately tap.

For example, Black (1970) defines deviance as any behavior for which there is a probability of punishment upon detection and further distinguishes four subtypes of criminal deviance. There are undetected crimes, which are measured by techniques such as the criminal victimization survey. There are crimes that have been detected but not yet, or perhaps ever, punished (measured by data such as "crimes known to the police"). There are crimes that have been both detected and punished (measured by official rates of arrest and conviction). The fourth type is crimes that are detected by the police through citizens' complaints but not formally recorded. Because no formal action is taken, this last type of crime—like undetected crime—does not appear in the official statistics.

To study this fourth type of crime (which is also measured by criminal victimization surveys), Black (1970) introduces yet another method that would allow him to identify the conditions under which crimes that have been reported go unattended by the police. He conducted field studies in which trained observers accompanied the police in three large American cities on their regular work shifts and recorded observations of the routine encounters between these officers and citizens who had telephoned complaints. Contrary to frequent charges, there was no evidence of racial discrimination. Crimes reported by blacks were as likely to be officially recorded by the police as crimes reported by whites. However, Black (1970) did discover that police were more likely to write an official report after investigating a complaint when the crime was a legally serious one, when the complainant clearly preferred the police to take action, when the suspected criminal was a stranger to the complainant (rather than a relative or an acquaintance), when the complainant acted in a deferent manner, and when the complainant was a white-collar rather than a blue-collar worker. Black (1970) concludes that the probability of a criminally deviant act being punished, even if detected, depended heavily upon who the victim was and how he (or she) presented a complaint to the police. Thus, the dark figure of unreported crime, to which we referred earlier, is accompanied by another equally dark figure comprised of crimes that victims report but the police choose to ignore.

## Applying the Multimedia Approach to All Research Stages

Empirical measurement is essential to determine the nature and frequency of social phenomena. Guesses and impressions obviously will not do. Important as it is, however, measurement is only one step, or stage, in the research process. To know what to measure and to choose the appropriate methods, one must both formulate a research problem to guide the investigation and develop a theoretical solution to that problem. To make actual measurements, data must be collected for appropriate samples of individuals, social settings, or groups. To see the measurements' implications for a problem and for the theories about it, the data must be assembled and analyzed in a systematic way. Finally, for the measurements and the conclusions they support to have an impact on knowledge, the research must be reported. Formulating research problems, building and testing theories, sampling, collecting and analyzing data, and reporting research results are—along with measurement—the major stages of the research process.

The decision to adopt a multimethod approach to measurement affects not only measurement but all stages of research. Indeed, multiple measurement is often introduced explicitly to solve problems at other stages of the research process as well as to answer more narrowly defined questions of measurement validity. These wider effects and uses of triangulation and other multimethod tactics need to be examined in detail, including the new challenges that the use of multiple methods poses for data analysis, for writing and evaluating research articles for publication, and for doing research in an ethical manner.

The promise of multimethod research, however, is far greater than its impact on any one stage of research. To apply the multimethod approach to any stage, it is usually necessary to analyze a social phenomenon's structure, setting, and constituent social processes far more fully than when only a single method is used. By enlarging the scope of the research to which it is applied, the multimethod perspective holds out the larger promises of more sociologically significant conclusions and greater opportunities for both verification and discovery. Moreover, we believe that the approach promises to alleviate some of the persistent dilemmas and conflicts in social research that now seem intractable and irremediable.

## Finding Consensus in a House of Many Mansions

It seems obvious that the point of research methods is to study substantive problems. But there is a strong tendency in all fields of social science for particular methods to be valued so highly by their users that they become ends in themselves, to be defended against rival methods and nourished by selecting only research problems for which they are well-suited. In 1957, in an exchange over the relative merits of participant observation and interviewing, Trow wrote an eloquent and frequently quoted exhortation against such methodological parochialism. We quote it again because it states the multimethod position well.

Every cobbler thinks that leather is the only thing. Most social scientists, including the present writer, have their favorite methods with which they are familiar and have some skill in using. And I suspect we mostly choose to investigate problems that seem vulnerable to attack through these methods. But we should at least try to be less parochial than cobblers. Let us be done with the arguments of "participant observation" *versus* interviewing—as we have largely dispensed with the arguments for psychology *versus* sociology— and get on with the business of attacking our problems with the widest array of conceptual and methodological tools that we possess and they demand. (Trow, 1957, p. 35)

Today, as in 1957, there are deep methodological divisions within the social sciences. Over time the arguments have not subsided. Nor do we seem as individuals to be any less inclined to follow our favorite methods where they lead. But some things have changed. Since the 1950s, the social sciences have grown tremendously. And with that growth, there is now virtually no major problem area that is studied exclusively with one method. While the social sciences have remained largely single method in approach at the level of the individual investigator and the individual research project, the sum of individual efforts has resulted in a multimethod approach to problems. In most substantive areas, surveys, experiments, field studies, and analyses of naturally occurring data stand side by side in the literature. This advance is clearly in the direction that Trow pointed. But like most advances, this one has, in its turn, created difficulties.

The development of multimethod social science disciplines within which individual researchers largely engage in single-method research poses serious problems of intellectual and social integration. As Wrong (1978) comments: "Never has social science seemed to be such a house of many mansions . . . past aspirations toward a single methodological canon or even toward unity of theory and research have dwindled" (Wrong, 1978, p. 28). Diversity can give a discipline varied strength, but it also can lead to incoherence, confusion, and fruitless controversy. For this reason, many social scientists feel the need to seek greater consensus. For example, Blalock (1978), a sociologist, writes the following:

Somehow we must . . . reach a much greater degree of *consensus* on our terminology and research operations. To some, this will seem to stifle innovation and impose orthodoxy. But an agreement on concepts or research operations does not by any stretch of the imagination imply agreement on empirical assumptions, nor does it restrict to any great extent the propositions we use to relate these variables. It seems that we already have enough concepts, variables, research topics, orientations, and theoretical positions to satisfy nearly everyone . . . A lack of diversity is not our problem, nor need we fear it will become so in the near future. But in order for this diversity to result in genuine culmination of useful knowledge, some greater semblance of order must—in one way or another—be created. (Blalock, 1978, p. 22)

## Order Without Orthodoxy

Few researchers, we think, would deny the need for greater coherence. The more pressing questions are how to achieve that coherence and how to do so without imposing an unwelcome orthodoxy? At present, the integration of the different and often conflicting views and empirical findings that result from diverse methods is undertaken mainly after the fact of research and usually at a very high level of abstraction. Only much more rarely is integration undertaken in the design of individual pieces of research. For the most part, we each seem to do and to publish our work in the faith and hope that somebody else will create a synthesis. We look to theoreticians to construct umbrellas of ideas broad enough to explain— or at least make comprehensible—all that our research has discovered and suggested. And we call upon methodologists both to trace logical pathways between our different roads of inquiry and to reassure us that these roads all lead in the same direction and may someday meet to produce more comprehensive knowledge of the social world.

The writings of theoretical and methodological synthesizers are among the most widely read and frequently cited works in the social science literature. Yet their proposed syntheses are as often as not rejected in favor of continued diversity. Their work often comes to be highly regarded in its own right, but only as an eloquent expression of still another school of thought. As a result, we now have so many orientations, viewpoints, and perspectives that the uninitiated might easily lose sight of the subject matter of the social sciences while laboring to distinguish correctly between the various approaches to that subject matter.

A major benefit of adopting the multimethod approach is that the approach begins the task of integration from the ground up by calling upon individual social scientists to integrate methods throughout the course of their individual investigations. In multimethod research, one must confront diversity and try to resolve contradictions from the outset. The challenge to state new problems (or restate old ones) in terms that make them susceptible to study by different methods, to find common ways of comparing and evaluating the results of different methods, and to reconcile the contradictions that the application of different methods might produce appears to us to be a very promising way to begin creating order without orthodoxy.

By emphasizing the value of individual multimethod research, we do not mean to deny that great benefits may also be gained by synthesizing a multitude of diverse single-method studies. Nor do we mean to imply that all individual research must be multimethod to make our knowledge about social life more coherent. The pressing need to coordinate methods by whatever means is the keynote of the multimethod perspective. It is immaterial whether coordination is achieved in one multimethod study or by comparing the findings of several independently conducted, single-method projects. Individual investigators using favored single methods and hoping to show the unique values of their methods can certainly reach multimethod conclusions by carefully building upon and correcting each others' work.

Interaction between colleagues—even colleagues of quite different methodological persuasions—can be a powerful integrative force. Examination of many scientific disciplines clearly shows that diverse single-method research does not preclude either a strong common focus on well-recognized research problems or efficient communication between scientists using different methods. For example, in epidemiological research, the results of experiments with human and animal subjects, clinical case studies, health surveys, and statistical analyses of medical records are often effectively coordinated to solve important medical puzzles, such as the relationship between cigarette smoking and lung cancer. However, when extensive cooperation among colleagues working independently is hard to attain (as appears to be the case in much of contemporary social science), then individual multimethod research has the great advantage of requiring only one investigator's will and ability to integrate the results of different methods.

## Styles of Research

Throughout this book we have very consciously referred to the general types of methods as *styles* of research. *Orientations, perspectives, strategies,* and other labels all similarly communicate the idea of differentiated ways of viewing the world and of going about the business of empirically investigating it. In addition, however, the term *styles* connotes an aesthetic dimension. Researchers' methodological preferences are not necessarily based entirely upon shared scientific criteria, nor upon a linear disciplinary development from more primitive classificatory and qualitative methods to more modern analytic and quantitative techniques. Instead, selection of methods is more likely to reflect researchers' different conceptions of what constitutes a *good* piece of finished social research—and although one might admire and praise the techniques of a different practitioner— the responsive inner smile to a *good* piece of research is more likely to be evoked by those styles that resonate with one's own methodological predilections.

To be *good*, it is not enough that a piece of research be done competently. It must also be considered important. "Moderns" might appreciate "primitive" techniques, and vice versa, but each might view the other's skills and efforts as wasted because the initial conceptions, questions, or problems to which the techniques were applied might appear trivial or obscure. Methodological styles reflect not just differences in technique (such as qualitative versus quantitative procedures) but also different views of the epistemology of science and its ultimate goals and contributions to human thought and endeavor.

These are not issues that are debated fully with every new piece of research. Training, socialization, role models, the structure of reward systems, and other aspects of the social organization of social science lead us to make different decisions as to which theoretical problems are important and which methodological styles are appropriate. Research styles are not simply the result of individual choice or idiosyncratic aesthetics. Rather, they are socially embedded in intellectual communities, networks of like-minded practitioners. The selective socialization, training, and proselytizing within these communities gives mutual support, but at the same time it perpetuates structural cleavages and conflicts among practitioners of different styles; or, at best, differentiated indifference.

## A Systematic Approach

There have, of course, always been a good many social scientists for whom Trow's earlier quoted exhortation was unnecessary—men and women who innovatively tailored their methods to their problems without undue regard for habit and convention. Some have formally identified their work as multimethod; others have not but have obviously made full use of various methods. There are also a great many social scientists who have perhaps made more limited and certainly less self-conscious use of multiple methods at one or more stages of their ostensibly single-method projects. For example, one reader of an early draft of this book remarked: "I was surprised to learn that I was using the MMP [the multimethod perspective] in my mailed questionnaire studies, not only when I pretested and interviewed nonrespondents but also when talking with officials in the target populations when designing the surveys."

Such researchers may be unaware of the general methodological perspective that their customary practices imply, but they do nonetheless use scientific common sense and readily employ supplementary methods to get information and insights that their primary method cannot provide. In other words, many social scientists are already (albeit implicitly) using the multimethod approach in their work. This is an important observation about current research practice because it means that the promise of multimethod research does not depend upon the risky business of doing something that has never, or only rarely, been done before. Instead, the promise is in doing more regularly, fully, and systematically what in the past we may have done only intermittently, partially, and perhaps haphazardly.

## Multimethod Projects

Multimethod research, considered in the broadest sense, includes any research that contributes in any way to gaining a multimethod view of social phenomena. However, actual multimethod projects are of special interest. They are either single studies or more complex programs of continuing research which systematically employ various combinations of field, survey, experimental, and nonreactive methods to address their research questions. This type of investigation is rapidly coming to be regarded as a research style in its own right—one as distinctive in its way as the more conventional styles upon which it builds. The application of different research methods to the same research problem in a single project is sometimes characterized, particularly in introductory methods textbooks, as either an extraordinary achievement or a mere ideal. For example, according to Babbie, "In the best of all possible worlds, your own research design should bring more than one research method to bear on the topic" (Babbie, 1979, p. 110). But the fact is that multimethod research is now discussed, planned, and conducted as a routine matter, part and parcel of normal social science.

Project-level multimethod research offers the distinct advantage of quick, close coordination and comparison of different methods and their findings. This approach is especially important in research areas with low social and intellectual integration. But we do not rashly assume either that the benefits of studying problems with multiple methods can only be attained at the level of the individual project or that such projects are in any sense substitutes for a discipline's collective inquiry. Quite the contrary, we think that the multimethod project has emerged as a research style precisely because the multimethod nature of contemporary social science has convinced many researchers that solutions to their research problems require more and different kinds of information than any single method can provide, and also that solutions based upon multimethod findings are likely to be better solutions—that is, to have a firmer empirical base and greater theoretical scope because they are grounded in different ways of observing social reality. Multimethod research is thus (in our view at least) an attempt to apply to our individual work lessons learned at the level of the discipline as a whole and thereby to enrich the collective effort to which we each contribute.

# Two

# A Healthy Skepticism About Theory and Method

S cientists are skeptics. In this chapter, we consider social research from the viewpoint of scientific skepticism. This position, which is central both to the logic and conduct of scientific inquiry, holds that scientific theories and methods provide at best only approximations to knowledge. As a result, scientists must closely and continually question the validity of their work. We will assess the ability of different methods (fieldwork, survey research, experimentation, and nonreactive research) to answer the kinds of questions that a scientific skeptic might pose. And finally, we consider the advantages for theoretically oriented research of adopting a multimethod approach.

## Orienting Theory Toward Research and Vice Versa

A major aim of social research is to build and to test theories of social phenomena. Theories are composed of abstract ideas, concepts, and propositions that can be thought of apart from any particular set of instances and in the absence of immediate empirical referents. Because of their abstractness, theories enable us to conceive of a variety of interpretations for any given set of data. However, these interpretations can contradict one another and might have quite different implications for action as well as for understanding. Moreover, the theoretical imagination is limitless. The theorist can conceive of infinite possibilities, including many that might prove to be sheer fantasy. For these reasons, theorizing requires the aid and the discipline of empirical research.

However, research equally requires the aid and discipline of theory. If we could not theorize, we would be unable to imagine that a situation might be other than it seems or that things might be different elsewhere. We would be bound to believe instead whatever the data "told" us, and data taken at face value can be very misleading, as the discussion in Chapter 1 about measuring crime illustrated. Police data, for example, purport to measure crime but can also measure victims' willingness to call the police and the quantity and quality of law enforcement. If police statistics show a marked increase in a community's crime rate, it might be that no more actual crimes were committed. Instead, citizens might have become more willing to call the police, or the police might have changed their record-keeping practices or become more vigilant—to mention but a few possible alternative explanations for the increase.

Of course, not all social research is primarily concerned with building and testing theories. Many studies are instead more concerned with fact-finding, often to aid in the formulation of social policies. Theorizing might seem less essential in such applied work—no more perhaps than an academic embellishment on data that already contain the relevant particulars. However, to interpret a body of data intelligently for any purpose, one must always entertain, and preferably test, alternative interpretations of that data's meaning. For example, to make effective policy recommendations, an applied researcher would clearly need to explore the different possible interpretations of crime data just as thoroughly as a more theoretically oriented researcher, albeit with a different end in view.

## Empirical Generalizations and Theories

In contrast to theorizing, data collecting is very down-to-earth. Empirical studies provide information as concrete as that found, for instance, in the news.

But while the news reports separate items telling who did what, when, where, and to whom, research findings are usually presented in the form of empirical generalizations. These generalizations summarize uniformities in the observed relations between variables. They are, as Wallace describes them, "brief but informationally heavy-laden" statements (1971, p. 26). For example, Archer and Gartner (1976) conclude in brief that civilian homicide rates tend to increase following wars. But this generalization is based upon an analysis of official homicide statistics for a sample of 50 nations that had been at war, as compared with another sample of 30 "control" nations that were at peace during the same period. Eighty instances, one generalization.

Because of the range of data supporting them, empirical generalizations are considerably more informative than most news items. Change in a single nation's homicide rate following a particular war might be newsworthy, but it might also be only a coincidence or a fluke. But such changes observed in many warring nations, especially in contrast with lack of change in peaceful nations, more firmly establish that there really is a regular and predictable relationship between these two variables of warfare and postwar homicide. However, despite their broader empirical support, even empirical generalizations like news items can be interpreted in a variety of ways. For instance, does the increase in officially reported homicides after wars really mean that more murders are committed, or does it mean instead that more suspicious deaths are being attributed to homicide than before? The data underlying an empirical generalization prove only that a uniform relationship between variables exists. It does not explain that relationship. Explanation requires theorizing beyond the immediate data and, in turn, new empirical tests of the resulting theoretical explanations.

Concepts and propositions are a theory's chief components. The concepts define the phenomena being investigated. The propositions tell how and under what general conditions those conceptually defined phenomena are thought to be related. Theories logically explain, and also predict, empirical generalizations. Theories explain existing empirical generalizations by logically and inductively subsuming these statements under appropriate theoretical concepts and propositions. And by the reverse process of logical deduction, theories predict empirical generalizations. For example, because murder is an instance of the phenomena defined by the concept of violence, and because in wartime societies officially condone violence against external enemies, the empirical generalization that homicide rates increase in postwar years can be explained by (and is predictable in terms of) the following propositions: (1) violence increases when customary prohibitions against it are weakened, and (2) official sanctioning of violence is a condition that weakens customary prohibitions.

Predicting an already known empirical generalization is, of course, no great feat. However, theories can also predict new empirical generalizations, which is more of an accomplishment. Theories differ in at least two important ways from the empirical generalizations that they are built to explain (Wallace, 1971). First, theoretical concepts are more abstract than the terms employed in empirical generalizations. The idea of violence, for instance, is considerably more abstract than the idea of murder, because although murder denotes a very specific act, violence denotes a much larger and more open-ended set of behaviors, including some that might never occur (e.g., the use of nuclear weapons by civilians). Second, theories contain concepts and propositions that are not contained in any of the empirical generalizations that they explain (for instance, in this example, the concept of "customary prohibitions against violence" and the proposition that "the weakening of these prohibitions increases the incidence of violence"). Because theorizing involves greater abstraction and introduces new ideas and assumptions into the analysis of a research problem, theories predict new empirical generalizations as well as explain existing ones. For example, because homicide is only one of many possible forms of violence, the foregoing theory predicts that not only murder but also other violent crimes and acts will be found to increase after wars. This ability to predict new generalizations is of central importance in theoretical inquiry. It provides the opportunity to test theories against new facts rather than using theories merely to interpret facts that we already know.

## Operationalization and Multiple Operationism

Theories often contain concepts and propositions that, for the time being at least, are empirically unmeasurable and untestable. For instance, all hypotheses alluding to the so-called dark figure of unreported crime *before* the invention of criminal victimization surveys were of necessity speculative because no research operations were in place to measure that figure. However, if they are to be tested, theories must ultimately be operationalized, or translated into terms that are sufficiently concrete to specify actual research operations for collecting data.

Ideally, the data collected would unambiguously test the hypothesis being investigated. But, as Webb, Campbell, Schwartz, and Sechrest (1966) have pointed out, every operationalization of an hypothesis is composed of theoretically irrelevant as well as theoretically pertinent elements. For example, police records and criminal victimization surveys are only partially relevant to hypotheses about the commission of crimes because both also simultaneously measure other phenomena, such as victims' willingness to call the police and survey respondents' reactions to being interviewed. The confounding of relevant and irrelevant elements obscures a body of data's actual significance for an hypothesis, since it means that the data are influenced by factors other than those specified in the hypothesis.

Because theoretical concepts and hypotheses are abstract, however, they can usually be operationalized in more than one way with different but still appropriate research operations. For instance, hypotheses involving the concept of criminal deviance, as Chapter 1 demonstrated, can be operationalized in terms not only of archival research but also in terms of surveys and field methods. The possibility of multiple operations for testing the same hypothesis is important because it permits tests that employ multiple measures. And if these are measures "which are hypothesized to share in the theoretically relevant components but have different patterns of irrelevant components" (Webb et al., 1966, p. 3), then—as Chapter 1 also demonstrated—the test results can be far more discriminating than if measures with similar irrelevant components were employed.

In some instances, of course, it is difficult to conceive of more than one mode of operationalizing an hypothesis. For example, it is hard to think of a practical alternative to official statistics for operationalizing hypotheses about international rates of homicide in different historical eras. However, theorizing offers an advantage in such instances. When an hypothesis or an empirical generalization is embedded in a theory, it is possible to derive from that theory other parallel hypotheses (in this case, hypotheses about other forms of violence) that are more susceptible to multiple research operations. The confirmation of these new hypotheses would support the original, more operation-specific hypothesis. For example, if both criminal victimization survey data and official statistics indicated increases in assault and other nonlethal violent crimes in postwar eras (or at other times when prohibitions against violence may have been weakened), that would provide added support to generalizations about homicide that derive from official statistics alone.

## Building and Testing Theories

Theoretically oriented research has two different but closely related aspects: theory building and theory testing. Theory building consists of either constructing new theories or adapting older theories to explain known but previously unexplained empirical generalizations. Theory testing, on the other hand, consists of logically deducing predictions from existing theories and stating these predictions as new hypotheses for research. The empirical tests of these hypotheses test the validity of the theory and, more indirectly, the validity of whatever other explanations the theory may have provided earlier. Should it be found, for instance, that violent acts other than murder fail to increase after wars, then one would question both the validity of the theory that led to that prediction and also the validity of explaining postwar homicide rates in terms of either that theory, or any other theory, that claims warfare is a sufficient condition for a general increase in violence.

A major problem in building and testing theories is that most empirical generalizations are logically consistent with a good many theories, and— as this implies—different theories lead to many of the same predictions. For example, the generalization that homicide rates increase after wars is consistent with the theory advanced previously. But it is also consistent with other theories: for instance, the theory that warfare produces veterans who acquire a habit of violence in the military, and it is these violent veterans who are responsible for increased domestic homicide rates. This alternative theory also predicts that many forms of violence, not just murder, will increase in postwar eras.

If every empirical generalization were logically explainable in terms of exactly the same set of theories, and if every theory implied exactly the same hypothesis, then theoretically oriented research would be futile because it would be impossible to distinguish one theory from another on the basis of empirical data. Fortunately, this is usually not the case. Instead, different sets of theories apply to different generalizations, and different theories imply different sets of hypotheses.

For example, the violent-veteran theory of postwar homicide implies that murderers will come disproportionately from those groups in the population who served in the military. By contrast, the earlier stated theory implies that all citizens for whom social prohibitions against violence are weakened as a result of war will become more violent, not just veterans. In fact, Archer and Gartner (1976) found that homicide increased not only among those who were eligible for military service but in other groups as well. Establishing this second empirical generalization narrowed the range of theories that might explain the initial generalization and also increased the plausibility of the initial theory.

Theory building and theory testing clearly require variety. In building theories, the more varied the empirical generalizations to be explained, the easier it will be to discriminate among the many possible theories that might explain any one of the generalizations. And in testing theories, the more varied the predictions, the more sharply the ensuing research will discriminate among competing theories.

## Validity and Verification

The better a theory explains and predicts empirical generalizations, the closer to the truth it is generally assumed to be. However, a theory's validity depends only in part upon its absolute power to explain and predict. The status of competing theories is equally important. As Campbell and Stanley (1963, p. 26) suggest, a well-established theory is one for which "few if any rivals may be practically or seriously proposed." Verification, therefore, centrally involves formulating and testing alternative hypotheses and theories. There are essentially three strategies: crucial experiments, multiple testing, and the earlier described procedure of multiple operationism.

Crucial experiments are studies designed to distinguish between specific competing hypotheses by generating findings that could be true only if all but one of the hypotheses or theories were false. If it were hypothesized, for example, that an increase in officially reported crime is attributable to an increase in reporting rather than to an increase in perpetration, then a comparison of criminal victimization survey data with police data for the appropriate time periods might provide the crucial data to determine which of these hypotheses is false. The strategy of the crucial experiment is to deduce opposing predictions from theories. For example, the two previously mentioned theories of postwar homicide led to the competing hypotheses that either all people are more prone to violence after wars or that only veterans become more violent. As we noted earlier, different theories often lead to substantially the same predictions. The crux of the crucial experiment is to make discriminating predictions.

Multiple testing, the second strategy, consists of deriving a large and varied set of hypotheses from a single theory. Unlike crucial experiments in which the hypotheses are considered to be rivals, the hypotheses in multiple testing complement one another, because all derive logically from the same theory. Deducing many different hypotheses from a theory provides for a more rigorous test of that theory's absolute predictive power than deriving only one or a few very similar hypotheses would do. But multiple derivations also provide a more stringent test of the theory's power relative to other theories. The larger and the more varied the pool of hypotheses, the more probable it is that only the theory from which those hypotheses were derived would predict them all, even though other theories might predict any one or a few of them. Because theories are not unique in their individual predictions, any single prediction is problematic. However, the more numerous and the more varied the predictions that one derives from a particular theory, the more nearly unique that theory's configuration of hypotheses becomes, and so the fewer plausible competitors the theory would have if those hypotheses were confirmed.

In contrast with crucial experiments, which involve deriving competing hypotheses from different theories, and multiple testing, which involves deriving multiple hypotheses from a single theory, the third strategy of multiple operationism involves multiple tests of the same hypothesis with each test operationalizing the hypothesis in a different way; for example, testing an hypothesis concerning crime with both police data and criminal victimization survey data. Just as the same prediction can follow logically from different theories, and different theories can explain any one empirical generalization, the same operational definitions can represent or be interpretable in terms of different hypotheses. Moreover, these rival hypotheses might stem from the terms of the operationalization itself. For example, any study today that operationalizes the concept of crime in terms of official police data must contend with rival hypotheses stemming from our knowledge of that data's deficiencies. If, however, different tests of an hypothesis employ different operationalizations and the test results agree, or converge, then the plausibility of rival hypotheses is greatly reduced.

A multimethod approach increases the feasibility of verifying or validating theories. Each type of research method, as we have illustrated, is limited in its ability to distinguish between competing hypotheses, to explore a theory's implications, and to operationalize hypotheses in contrasting ways. Multiple methods facilitate the design of crucial experiments, the derivation of multiple hypotheses, and the definition of multiple operations.

## A Healthy Skepticism

Whenever we theorize, we naturally hope that our ideas will prove to be more nearly right than wrong. However, only by trying to prove ideas wrong can it be determined how nearly right they can be. As Campbell and Stanley (1963, p. 35) have stressed, even the findings of "true" experiments, regarded by many as the ultimate verificational instruments, "never 'confirm' or 'prove' a theory—rather, the successful theory is tested and escapes disconfirmation. An adequate hypothesis is one that has repeatedly survived such probing—but it may always be displaced by a new probe." To suggest that any hypothesis or theory can be displaced, no matter how strong the evidence for it now appears, risks sounding like a manufacturer nervously disclaiming responsibility for a product. However, scientific knowledge is composed not of eternal truths but rather of those empirical findings and theories that have gained sufficient acceptance among scientists to be taken as the pertinent intellectual context for their current work. The strongest conditional guarantee that can be given, therefore, is the promise of continual research to determine how far, and in what ways, currently accepted knowledge might be wrong.

Because scientific knowledge is provisional, or contingent upon the results of studies yet to be done, skepticism plays a legitimate and important part in research. Only by closely and continually questioning our work, and by doing research designed to answer those questions, can we test our present ideas' empirical foundations and break ground to build new theories. But to promote rather than impede inquiry, skepticism must be counterbalanced by recognition that the ultimate test of a theory's validity is its ability to function well when employed in later studies—no matter how poorly, or well, its author might have answered earlier criticisms. "A theory is validated, not by showing it to be invulnerable to criticism, but by putting it to good use, in one's own problems or in those of coworkers. Methodology . . . should say no more than this about a questionable theory: if you can do anything with it, go ahead" (Kaplan, 1964, p. 322). This is a formula for healthy skepticism—criticism that is constructive in the sense that it shows how new research can build upon promising ideas from past work and improve upon doubtful ones.

Certainly not all the questions that a skeptic might ask are equally constructive. One type to be strenuously avoided is the question that is unanswerable because it assumes the existence of an impossible state of affairs. For example, who can say, and so why ask, what the rate of crime (or any other phenomenon) would be if it were measured with an error-free instrument. There are no such instruments. And in the words of Hume, "the notion of any correction beyond what we have the instruments and the art to make is a mere fiction of the mind, and useless as well as incomprehensible" (quoted by Kaplan, 1964, p. 202). But at the same time, we must not underestimate "the instruments and the art" that we do have.

The array of methods available to social scientists today makes it feasible to ask a good many questions without risking unhealthy skepticism.

## The Skeptic's Questions

The most persistent skeptics are of course social scientists themselves, who might quite properly raise a number of different kinds of questions. Some of the most important and frequently asked questions are based upon an ideal but widely shared conception of theory. First, a theory should logically explain existing empirical generalizations and yield precise and accurate predictions of new generalizations. Second, it should explain and predict better than other theories. Third, it should explain empirical findings in substantive terms, not as artifacts of the methods employed to obtain them. Fourth, it should apply to complex real life settings as well as to more highly simplified and tightly controlled research contexts. Fifth, it should be generalizable to well-defined and relevant universes and populations beyond the boundaries of the particular studies in which it was built and tested. Sixth, it should infer causal relationships between the phenomena being investigated. And seventh, it should define those phenomena in validly measurable terms appropriate to the explanations and predictions made. These seven properties are the basis for a healthy skepticism about theoretically oriented research because they are the standards that social scientists strive to meet.

First, are *questions of absolute theoretical adequacy.* These ask how well does a theory account for empirical findings, and how thoroughly have a theory's empirical implications been explored? Unexplained empirical generalizations, theoretically anomalous findings, and outright contradictions all indicate possible shortcomings in a theory. Also, because a few findings can be adduced for nearly any theory that is neither hopelessly abstract nor blatantly false, and because a good many theories might be equally consistent with a few similar facts, we must also ask how numerous and how diverse the theory's successful explanations and predictions are.

Second, there are *questions of relative theoretical adequacy*: Are there rival theories that are equally consistent with the theory's explanations and predictions? If there are a great many discrepancies between a theory and the data that it purports to explain and predict, then even a nonskeptic will suspect that another theory might be more appropriate. When the fit between a theory and data is loose, the question is which other theory might fit the data better? When the fit is tighter, the question is which alternative hypotheses and theories have been eliminated and which remain plausible alternatives? As Kaplan rightly stresses, "What must in any case be taken into account in assessing a theory's validity is the set of alternatives to it in conjunction with which it is being considered. That a theory is validated does not mean that it is probable, in some appropriate sense, but only that it is more probable than the other possible explanations" (Kaplan, 1964, p. 315). Because validity is a relative rather than an absolute judgment, estimates might vary depending upon the context in which a theory is built and tested. Therefore, it is always appropriate to ask which "set of alternatives" has been considered and whether that set includes the most strongly competing hypotheses.

Some rival hypotheses represent competing theoretical viewpoints that suggest different substantive interpretations of data. But methodologically based hypotheses are in many instances equally powerful rivals. Alternative hypotheses based upon suspected methodological influence or bias are especially irksome, because until they are disconfirmed they cast doubt upon some or all of the substantive theoretical conclusions that might be drawn from the data. Third, therefore, are *questions of methodological bias*: To what extent, and in what ways, may the empirical findings to be explained have been influenced by the method, or methods, used to obtain those findings? Webb et al. (1966, pp. 12–32) have identified a number of common sources of method-related error that might give rise to rival hypotheses. These sources of error include a variety of reactive measurement effects (the guinea pig effect, role selection, measurement-induced changes, response sets, and interviewer effects); changes in the investigator or the measuring instruments over the course of the research; and the selectivity of different methods in giving access to different kinds of persons, situations, events, times, and places.

Fourth are *questions of measurement and conceptualization*. These ask how well have the phenomena defined by the theory's concepts been measured, and how appropriate are those concepts to the explanations and predictions that the theory is intended to provide? Ideally, measures of theoretically related phenomena should correlate highly with one another, but not with measures of theoretically unrelated or irrelevant phenomena. When different measures of the same phenomenon fail to correlate, or when the measures correlate poorly with measures of other phenomena to which they are supposedly linked, or correlate well with measures of concepts to which they are supposedly unrelated, then one must be skeptical about either the validity of measurement, the appropriateness of the conceptualization, or both.

Fifth are *questions of causal inference.* These ask how clearly has research demonstrated the cause-and-effect relationships that the theory's propositions imply? To establish a causal relationship between variables, it is necessary to show that the variables are associated (or covary), that the supposed cause (or independent variable) in fact occurs before the supposed effect (or dependent variable), and that the observed association between the two is not actually attributable to the influence of some third variable. When a correlation is found to be the result of a third variable's influence, the correlation is said to be spurious. For example, in the past some studies employing police statistics found social class to be correlated with juvenile delinquency. But it now seems likely that the correlation was spurious, the result of police practices that made it more probable that lower status offenders' crimes would be detected and recorded.

Ideally, research would control for the effects of all the relevant variables except those whose relationships are being considered. But as Campbell (1957) has demonstrated, complete control is impossible to attain even in true experimental designs. The suspected influence of uncontrolled third variables is therefore a prime source of rival hypotheses. However, to question causal hypotheses constructively, more than a suspicion is required. One must say as precisely as possible which third variables need to be controlled and why they are relevant. Some variables are specific to particular research problems and so need to be taken account of only in special cases. The phases of the moon, for instance, might be pertinent to investigations of the effects of illumination on social behavior, but are irrelevant to most studies. However, other variables so commonly affect behavior that failure to control for their possible influence is nearly an automatic reason to question research findings. For example, Campbell (1957) has shown the need to control for the effects of history (or the larger events, such as wars and elections, that transpire during the research), maturation (or natural changes associated with the passage of time), and testing (or the very act of research itself).

Sixth are *questions of generalizability.* These ask how far and with what degree of accuracy can the empirical findings pertinent to the theory be generalized beyond the particular situations that have been investigated? To frame these questions precisely, one must examine both the research samples and the universes or populations from which these samples were drawn. (For instance, were the subjects volunteers from college classes or a randomly drawn sample of the members of a community?) It should then be asked whether the sampled universe is appropriate to the theory being considered (a theory of humankind's propensity for violence that is based on data for men only would be questionable, for example) and how well does the sample represent the universe that it taps (thus, a sample of male members of pacifist organizations would be a biased sample of males as well as of humankind)? Finally, a method-related question asks whether the experience of participating in the study may have affected subjects in such a way that they may no longer be regarded as representing the population that they were selected to represent. If the mere act of being recruited as respondents in a criminal victimization survey heightened people's awareness of crime as a social problem, for instance, and if this greater concern affected their responses, then the survey would be of questionable generalizability to the uninterviewed population.

Finally, there are *questions of theoretical realism.* Most social scientists agree that the long-range goal of social research is "to develop theories which 'work' in the real world of complex, overlapping social relationships" (Leik, 1972, p. 11). Yet all research involves simplification, both in observing and theorizing about the social world. Even the most meticulous ethnographers observe selectively and edit their descriptions of social life. And social scientists who build and test theories simplify even more, deliberately narrowing their observational and conceptual focus to sharpen the view. It is impossible to observe and record everything, and, even if we could, we would not know what it all meant. Similarly, without becoming hopelessly complicated, no theory can include all the concepts that might possibly aid our understanding. "Put simply, the basic problem faced in all sciences is that of how much to oversimplify reality" (Blalock, 1964, p. 8). The necessity of simplification is undeniable, but nonetheless it is legitimate to ask how has that inevitable simplification affected the resulting theories' realism?

## An Assessment of Four Research Styles

The methods of fieldwork, survey research, experimentation, and nonreactive research are the means at hand to answer the skeptic's questions. Each of these different types of method promises to answer a few of these questions quite well, but none promises to answer all with equal ease and certainty. An assessment of the four research styles also reveals that, in fact, none fully lives up to its promises.

To qualify as a scientifically useful mode of inquiry, a research method must, at the minimum, be able to address questions of measurement and theoretical adequacy by providing the information needed to measure variables and test hypotheses. Each of the four types of methods does that. However, none of the methods can provide the data required to measure all the variables and test all the hypotheses that might possibly be pertinent to determining a theory's validity. Rather, each type gives access to some variables and hypotheses while failing to give access to others.

Fieldwork, for example, gives access to variables and hypotheses that pertain to relatively confined natural social settings, such as communities and organizations, but fails to give access to those that pertain either to past eras or to large contemporary populations (for instance, hypotheses about national public opinion). Surveys can provide information about such populations but only about topics on which respondents are able and willing to report verbally. Experiments, by contrast, can study nonverbal behavior but are generally limited by ethical and practical constraints to relatively low-impact variables and hypotheses. (For instance, few experimenters would condone, and few subjects would agree to join, experimental studies of homicide.) Finally, the nonreactive approach is in principle widely applicable, but it is in fact limited on the one hand to variables and hypotheses for which appropriate naturally occurring data (such as historical records) can be found, and on the other hand to those for which ethical opportunities for unobtrusive observation exist.

Fieldwork promises realistic theories that do justice to the complexity of actual social life. It is distinguished from other styles of research by the fact that the fieldworker personally enters natural social groups and settings and studies them, as far as possible, in their full and natural state. In studying these groups and settings, fieldworkers often employ multiple data-collecting techniques. For example, participant observation, informant interviewing, surveys of group members, and analyses of documents and records are often combined. However, these different techniques are usually adapted to the basic stylistic strategy. Thus, techniques such as experimental manipulation and control that would alter the natural flow of events, a survey of the larger population rather than of the particular group's members, or an analysis of historical records pertaining to groups other than the one being studied, are generally avoided on the grounds that they would either interfere with or be irrelevant to the fieldwork strategy, even though they might be highly pertinent to the wider theoretical problem. Nevertheless, fieldwork is inherently (if not quite fully) multimethod and derives its strength as much from its flexibility in data collecting as from its unique strategy of observing natural events firsthand.

Most field research focuses on only one or a few groups, or upon a relatively small sample of individuals. This frees resources and also allows fieldworkers to develop not only an inside knowledge of the group but also the necessary rapport with subjects to conduct intensive multifaceted studies. However, this small scale also leads to questions about the representativeness of fieldwork's findings and whether so few cases can provide a broad enough basis for testing as well as forming hypotheses. Fieldwork's emphasis on observing natural sequences of events precludes the use of experimental techniques, and its small case base precludes some statistical modes of causal analysis as well. Finally, fieldworkers' close contact with subjects always raises questions about the researchers' influence on events and about subjects' reactions to the researchers' presence.

Survey research promises high generalizability. The survey strategy of statistically sampling populations permits survey researchers to say with a known degree of confidence how well a particular sample of subjects represents the population from which it was drawn. A theory built and tested with survey data, therefore, has a better known range of applicability as to subjects (or other units of sampling) than one based upon nonsurvey data. However, the generalizability of survey data is purchased at the price of results that are often questionable in other ways. First, most surveys rely upon highly structured verbal reports, either questionnaires or fixed-choice interviews. This leaves little room for maneuvering into areas of social life about which respondents are unwilling or unable to report accurately, or that have a structure as yet unknown to the investigator. Second, surveys always involve a high risk of reactive measurement effects. And third, although sophisticated techniques of statistical analysis can often be applied to make causal inferences from survey data, the absence of experimental control over supposed independent variables, and the fact that most surveys are cross-sectional rather than being conducted over time, complicates the task of distinguishing correlations between variables from truly causal relationships.

Experimentation, more than other styles of research, promises clear causal inferences. Its strategy is to manipulate exposure to an hypothesized cause while controlling for the contaminating influence of other possible causes by the use of control groups and by the random assignment of subjects to control and of experimental situations. These arrangements are intended to maximize "internal validity," which means confidence that the independent variable did in fact "make some significant difference in this specific instance" (Campbell, 1957) and that the observed effects are not really the result of some uncontrolled and perhaps unknown variable that is the true cause. However, to gain causal clarity, experiments must frequently sacrifice realism and generalizability to nonexperimental populations and situations (or "external validity"). Furthermore, although it is possible to design experimental controls for many types of testing and measurement effects, the risk of such effects is high.

Finally, nonreactive research, which employs the strategy of searching out naturally occurring data and opportunities for unobtrusive observation, promises freedom from the reactive sources of error that threaten the other styles. The investigator plays neither an active nor an overt role in eliciting information from subjects. Instead, the subjects themselves generate the data while acting as normal members of society, rather than as participants in social research. However, the passivity that the style imposes on the researcher precludes much of the flexibility, precision of generalization, and control over the conditions of causal inference that the other styles afford. The nonreactive researcher is in much the same methodological straits as the spy, with the added restraints of ethics and the law.

None of these four styles of research can fully deliver on its promises. For example, fieldwork's realism is restricted by its small scale, which makes it difficult for fieldworkers to examine the complexities of larger social structures. The ability of survey research to generalize is limited by the ability to define theoretically relevant populations that can readily be sampled and questioned. The causal clarity of experimental research ends when there are confounding influences present that cannot be eliminated by control and randomization. And nonreactive studies' freedom from reactive measurement effects can never be taken for granted. Even in historical research, the possibility exists that the documents, statistics, etc., that comprise the historical record have been altered or edited in anticipation of scrutiny.

## The Multimethod Approach: A Fifth Research Style

The four research styles that we have just assessed represent the conventional methodological options for theoretical inquiry. The multimethod approach, which is in effect a fifth style, provides an additional option: the possibility of employing not just one type of method per study but instead a strategically selected set of methods. As the following considerations suggest, this approach has a number of advantages for theoretically oriented research.

First, theories do not respect conventional methodological boundaries, nor should they be required to do so. For instance, a single theory may predict or explain observed patterns of behavior, frequency distributions of attitudes in large populations, particular experimental effects, and events from earlier historical eras. To assess fully the validity of the theory, these different kinds of predictions, explanations, and variables should be studied, even if the studies require different types of research methods. The strongest confirmation of a theory comes, after all, from research that studies numerous and varied hypotheses and employs multiple measures of the theoretical concepts involved. The employment of multiple research methods adds to the strength of the evidence.

Second, almost any theoretical problem of importance is the subject of repeated investigations. The continuing nature of theoretical inquiry most often involves methodological replication—applying the same type of method in successive studies. However, the very fact that a particular type of method has been used before, and especially its repeated use, may be a good reason to use a different type of method in a new study. For example, Webb et al. (1966) were particularly concerned that the many advantages of survey research might cause researchers to overrely upon this one type of method, thereby making social research especially vulnerable to the kinds of reactive errors and content and population restrictions associated with interviews and questionnaires. They suggested greater use of nonreactive methods in conjunction with surveys as a corrective. Nonreactive methods are no freer than other types of research methods from general sources of error. But as one component of a multimethod design, nonreactive methods are especially useful because of their relative freedom from the specific sources of reactive error that threaten other methods.

It is instructive to note that Webb et al. (1996) urged greater use of nonreactive methods at about the same time as some other social scientists were urging the use of criminal victimization surveys as a corrective for overreliance upon flawed archival police data in the study of crime. The lessons here are clear: (1) Overreliance upon any one type of method, no matter how great its advantages in other respects, is problematic because it fails to guard against the specific sources of error which threaten that method; and (2) which additional methods to use in multimethod inquiry depends heavily upon which methods have been used previously, with the general rule being: Do something different.

Methodological replications, however, are important, too. Although they entail the risk of monomethod bias, they test the reliability of particular methods and findings, and provide methodological continuity with past work. For this reason, Campbell (1957) has proposed "transition experiments." These are multimethod studies (which may involve methods other than experimentation) that incorporate both a conceptual replication of earlier studies—a study of the same ideas with a different type of method—and a methodological replication. The conceptual replication guards against the threat to validity of monomethod bias, whereas the methodological replication serves to test the reliability of earlier findings and establishes a contemporary benchmark against which to compare the findings from the conceptual replication. Transition studies are especially appropriate if considerable time has elapsed between the current research and the studies being replicated. In that event, failure to replicate the earlier findings might be attributable to substantive social change in the interval between studies rather than to either unreliability (in the case of methodological replication) or the use of a different research method (in the case of conceptual replication). Transition studies help to sort out these different interpretations by providing a comparison between the two types of replication as well as a comparison with past studies.

Third, realism, generalizability, accurate causal inference, and freedom from reactive error are all desirable research objectives. However, if different types of research methods are relatively specialized with respect to these objectives, as the foregoing assessment of methods suggests, then there is good reason to doubt that inquiries that rely solely upon one type of research method will be able to accomplish all the objectives equally well. And indeed, perhaps the most common criticisms of social research are that nonfield studies tend to be artificial and overly simplified, that nonsurvey research tends to be weak in generalizability, that nonexperimental research lacks causal precision, and that reactive methods are prone to reactive error and are restricted to cooperative subjects and contemporary events.

To be sure, there are compensatory techniques designed to cope with the inherent limitations of each research style. For example, statistical analysis of survey data is intended to compensate for a survey's lack of experimental control. But for the most part, each style remains preeminent in its strengths. Although nonexperimental researchers, for instance, devise ingenious means of determining whether variable X caused variable Y, or vice versa, experimentalists—as Aronson and Carlsmith (1968) point out—have a simple solution to the problem: "the experimenter knows what caused variable X—he did" (Aronson & Carlsmith, 1968, p. 8).

The skillful use of a single type of method may therefore approximate the strengths of other types of methods, but the results will generally be less compelling than if each type of method were actually employed to do what it promises to do best. Therefore, there are obvious advantages in combining methods that have different but complementary strengths. For instance, one can test an hypothesis both experimentally for causal precision, and also with survey data to determine the generalizability of the hypothesis to the larger nonexperimental population. Because methods are specialized, "we often," as Zelditch (1962) observed, "treat different methods as concretely different types of study rather than as analytically different aspects of the same study" (Zelditch, 1962, p. 576). However, the multimethod approach integrates, at the very concrete level of individual studies and research programs, the various empirical implications of a theory by combining the research methods that are best adapted for studying each empirical implication.

Fourth, although each type of method is relatively stronger than the others in certain respects, none of the four methods is so perfect, even in its area of greatest strength, that it cannot benefit from corroboration by other methods' findings. Nor is any method so imperfect that it cannot provide some degree of corroboration even in areas of relative weakness. For instance, Blalock (1964) has suggested the usefulness for clarifying causal inferences of supplementing experimental with nonexperimental studies because "the same confounding influences are less likely to be operating in both studies" (Blalock, 1964, p. 131).

Sieber (1973) has also illustrated the principle that relatively strong methods can be aided by relatively weak methods and vice versa. He has demonstrated that survey research can contribute to fieldwork by helping to establish the generality of field observations, but that fieldwork may likewise cross-check a survey's accuracy by means of informant interviews. This contribution can be especially valuable in the event of low survey response rates. The generalizability of survey results depends not only upon the sampling techniques but also upon respondents' willingness to cooperate. If respondents fail to respond, then the researchers must question the survey's findings because those respondents who fail to answer may be significantly different from those who do. Informant interviews can check the inferences made from low response surveys. Sieber has also demonstrated that although fieldwork can improve the realism of surveys by providing empirically grounded theoretical frameworks for survey research, surveys can likewise improve upon fieldwork's theoretical realism. For instance, a survey can aid in guarding against the "holistic fallacy," "a tendency on the part of field observers to perceive all aspects of a social situation as congruent" (Sieber, 1973, p. 1354), whether they are or not.

Fifth, the need for corroboration by different methods is underscored by the fact that very often in social research the ideally appropriate method to study a particular research problem is infeasible. For example, the ideal method for testing causal inferences is experimentation. But practical and ethical constraints so severely limit this method's use that many (probably most) causal hypotheses are not now studied experimentally. Or if they are studied experimentally, the experimenters operationalize their hypotheses in ways that call the realism and generalizability of their results into question, much as when medical researchers experiment with animals rather than humans.

Campbell and Stanley's (1963) discussion of quasiexperiments, and in particular the "patched-up" quasiexperimental design, provides a prototype for multimethod investigations in which none of the feasible methods alone promises very compelling evidence. Like many multimethod tactics, this one involves adopting in a single investigation a procedure that is more often used with independently conducted studies. They demonstrate how one imperfect method may eliminate one or a few plausible rival hypotheses; then how by patching together several such methods in the same project a variety of rival hypotheses may be disposed of, leaving only one hypothesis as the most promising. "The appeal," they write, "is to parsimony. The 'validity' of the experiment becomes one of the credibility of rival theories" (Campbell and Stanley, 1963, p. 36).

In this context, the advice of Webb et al. (1966, pp. 174–175) for selecting research methods seems especially appropriate. They observed that the conventional wisdom about the choice of research methods is to ask which single method will be best-suited for my research problem? They urged that instead we ask "Which set of methods will be best?" And they defined best as a series of methods that "with a reasonable expenditures of resources" will allow us to test the most serious rival hypotheses involved in solving the problem.

Sixth, a research problem's stage of development, either its historic stage in the discipline or the stage in a particular project, is often cited as a rationale for choosing one research method over another. It is usually suggested that as a discipline matures or as a project progresses, problems become more sharply defined and a natural progression of methods occurs: from exploratory field studies and analyses of naturally occurring data toward increasing use of surveys and experiments to verify theories. In fact, however, inquiry is not as unidirectional as this model implies. Research is rarely so orderly, either in disciplines or individual projects, that exploration is required only at the beginning and verification only at the end. There are usually impressions that need to be checked and assessed accurately at the outset, and surprising findings to be explained and explored in the aftermath. Nor are these methods so specialized that they can be applied only in a given phase of research. For example, Sieber (1973) has demonstrated the mutual benefits of integrating field and survey methods in both exploratory and verificational phases of research.

Finally, employing different types of methods helps to guard against and to correct for inherent methodological biases, either for or against certain types of theories. In obvious but also more subtle ways, research methods can shape the types of theories that we build, and even the outcomes of our tests. For example, it has often been suggested that surveys tend to favor atomistic social theories by focusing upon statistically drawn samples of individual respondents rather than upon intact social groups and the cultural context, as fieldwork does. However, Sieber (1973) has suggested that fieldwork might be biased toward holistic theories, owing to its roots in anthropological studies of small, isolated, and so relatively homogeneous communities.

Experiments and surveys may also involve biases toward different kinds of theories. Experiments strongly imply the possibility of strong cause-and-effect relationships between phenomena because true experimental design does everything possible to make such relationships evident if they are present. By contrast, a survey study of the relationships between those same variables in a natural population may also hypothesize cause and effect, but survey techniques do nothing to make causation more evident than it naturally is in that population, thereby usually implying a much weaker causal theory. In these ways, methods may heavily influence the likelihood that one type of theory rather than another will be formulated and may well influence the probability that a theory will ultimately be accepted or rejected.

# Three

## Formulating Research Problems

R esearch problems are questions that indicate gaps in the scope or the certainty of our knowledge. They point either to problematic phenomena, observed events that are puzzling in terms of our currently accepted ideas, or to problematic theories, current ideas that are challenged by new hypotheses. This chapter first looks at the role of such questions in the research process, and especially the ongoing debate among social scientists as to when and how problems should be formulated. Second, we consider methodology's effect on defining problems and how the multimethod approach can be used to focus research more sharply upon the substance of research problems. Finally, we consider the role of theory in problem formulation and how the multimethod approach integrates theory and research more closely in posing these research questions.

## The Role of Research Problems in the Research Process

The problems of everyday life are difficulties to be avoided, if possible. Research problems are eagerly sought after. The difference is that research problems represent opportunities as well as trouble spots. Because scientific knowledge is provisional, all empirical findings and theories are in principle problematic and are, therefore, subject to further investigation. But in addition to seeking more exact confirmations of existing claims to knowledge, research has the equally important goal of generating new claims. Problem formulation is the logical first step toward this goal. As Northrop (1966) writes, "Inquiry starts only when something is unsatisfactory, when traditional beliefs are inadequate or in question, when the facts necessary to resolve one's uncertainties are not known, when the likely relevant hypotheses are not even imagined. What one has at the beginning of inquiry is merely the problem" (p. 17).

The formulation of research problems also has an important social function. As Merton, Broom, and Cottrell (1959) suggest, researchers must justify the demands for attention and other scarce resources that research makes: "In conferring upon the scientist the right to claim that a question deserves the concerted attention of others as well as himself, the social institution of science exacts the obligation that he justify the claim" (p. xix). Achieving significant research results is perhaps the most powerful justification for such claims, but this type of justification can be offered only after the fact and only in the event that the research is successful. A compelling research problem, by contrast, must marshal support in advance of research and, if it is sufficiently compelling, can even sustain that support through the sometimes fruitless periods that researchers experience.

However, despite research problems' logical priority in inquiry, and their importance as a priori justifications, a problem's formulation, as John Dewey stresses, is in fact a "progressive" matter. Dewey means that problem formulations are themselves problematic and so require continual attention to assure that the questions being asked will direct research toward the desired end: "If we assume, prematurely, that the problem involved is definite and clear, subsequent inquiry proceeds on the wrong track. Hence the question arises; How is the formation of a genuine problem so controlled that further inquiries will move toward a solution?" (quoted by Northrop, 1966, p. 13).

## When and How to Formulate Problems: A Debate

It sometimes seems that there is little about which social scientists agree, and the most effective procedure for formulating research problems is no exception. In particular, there has been considerable debate over whether or not it is important to define problems explicitly in advance of research and to show how they are linked to prior work. Many social scientists hold that research problems should be formulated by carefully analyzing as much of the relevant research literature as possible, formally stating the problem and the major hypotheses that the literature suggests, and only then collecting the data. Their intention is to give research a clear and firm justification and to encourage hypothesis testing. This will ensure that each new study does its utmost to add in an orderly fashion to the sum of knowledge. However, there are many other social scientists who are equally convinced that this style of formulating problems tends to stifle questions and prevent discoveries that a more open-ended approach might stimulate.

This latter group argues instead for letting problems and hypotheses emerge throughout the research process, pushed forth by new empirical observations that encourage the researcher to ask new questions and build new theories. For example, Schatzman and Strauss (1973) write:

> The automatic use of formally stated hypotheses, and of statements of "the problem" may make it easier to program action, but it will also limit the kinds of experience that he (the researcher) will tolerate and deal with. In original research there is less likely to be a conceptual closure to inquiry, for as the work of discovery continues and new kinds of data are conceptualized, new problems and hypotheses will emerge. Consequently far from putting a closure on his new experience the researcher will modify his problem and hypotheses—if indeed he ever stated them explicitly—arrange to handle new ones simultaneously with the old, or do so in serial order. This is how the relationship between the observer and the observed object is altered, and how it becomes possible for new questions to be asked and answered through research. (pp. 12–13)

Stating the problem early and in a highly structured form may indeed lock the researcher into a fixed stance with respect to the situation being observed, and it may also block the emergence of new ideas that might be stimulated by new experience. But open-endedness may have costs as well. For instance, Huber (1973) argues that letting the emergent features of each new research situation continually exert pressure to redefine problems and hypotheses tends to bias the emerging theory in the direction of the status quo. It gives undue weight to the particular situation being studied at the moment, diverts attention from the problems posed by other theories, and interferes with theory-testing because the same data obviously cannot be used both to form and to test an hypothesis. In this view, prestated problems and hypotheses do much more than make it "easier to program action" (as Schatzman and Strauss [1973] suggest). They discipline research in the interest of testing theory, accumulating knowledge, and achieving a theoretical standpoint independent of the time and place in which researchers presently find themselves.

## Overcoming Methodological Constraints on Problem Formulation

Both sides in the foregoing debate clearly have merit. However, in practice the decision as to when and how research problems should be defined usually depends less upon the perceived merits of one or the other of these procedures than upon the research style selected. Methods differ in their abilities to predict the kinds, quantities, and quality of the data that may be available in any given instance. For example, survey researchers or experimentalists can usually say with more certainty than fieldworkers whether or not the data pertinent to a particular research problem can be readily collected. Fieldwork offers the possibility of many data sources, but it is usually hard to say in advance which data will actually be obtainable. Similarly, Selltiz, Jahoda, Deutsch, and Cook (1959) note the need to take a "wait-and-see" attitude in the use of nonreactive data sources such as statistical records: "The use of such data demands a capacity to ask many different questions related to a research problem. . . . The guiding principle for the use of available statistics consists in keeping oneself flexible with respect to the form in which the research questions are asked" (p. 318).

Furthermore, as we will discuss in greater detail in Chapter 4, an empirical search for problems is considerably less expensive with some methods than others. Exploratory experiments and surveys are certainly feasible, but pilot field studies and searches through archives generally cost less, except perhaps for the researcher whose personal expenditure of time and energy usually "fund" such studies. Moreover, discoveries arise in different ways for different methods. Fieldworkers and nonreactive researchers are more likely to make discoveries as a result of finding new data sources and examining new situations; while survey researchers and experimentalists are more likely to make discoveries through innovations in techniques of study design, sampling, or data analysis, which can generate unexpected (serendipitous) findings by more precise tests of hypotheses.

Different research styles thus exert different constraints on formulating problems: open-ended constraints in response to the immediate research situation for fieldwork and nonreactive research or more programmed constraints for surveys and experiments. The multimethod strategy provides the opportunity to overcome these methodological constraints upon problem formulation and thereby gain the advantages of each approach while compensating for its disadvantages.

Sieber (1973), for example, notes Stinchcombe's (1964) reliance upon about six months of fieldwork among the teachers and administrators in a high school to formulate the hypotheses that guided Stinchcombe's analysis of survey data from the same school. Sieber (1973) concludes that "an optimal schedule for theoretical survey research would include a lengthy period of fieldwork prior to the survey" (p. 1346). He further observes that although he could find in the literature few other examples of this practice of deriving a survey's guiding theory from fieldwork, it may be quite common, since "Often, only passing acknowledgment is made of prior personal familiarity with the situation, a familiarity that has produced rather definite ideas for research" (p. 1345). Sieber (1973) cites, for instance, Lipset's (1964) autobiographical account of how the childhood experience of his father's membership in the International Typographical Union, along with the classic works of Robert Michels and Alexis de Tocqueville, influenced the research problem that Lipset and his colleagues formulated and tested in the classic survey study, *Union Democracy* (1956). If, as Dewey suggested, the correct formulation of research problems is crucial to their solution, then it is critical that no source of potentially valid information—no matter how "unscientific" it may seem—be ignored.

Furthermore, Sieber (1973) demonstrates how despite "an historical antagonism between proponents of qualitative fieldwork and survey research," integration between these two research styles has been achieved in numerous studies (p. 1335). He shows how fieldwork has been employed to define the theoretical structure of problems later studied in surveys, to define and gain greater knowledge of the problem-relevant populations for surveys, and to reformulate problems by aiding in the interpretation of surprising survey findings and statistical relationships between variables. He likewise shows how surveys have been used to define and pinpoint relevant cases for fieldwork, to verify and establish the generality of field observations, and to cast new light on "hitherto inexplicable or misinterpreted" observations.

## Generating Versus Verifying Theories

The issue of when and how to formulate research problems is closely related to another issue: the relative importance of generating new theories versus the verification of existing theories. Both building and testing theories empirically, as Chapter 2 explained, are important research activities, but they serve very different functions in scientific inquiry. Since at least the 1960s, the appropriate balance between these two aspects of research has provoked considerable controversy in the social sciences.

For example, Glaser and Strauss, writing about sociology in 1967, observe: "Verification is the keynote of current sociology. Some three decades ago, it was felt that we had plenty of theories but few confirmations of them—a position made very feasible by the greatly increased sophistication of quantitative methods. As this shift in emphasis took hold, the discovery of new theories became slighted and, at some universities, virtually neglected" (p. 10). Glaser and Strauss (1967) argue that the emphasis on verification of existing theories kept researchers from investigating new problem areas; prevented them from acknowledging the necessarily exploratory nature of much of their work, encouraged instead the inappropriate use of verificational logic and rhetoric; and discouraged the development and use of systematic empirical procedures for generating as well as testing theories. To compensate for the overemphasis upon verification, Glaser and Strauss urged that research designed to build empirically "grounded" theories must be recognized as a legitimate social scientific pursuit independent of verification. They saw no necessary logical conflict between empirically building and testing theories. But they felt that the social and the psychological conflicts "reflecting the opposition between a desire to *generate* theory and a trained need to *verify* it" (p. 2) were so strong that clear designation of theory building as a proper research goal was essential: "when generating [theory] is not clearly recognized as the main goal of a given research, it can be quickly killed by the twin critiques of accurate evidence and verified hypotheses" (p. 28).

If we accept that generating theories empirically is not a substitute for empirical verification, then building theories without immediate regard for testing poses no special logical problems. However, it may complicate matters methodologically. One serious complication is that theories are often built empirically using research methods that are different from the methods required to verify them.

Each style of social research can be employed either to generate or to verify theories. But in fact, purely generational studies tend to rely more upon fieldwork or nonreactive data sources than upon experiments or surveys, and often more upon qualitative than upon quantitative observation and analysis. The transition from generational to verificational research may therefore involve a methodological shift as well as a change in the focus of problem formulation. As Chapter 2 suggested, studying a theory with different research methods provides an opportunity for fuller examination of that theory. However, employing a new or different method also creates difficulties. It may be far from obvious how, for instance, concepts and propositions developed through qualitative field studies may be measured and operationalized in terms suitable for quantitative surveys or experiments—or vice versa, how to design a field study to test a theory deriving from surveys or experiments. There may also be questions about the appropriateness of the new method to the theory's content, or about whether or not operational hypotheses that can be tested with that method do in fact adequately represent the theory and so provide a fair and full test.

Bernstein, Kelly, and Doyle (1977) encountered these kinds of difficulties in formulating and testing hypotheses derived from symbolic interactionist theories of deviance. These were theories that had been generated largely in qualitative field studies. Bernstein et al.'s strategy was to combine qualitative field observation with quantitative analysis of interviews and court records collected for a larger sample of criminal defenders. This multimethod approach, which is an example of the transition study described in Chapter 2, allowed them to use the fieldwork data to aid in both the design and the interpretation of the survey and archival segment of their study. The approach also permitted them to be open and sensitive to the kinds of firsthand field observations that had prompted the initial theories. They thereby retained descriptive realism without sacrificing either the quantitative precision required for verification or the generalizability provided by their larger sample.

## The Empirical Unfolding of Research Problems

Once a study is published, it is in many ways irrelevant whether the research problem prompted the study or instead emerged from it. With publication, the study's problem enters the public domain and becomes the responsibility not only of the study's author but of all who are professionally interested in that research area. At that point, the key issue is what to do with the problem next. Research into a problem does not end with a single study. Nor is there truly a final formulation of a problem any more than there is a final solution. All research, as Chapter 2 suggested, involves some simplification of the problem being investigated. This is unavoidable given the limitations on our resources, theories, and methods. However, each of a discipline's separate new studies, or each phase of study in an individual's research program, reveals new aspects of the problem by addressing issues (such as those raised by the "skeptic's questions" in Chapter 2) that earlier research could not address.

The two modes of formulating research problems that we have just discussed differ in that one looks to past studies while the other looks to ongoing work. But the two are similar in that both rely upon empirical inquiry rather than upon nonempirical procedures, such as speculation or the purely logical analysis of ideas. This means that whether research problems emerge from current research or instead derive from earlier work, research methods are directly implicated in the process. Every empirically based research problem has a methodological as well as a substantive component, and this methodological component may equally influence our perceptions as to which particular phenomena and theories are problematic. One of the central questions to be posed, therefore, is how do the methods employed in research directly affect the formulation of research problems?

## The Substantive Importance of Methodology

Deutscher (1966), for example, posed this question of methodological influence by revealing one of the major simplifications of social policy research conducted through the early 1960s. He noted the very heavy reliance upon survey research at that time and suggested that this reliance upon surveys led social scientists to oversimplify research problems by assuming that verbal responses reflect behavioral tendencies. Deutscher observed that only by making this assumption were researchers, who were studying issues such as racial and ethnic discrimination, able to make causal inferences about behavior solely on the basis of questionnaire and interview data. However, he stressed that this assumption neglected a central problem that had begun to emerge from exploratory field studies as early as the 1930s: People's words and deeds frequently do not agree. To correct this oversimplification, Deutscher urged both that this neglected problem of "attitude versus action" must be formulated more systematically and that a new research technology, a multimethod approach, must be developed to capture both attitudinal and behavioral aspects of policy problems.

The problem of attitude versus action is now a major topic of multi-method research. But when Deutscher addressed this problem in 1966, the topic was relatively unexplored. New areas of inquiry, where little is presumably yet known, promise productive research problems. However, the actual formulation of the problems may be more difficult than in more developed areas in which consistent bodies of empirical generalizations and theories have already been established. This became evident when Deutscher (1966) set about formulating the problem of attitude versus action:

> We still do not know much about the relationship between what people say and what they do—attitudes and behavior, sentiments and acts, verbalizations and interactions, words and deeds. *We know so little that I can't even find an adequate vocabulary to make the distinction!* Under what conditions do they say one thing and behave exactly the opposite? In spite of the fact that all of these combinations have been observed and reported few efforts have been made to order these observations. (p. 242)

As research into a problem proceeds with researchers posing it in different ways, the problem ideally (as Dewey implied) unfolds to reveal new dimensions that facilitate the problem's solution. The variety of available research methods is a key element in this process in that it provides researchers with a multifaceted empirical view of the phenomena and of the theories in question. This enables researchers to formulate problems in a manner that does greater justice both to the complexity of social phenomena and to the complex implications of our theories. For example, Chapter 1 demonstrated how the variety of methods now employed to measure crime led to a more discriminating conceptualization of the phenomenon of criminal deviance. And Chapter 2 illustrated how the employment of multiple methods allows researches to consider more fully a theory's empirical implications.

However, employing a variety of methods also complicates the process of problem formulation because different types of research methods very often provide conflicting answers to the same research questions. For example, Deutscher (1966) found the problem of attitude versus action to be complicated by the fact that experimental studies generally reported greater consistency between subjects' words and deeds than did observational field studies. When such methodologically linked contradictions appear in the course of a problem's development, the suspicion is that they may derive from theoretically irrelevant characteristics of the different methods employed rather than from the substantive complexity of the problem. Inconsistent findings require reformulations of research problems. When these inconsistencies reflect unanticipated substantive complexity, then concepts and propositions must be recast to take account of that complexity. But although more complicated theories are sometimes necessary to achieve theoretical realism, simplicity is preferable. And if, in fact, contradictory research findings are attributable to methodological influences and can be shown to be consistent with existing theories, once those influences have been taken into account, so much the better.

The substance of social life is certainly diverse enough to generate inconsistent findings, but the methods of social research are also diverse. Only by analyzing the methods employed to obtain research findings can it be determined which source of inconsistency any given set of findings reflects. For example, Hovland (1959) observed that textbooks summarizing the effects of communication on opinion-change in the 1950s often reported substantive contradictions in research findings without regard to differences in methodology, despite the fact that stronger effects were generally found in experiments than in surveys. However, Hovland found that upon closer inspection these apparent contradictions might be explained in terms of the idiosyncrasies of these two different types of methods and might not require new theoretical explanations. In sum, although the exclusive use of a single type of research method can oversimplify research problems, the use of different types of research methods, without systematic comparisons of their results and an understanding of possible methodological influences, can make problems appear to be more complex—or complex in different ways—than they really are.

## Research Questions Stemming From Multimethod Research

Multimethod research can help in sorting out substantive and methodological issues. But not even this approach can provide totally method-free results. No research style can do that; *what* we know is always shaped in part by *how* we came to know it. Multimethod studies may be expected, therefore, to spawn as well as to aid in answering research questions. A major problem is how to proceed with inquiry once it has been discovered that two or more methods' findings diverge. As we said in Chapter 1, convergent results from different methods increase confidence in each method, but contradictory results call for reanalysis of the methods, both in relation to one another and in relation to the original research problem. (We shall see in Chapters 6 and 7 that under some circumstances convergent findings also raise questions, but it is best to examine one source of problems at a time.)

When contrasting different methods' results, there are two general classes of potential research questions that emerge in particular. The first is whether quite different styles of research really study the same phenomenon in anything but name. The second is whether different variants of the same research style will yield the same results. Let us consider the types of potential research problems that emerge from multimethod research in connection with these two issues.

In Chapter 1, we saw that crime data from official statistics and from criminal victimization surveys might measure quite different aspects of criminal deviance. Hindelang, Hirschi, and Weis (1979) have considered still another survey method of measuring crime (the self-report method), which has also often been found to give results different from those obtained with official statistics. They find that many of the apparent discrepancies may stem from a failure to recognize that these two methods may tap quite different domains of crime (trivial versus major crimes), which may have quite different social correlates.

The self-report method of measuring crime, most commonly used to measure juvenile delinquency, calls upon respondents to report their own offenses rather than offenses committed against them, as in criminal victimization surveys. The method is essentially a technique for estimating delinquency in nondelinquent populations; that is, among juveniles not officially labeled as deviant by arrest or conviction. It provides data to study possible correlates of self-reported delinquent behavior, irrespective of whether or not that behavior was previously identified in official data sources, which are often suspected of measuring official action more nearly than deviance. With self-report data it is possible to estimate how (if at all) social factors such as gender, race, or social class are related to delinquent behavior, when the possibly contaminating influences of official detection and recording practices are eliminated.

Self-report studies, like criminal victimization surveys, were intended to resolve the crime-measurement problem. But the result was quite different. Instead of confirming the findings of earlier methods, the self-report studies often produced divergent findings. For example, Tittle, Villemez, and Smith (1978) report that in 35 studies of the relationship between social class and crime, those studies conducted before 1964 (using self-report data) consistently show no relationship, while those using official data show a negative relationship; and that in studies done after 1964 no relationship between class and crime was found in either type of study. These findings led Tittle et al. (1978) to conclude that the often assumed relationship between social class and crime was a myth, probably based upon the tendency for police data to overreport the crimes of lower class offenders.

However, Hindelang et al. (1979) argue that the discrepancies between the two types of studies may themselves be an illusion, largely reflecting the tendency for self-report measures to include many more minor offenses than do measures of delinquency based upon official statistics—trivial offenses that may in principle be chargeable but in fact are "almost by definition outside the domain of behavior that elicits official attention" (p. 996). Their argument underscores the point, made earlier with respect to uncoordinated single-method studies, that methodological diversity may create an impression of contradiction and inconsistency where none exists. But their argument suggests a second equally important point: Special care must also be taken in designing multimethod investigations to ensure that convergence between different methods' findings will be evident if it is present, not masked by incomparable data.

To bolster confidence that convergent findings are not the result of the methods' shared biases, the multimethod strategy calls for methods whose weaknesses differ. But to make convergence as evident and as likely as possible, the multimethod strategy also calls for methods whose strengths coincide in relation to the research problem. If methods fail to complement one another, then divergent findings have problematic significance, as Hindelang et al. (1979) suggest in the case of self-report studies. "Regardless of how often it is said that self-reports measure primarily trivial offenses . . . it is easy to forget that they do. Self-report offenses are routinely treated as equivalent to official offenses in comparing correlates of delinquency. . . . When the results using the two criteria are inconsistent, it seems to follow that one or both measurement procedures is faulty. An alternative interpretation remains: it may be simply inappropriate to compare the correlates of trivial and serious offenses" (p. 997). They conclude that "explicit attention to seriousness and content issues across methods must precede comparisons of their results" (p. 1010).

Dunaway, Cullen, Burton, and Evans (2000) have done more research specifically designed to help clarify these issues. They conducted a self-report mail survey of the general population aged 18 and over living in an urban area in the Midwest, inquiring about serious crimes (including violence) as well as lesser offenses. Their study thus focused on adults rather than juveniles and a fuller range of offenses than covered in earlier studies of juvenile delinquency. They describe their effort as follows: "The goal of the current study has been to add an additional piece to solving the class-crime puzzle. In particular, we offer the conclusions that among the general adult population social class appears to be weakly related to involvement in self-reported criminality, but that evidence exists to suggest that that this relationship is specified by race and type of crime (violence)" (p. 611). However, they recognize that no single study such as theirs will resolve the empirical issues. And they urge that in "the under researched area of adult crime, we may need carefully designed, sustained research on class that uses multiple methods across diverse samples" (p. 611). But they suggest also that the current state of the research, unresolved as many issues may be, presents a theoretical problem that needs to be addressed: "those researchers wishing to construct class-based theories of crime must confront why class position, even if related to serious crime, is only modestly implicated in the causation of less serious offenses" (p. 620).

Brannon, Cyphers, Hesse, Hesselbart, Keane, Schuman, Viccaro, and Wright (1973) pick up the problem of "attitude versus action" as it stood in the early 1970s. They note that most studies at that time had reported either negative or mixed relationships between what people say and do. But they also note that these studies had not "concentrated on the validity of typical survey questions in general populations." They carefully observe that although this failure does not invalidate the evidence from the earlier studies, it does leave us "uncertain of their implications for the validity of standard cross-section attitude surveys" (p. 625). Their remedy was to pose their questions about substance and method jointly and to design a multimethod study in which a typical attitude question on the important social policy issue of "open housing" was embedded in a larger survey. The survey was then followed three months later by a field experiment designed to test respondents' willingness to act in a manner consistent with their earlier expressed attitudes. Brannon et al. (1973) report an overall high level of consistency between the survey responses and the later experimental findings. However, they conclude not simply that "attitudes and actions are consistent" but rather they use their findings as the basis for stating three hypotheses to explain why *in this instance* attitudes and actions were found to coincide.

The study by Brannon et al. (1973), like Hindelang et al. (1979), in addition to illustrating how to develop specific multimethod research questions, illustrates an important general point about multimethod research. Generic labels for research methods, such as those that we introduced in Chapter 2, conceal a great deal of species variation among the actual research techniques that compose the style designated by each label (fieldwork, survey research, etc.). For example, a *survey* may refer either to a questionnaire study of a convenient sample of college students conducted by a faculty member in a college classroom or to an interview study conducted by a team of paid interviewers in the households of a cross-sectional sample of a city's population. (Similarly, Campbell and Stanley [1963] have demonstrated the variety of "experiments.") Broad classifications of methods are useful for purposes of general discussion, and they are important to the analysis of research when they designate groups of techniques that are thought to have common strengths and weaknesses. But if the labels are used without regard for the underlying variations in techniques, they can easily lead to mistaken inferences. In all cases, it is an empirical question whether the findings from a given form of a method correlate well or poorly with a given form of another method.

## The Role of Theory in Problem Formulation

Theory plays a dual role in research. On the one hand, new theories solve research problems by accounting for unexplained phenomena and by superseding questionable older theories. On the other hand, existing theory guides researchers in formulating research problems. In determining whether and in what respects a phenomenon or a theory is problematic, researchers consider the context of accumulated theoretical as well as empirical knowledge. And only those phenomena and theories that appear to be problematic when viewed in that context are then studied. Ideally, at least, formulating problems in this manner ensures the orderly advance of knowledge because new research is aimed at solving problems left unsolved in past work rather than being aimed at either totally new or theoretically irrelevant problems.

The guiding role of theory in problem formulation is obvious in verificational studies. But while less obvious, it is equally important in exploratory research. To a large degree, preexisting theories define both the territory to be explored in the search for problems and the nature of the new facts one hopes to discover. Of course, opinions differ about how explicit the theoretical background of exploratory research should be. Some recommend spelling it out in nearly as much detail as in verificational research, stating exactly what existing theory leads you to expect and why. Others object to granting existing theory such a directive role and prefer instead to work with general theoretical orientations that sensitize the investigator to important but less precise categories of data. Closure in either the definition of concepts or the statement of hypotheses is avoided in favor of more open "sensitizing concepts" and the "suspension of expectations." In the first view, new problems and hypotheses emerge from the confrontation between old theories and new data, much as in verification. In the second view, new problems and hypotheses emerge from the confrontation between the data and a theoretically oriented and sensitized investigator.

## Decentralized Theorizing and Cumulative Knowledge

In contrast with an earlier time, when Glaser and Strauss (1967) criticized the overemphasis on verification in social research, many social scientists now do their own theorizing in the course of their research, rather than testing others' theories. As Freese (1972) has suggested with respect to sociology, there is now widespread acceptance of two premises: "(1) sociological investigations should consist of constructing and testing theories; and (2) theory construction is not the exclusive province of an intellectual elite, but is the proper responsibility of each sociologist when he defines some social phenomenon as problematic" (p. 473).

If individual researchers are to be their own theoreticians, however, then each must also accept some responsibility for synthesis; otherwise, we risk inundation by idiosyncratic theories that may be firmly grounded in their authors' research but that are of problematic significance in the larger scheme of things. Verificational research, which by its very nature draws upon and feeds back into a larger body of knowledge, is the conventional way in which researchers in the past assumed this responsibility. However, today we need models of synthetic problem formulation for researchers who want instead to generate theories. We, therefore, conclude this chapter with two such models: *paradigmatic pragmatism* and *mixing metaphors,* which take into account both the role of theory and the role of method in defining research problems.

## Paradigmatic Pragmatism

It has become increasingly clear that research methods cannot be assumed a priori to be neutral or atheoretical tools. For example, Walton (1966) demonstrated that the different theories of community power held by political scientists and sociologists might well be a consequence of the fact that researchers in these two disciplines have characteristically studied community power with different types of methods. And Perrucci and Pilisuk (1970) have further shown that the method employed to study community power may not only determine which theory one accepts but may also determine which theories one can formulate and test.

More generally, Ritzer (1980) has posited systematic links between theoretical styles (or paradigms) and research styles (or methods):

> Those who accept the social facts paradigm tend to use questionnaires and/or interviews when they do empirical research. . . . Those who accept the social definition paradigm tend to use the observation method in their research. . . . The choice of methods is, of course, made necessary by the nature of the social definition paradigm. . . . All of the methods discussed in this book *could* be used by the social behaviorist . . . [but] . . . the behaviorist almost invariably uses the experimental method. (pp. 67, 125, 177–178)

However, Platt (1996), in her historical study of sociological methods, has cautioned against assuming tight connections between general theoretical orientations and particular types of method. She concludes that "the link between theory and method has been a loose one. It does not follow that it is insignificant, or equally loose in all cases, but it is clear that we need to look elsewhere to explain both the origins of particular methods and the choice of method made in particular projects" (p. 123).

To the extent that theoretical styles and research styles are systematically linked, it may be expected that researchers will pose problems that are compatible with their own particular theoretical orientations and with the methods linked to those orientations, and will ignore problems that are either theoretically or methodologically incompatible. Specific theories and methods may be associated for at least two reasons. First, certain methods may be better suited for gathering data on specific types or classes of variables, and these variables may in turn suggest certain types or classes of theoretical concepts and propositions more readily than others. Second, certain theories may contain concepts and propositions that imply types or classes of variables that in turn recommend certain methods as being more appropriate than others. Both of these reasons imply that the form in which research problems are initially posed may be shaped by methodological or theoretical commitments, but neither implies any necessary linkage between or limitation by singular methods and singular theories.

And it is also to be expected that researchers working in different theoretical and methodological styles will frequently disagree about the relative importance of particular research problems and even as to whether particular phenomena or theories are problematic. For example, survey researchers who assume a "common understanding" about questionnaire items are often criticized by phenomenologists (e.g., Cicourel, 1962) who regard such understandings as highly problematic. And human ecologists and demographers who study the relationships between resources and population characteristics are criticized by conflict theorists for ignoring concepts and variables pertaining to political power and governmental structures.

Such debates will and should continue until the issues are resolved. However, the pragmatism of employing multiple research methods to study the same general problem by posing different specific questions has some pragmatic implications for social theory. Rather than being wedded to a particular theoretical style, its pet problems and questions, and its most compatible method, one might instead combine methods that would encourage or even require the integration of different theoretical perspectives to interpret the data. If hypotheses and variables that have been previously isolated each within their own theoretical systems are instead empirically interrelated in the same study, then conceptual linkages between different theoretical systems are more likely to follow.

Sandole's (1999) multimethod and multiparadigm study using simulation-generated, archival, and survey data to investigate violent ethnic conflicts in the post cold war era provides a good example of research that tries "to achieve not only the 'normal science' type . . . of *additive cumulation,* whereby one refines and expands what one already knows, but the potentially 'extraordinary science ' type of *additive cumulation . . .* whereby one goes beyond what one already knows, perhaps shifting or combining paradigms in the process" ( p. 192).

## Mixing Metaphors to Generate Research Problems

"A stitch in time gathers no moss" may make little sense as a homily, but if one struggled to make sense of it, then a new meaning or insight might be generated from two common sayings. Mixed metaphors, crossovers of theories, or applications of a theory developed in one sub-field to another may provoke new questions, provide useful insights, and suggest new ways of looking at phenomena. Becker's (1963) work on deviance, for example, can be seen as an application of Mead's (1934) concepts and propositions of identity formation in social psychological development to the area of deviance, as can his application of Hughes' (1960) research on work and occupations to the development of concepts and propositions on "deviant careers." "Night as Frontier" (Melbin, 1978), "Neighborhoods as Fashion," and "Cities as Organisms" are but a few obvious examples of analyses based on the conscious use of metaphorical thinking. Theories of stratification also contain metaphorical concepts related to the physics and chemistry of geology (such as strata, crystallization, and permeable and semipermeable boundaries). And the economist Lester Thurow (1996) has borrowed the geological concept of plate tectonics and combined it with the evolutionary biology concept of punctuated equilibrium to explore the future of capitalism: "Today the world is in a state of punctuated equilibrium—which is being caused by the simultaneous movement of five economic plates. In the end a new game with new rules requiring new strategies will emerge. Some of today's players will adapt and learn how to win in the new game. They will be those who understand the movement of the economic tectonic plates. They will become the top-of-the-food-chain, 'fittest' individuals, business firms, or nations. Historically, they will come to be seen as the economic equivalent of mammals" (p. 8). Early social scientists, of course, also drew heavily on biological or anthropomorphic metaphors—for example, the work of Spencer (1898) and Durkheim (1897/1951). The early Chicago School of Sociology likewise drew heavily upon biological metaphors, especially in its human ecological theories of cities.

The systematic use of metaphorical thinking is closely related to argument by analogy. Analogous thinking requires seeing similarities among disparate entities and asking whether what is known to be true about the one may be generalized to the other. Posing metaphorical questions is not simply a word game, but enters centrally into the social scientist's paradigmatic view of the world, of what is problematic about that world, and of how to conduct empirical research to understand those problems. According to Kuhn (1970), "puzzle solving" is a characteristic of normal science. Rather than employing explicit rules that define problems and their solutions, scientists work by example, analogy, or metaphor, applying exemplars from one situation to another:

> The resultant ability to see a variety of situations as like each other . . . is, I think, the main thing a student acquires by doing exemplary problems . . . After he has completed a certain number, which may vary from one individual to the next, he views the situations that confront him as a scientist in the same gestalt as other members of his specialists' group. (p. 189)

The legitimacy of the use of exemplars or analogies is ultimately based upon the community of practicing scientists accepting such models. For example, biological analogies have been widely accepted within sociology, whereas models from physics have not. *Social physics* was offered by St. Simon as an alternative label to sociology as a name for the discipline, but only a few analogies from physics are to be found in research. One such is Samuel Stouffer's (1940) *gravity model* (inverse square law) that relates the amount of geographical mobility between cities to the distance between them.

New metaphors and new concepts suggest new variables and new methods—new questions and new data to answer them. As in the parable of the blind men and the elephant, the metaphor used to describe a phenomenon (it is *like a snake* said the man holding the trunk, *like a tree* said the one holding a leg, etc.) depends partially upon the aspect of reality one happens to get hold of. But metaphorical depiction of reality is also determined by the method of observation one uses. Hearing an elephant, one might liken it to a trumpeter swan; or tasting a juicy, rare elephant steak, one might liken it to a cow. In short, metaphors are often (some say always) used to define reality, and metaphors are in part measurement and method specific. Mixing metaphors can suggest new questions requiring new methods, and mixing methods can generate new questions leading to new metaphors.

# Four

## Collecting
## Data With
## Multiple Methods

"S cientific observation," Kaplan writes, "is deliberate search, carried out with care and forethought. . . . It is this deliberateness and control of observation that is distinctive of science" (Kaplan, 1964, p. 126). Researchers control the process of observation or data collection by means of both theory and method. Theories determine the kinds of information that are required by defining the phenomena and hypotheses of interest. Methods determine how the necessary information will be obtained by defining appropriate data-collecting procedures. In this chapter, we first consider the different data-collecting procedures employed by different research styles. Second, we consider how multimethod research differs, depending upon whether the primary objective is to obtain information for validation or for exploration. Finally, we analyze different research styles' relative costs and benefits for collecting usable data and consider the costs of multimethod data collecting.

### A Variety of Data-Collecting Methods

Each style of social research has a purpose for which it is particularly well-suited. Fieldwork's purpose is to observe behavior in natural settings in order to construct realistic theories, ideas that "work and fit" (Glaser & Strauss, 1967, p. 3) when applied and tested in the field. Survey methods have been developed chiefly to study population distributions of attitudes, opinions, and reported behaviors, and to form and test hypotheses about the relationships between those kinds of variables. The experimental method, by contrast, is intended specifically to test causal hypotheses. And nonreactive methods have the dual purpose of collecting data unobtrusively to minimize subjects' reactions to being observed and in circumstances that prohibit fieldwork, surveys, or experiments.

To collect data, one must decide upon and gain access to a research site, select and enlist the cooperation of a sample of subjects, devise and apply measurement techniques, and establish and follow a schedule of observation that specifies when, where, for whom, and by whom particular variables are to be measured. To accomplish its special purpose efficiently, each research style treats these four operational requirements of data collecting differently. The particular requirement that is most central to each style's purpose often determines how the other requirements are met.

For instance, to achieve realism, fieldwork stresses above all that the research site must exemplify the natural social environment in which the phenomena being studied occur "a human field in its natural state; that is, in its own time and place, and in its own recurrent and developing processes" (Schatzman & Strauss, 1973, p. vi). Sample, observational schedule, and measuring techniques all largely follow from this requirement in a pure field study. Data are to be collected from the field setting's indigenous inhabitants (who may comprise a very biased sample of the larger population) and on a schedule determined jointly by the natural flow of events and the fieldworker's increasing awareness and emerging theory of those events. And although fieldworkers may employ a variety of measurement techniques, the most characteristic ones are participant observation and informant interviewing, because they promise an inside view.

Survey research, in contrast to fieldwork, focuses on the population in which the phenomena being investigated occur rather than on the social setting in which they are embedded. To achieve generalizability to the relevant population, this method gives sampling procedures top priority. Site, scheduling, and measuring techniques are typically adapted to the goal of efficiently studying a statistically fair sample. This is why most surveys employ short, highly structured interviews or questionnaires; contact respondents once rather than scheduling repeated interviews; and make use of the most convenient sites (for instance, telephone interviewing, which is now common).

Experimentation's focus on testing causal hypotheses requires careful scheduling. Observation must correspond with the hypothesized causal order of the phenomena being studied (that is, changes in the independent variable must be observed before changes in the dependent variable) and must also conform with the logic of experimental design in order to control for rival causal factors). Unless the hypothesis specifies a particular target group, experimenters usually choose their subjects with more consideration for their ability and willingness to participate in the experiment and conform to its schedule than for their representativeness of a larger population. The research site (the laboratory) is designed to maximize the independent variable's impact rather than to simulate either real events or natural settings. As Aronson and Carlsmith (1968) write: "It is the major objective of a laboratory experiment to have the greatest possible impact on a subject within the limits of ethical considerations and control. In effect, the experimental situation and operations must hit the subject squarely between the eyes" (p. 24). Experimental measurements are designed to detect changes in response to manipulation of the independent variable to determine if this "treatment" has its predicted effects and are usually meaningful only in the context of the experiment.

Nonreactive research centers around the use of two kinds of measuring techniques: unobtrusive observation, in which subjects are unaware of the researcher's activities; and indirect observation, in which the researcher studies archives, artifacts, and other naturally occurring data sources. By comparison with more overt and direct measuring procedures, these nonreactive techniques entail less risk that subjects will react abnormally to measurement and do not require subjects' knowing cooperation with the researcher to generate data. This method serves to reduce the risk of errors stemming from the effects of observation and from the bias of studying only living, competent, and cooperative subjects.

Unobtrusive observation is mostly conducted in the context of either fieldwork, experimentation, or (although more rarely) surveys rather than as a method in its own right. The site, sample, and observational scheduling of these studies must then be adapted to the requirement of concealing measurement. However, indirect observation, while also useful as an adjunct to other methods, is frequently employed independently and is the principal method of archaeologists and historical researchers. It involves searching for sites in which artifacts repose or records are stored, a schedule determined largely by the vicissitudes of the search, and reconstruction of the populations and samples to which the found data apply. (For instance, do police records of crime apply equally to all segments of the population?)

## Composite Methods

In addition to the four basic research methods, a number of more eclectic methods are possible, which are composed of elements borrowed from the basic styles. A leading example is the field experiment, which combines a field setting and sample with an experimental schedule of observation and measurement. Under favorable conditions, each basic research method can accomplish its special purpose with relative effectiveness and efficiency. But as Chapter 2 suggested, each method is also either relatively ineffective or inefficient at accomplishing other purposes. Composite methods are designed to compensate for the basic methods' limitations. Field experiments, for instance, try to compensate on the one hand for fieldwork's relative causal imprecision, and on the other hand for the artificiality of laboratory experiments. In effect, the field experiment is an attempt to achieve both fieldwork's realism and experimentation's causal precision with only one method and with only one round of data collecting—instead of two or more, as in multimethod research.

Compared with the simpler basic methods, composite methods obviously have some advantages. However, these eclectic methods also have some disadvantages. One serious disadvantage is that in trying to achieve multiple research purposes simultaneously, composite methods compromise some of the basic methods' sources of strength. For instance, in striving for both realism and causal precision, field experiments lose the more rigorous control of the laboratory experiment and the greater flexibility in data collecting of the pure field study.

Furthermore, as a rule, the more exclusively research is controlled for a particular purpose, the more efficiently the relevant data can be collected. For instance, laboratory experiments can provide very precise causal data at a relatively modest price by focusing exclusively upon the issue of causation. But for an experiment also to address issues of realism and generalizability may sharply increase its costs in money, time, and effort;

because the field is rarely as convenient a site as the lab, and population samples are considerably harder to obtain than convenience samples of students. This rule suggests not only that each of the basic research methods is likely to achieve its own special purpose more efficiently than any one of the other methods with a different purpose but also that each method is likely to be more efficient than composite methods with multiple purposes.

Compared with multimethod research, a major disadvantage of composite methods is that they fail to provide the opportunity for triangulated measurement and hypothesis testing, and the protection against monomethod bias, which the multimethod strategy provides. Despite their greater complexity, composite methods generate only one methodologically distinct data set per study. Because of this, they provide no basis for cross-method comparisons if they are used alone.

## Quantitative and Qualitative Methods

Much recent writing on multimethod research chiefly contrasts quantitative with qualitative methods (much as early sociologists did with "statistics" versus "case studies") rather than considering the fuller range of research methods discussed previously. The distinction between quantitative and qualitative styles and the mixing of these styles is certainly important (Tashakkori and Teddlie, 2003). But to focus on it exclusively ignores a wider range of methodological problems and opportunities to solve them. The multimethod strategy calls for the use of multiple methods with complementary strengths and different weaknesses in relation to a given set of research problems. But these criteria don't imply that one must always employ a mix of qualitative and quantitative methods in each project. This may sometimes be the case, but some research problems might be better served by combining two different types of quantitative methods (e.g., a survey and an experiment), or of qualitative methods (e.g., a field study and textual analysis of archival documents). In short, the multimethod strategy focuses more on the particular problem's demands than on some particular set or combination of methods.

Moreover, the classical quantitative versus qualitative distinction crosscuts the four styles just described and may produce variants and offshoots of each of these styles. That is, fieldwork includes both qualitative participant observation and quantitative case studies. Survey research employs both statistical samples and qualitative focus groups and may qualitatively as well as statistically analyze data from respondents. Nonreactive research includes not only quantified unobtrusive measurement and statistical analysis of records but also narrative historical research and textual analysis of documents. And there is even qualitative experimentation of a sort, such as ethnomethodologists' "breaching experiments," in which the experimenter creates and presents to participants unusual situations to study how people reconstruct everyday social reality when it has been disrupted. The four styles are more importantly distinguished by their different strategies than by their data format or mode of analysis implied by an oversimplified qualitative versus quantitative distinction.

## Deciding Which Types of Data to Collect

The distinguishing feature of multimethod research is that it generates multiple data sets about the same research problem; each set being collected with a different type of method. The number of social science methods being practiced implies that there is a considerable body of information potentially available about any research problem, a body comprising at least as many sets of data as there are types of data-collecting instruments. Single-method studies obviously provide smaller samples of this information than multimethod studies. However, the chief advantage of the multimethod approach is not the quantity of data that it provides but rather the data's diversity and the opportunities for comparison that this diversity affords.

Data collecting in multimethod research, as in single-method research, is a selective process to be controlled primarily by the researcher's theoretical formulation of the problem and only secondarily by methodology. The multimethod approach does not imply that because there are a number of different types of methods, all the types must be employed in every study. Which and how many methods are to be employed in a multimethod study depends upon the information required to shed light on the problem being investigated.

Consider, for example, the problem posed by a causal theory grounded in firsthand field observations of events in some natural social setting. Such a theory will closely fit the observed facts because the researcher has built the theory with those facts in mind. But the theory will also raise a host of questions. Some of these questions will have to do with the theory's validity. For instance, are the theory's hypotheses generalizable to the larger population and to settings other than the one in which they were formulated? Will the theory's causal implications hold up when tested under more strictly controlled and predictive conditions? And did the fieldworker's presence alter in any significant way the natural course of the observed events? Other kinds of questions will be more exploratory in their intent. For instance, might other types of data reveal different facets of the phenomena being investigated: suggest new variables, concepts, and propositions that would improve the theory?

Many of these questions might better be answered by next employing a survey, an experiment, or a nonreactive method instead of doing additional fieldwork. However, rather than pursuing all these lines of inquiry at once, the problem can be made more manageable by focusing on those issues to which the researcher gives highest priority. For example, if causal validity is the key concern, then an experiment might be the next step. But if exploration of the theory's capacity to explain historical as well as contemporary events has higher priority, then an archival nonreactive study would be more in order. The operative assumption here is that low-priority issues may be worth pursuing only if high-priority issues are decided in the theory's favor.

## Validation Versus Exploration

Multimethod research tests the validity of measurements, hypotheses, and theories by means of triangulated cross-method comparisons. Triangulation requires multiple sets of data speaking to the same research question from different viewpoints. The researcher infers validity from agreement between the data sets and invalidity from disagreement. To support these inferences, the data must be collected with truly different methods that are employed independently of one another but that are focused as tightly as possible upon the particular question being investigated. Otherwise, convergence (or agreement) may indicate instead a shared methodological bias, and divergence (or disagreement) may represent either an irrelevant or a poorly focused comparison. Exploratory multimethod studies, on the other hand, may adopt a very different attitude toward data collecting. Rather than insulating methods from one another to ensure independent cross-validation, exploratory studies may deliberately foster interdependence and interaction. And instead of maintaining a tight comparative focus, researchers may deliberately seek sharp contrasts.

## Independence

Multimethod research entails a risk that the prior use of one method will affect the next method's observations. One type of methodological effect is influence upon the subjects. For example, when Brannon, Cyphers, Hesse, Hesselbart, Keane, Schuman, Viccaro, and Wright (1973) conducted both a survey and a field experiment to study the relationship between subjects' expressed attitudes and their subsequent actions, the experimental subjects' behavior might have been affected by their earlier experience as survey respondents. To control for this possibility, Brannon et al. (1973) employed alternative forms of the interview and conducted the experiment not only with the survey's actual respondents but also with subjects from the original survey sample who had not been interviewed. This procedure both insulated a portion of the experimental sample from the possible effects of interviewing and also provided comparisons to check for such effects.

Another type of methodological effect stems from the possibility that one method will influence another method's application through the investigator rather than through the subjects. In purely exploratory research or research designed to generate theories, the use of multiple methods is intended to alter the investigator's view of the data: "The different ways of knowing about a category virtually force him [the researcher] to generate properties as he tries to understand the differences between the various slices of data, in terms of the different conditions under which they were collected" (Glaser & Strauss, 1967, p. 66). However, in verificational research, the learning and discovery that are highly prized in exploratory work can be a serious source of methodologically induced error. "Although we usually think of difficulty only when the instrument (the investigator) weakens, a difference in competence between two waves of interviewing, either *increasing or decreasing*, can yield spurious effects" (Webb, Campbell, Schwartz, & Sechrest, 1966, p. 22). If, for example, tests of an hypothesis with two methods administered by the same researcher gave very different results, it might be that the experience gained with the first method led the researcher to use the second method differently, and perhaps better, than the first. An advantage of multimethod studies is that when multiple tests are designed and performed by the same investigator in a short period of time, the same level of knowledge and skill are more likely to inform each test.

## Insulation

There are at least four techniques that are frequently employed, either alone or together, to insulate subjects from the effects of multiple waves of data collecting. These techniques are deception, the combined use of reactive and nonreactive methods, the sequencing of methods, and multiple or partitioned samples. Deception, no matter how well-intended, always raises ethical questions. Nonetheless, deception plays a part in much social research. Misrepresenting a study's purpose, disguising the investigator, and even concealing data collection from subjects have long been standard procedures. Deception is usually employed when honesty might either bias subjects' responses or discourage subjects from cooperating. In multimethod research, deception can sometimes also be used to conceal the fact that multiple observations or measurements are being made and thereby eliminate the effects that this knowledge might have upon subjects. However, aside from ethical objections, deception is of limited utility as a technique for insulation because it cannot guarantee that a researcher's acts, as opposed to subjects' *awareness* of those acts, will be free of effects. For instance, interviewing subjects can influence their later behavior in an experiment even if they are unaware of either the interview's real purpose or the connection between the interview and the experiment. Fortunately, there are several other techniques that are more effective and less ethically debatable.

Insulation is an important reason for combining reactive and nonreactive methods. Official statistics, archives, and other naturally occurring sources of data can often be examined with little risk of affecting concurrent fieldwork, surveys, or experiments. Furthermore, data collection can often be sequenced, or scheduled, so that the data that are most vulnerable to influence (usually data from reactive methods) are collected first. For example, organizational researchers who plan both to conduct a survey and to analyze official records, but who fear that knowledge of their access to records might influence respondents, would obviously do well to conduct the survey first and request access to the records later. Insulation is, of course, not the only consideration in sequencing methods, and these other considerations may be of overriding importance. For instance, gaining access may dictate the use of one type of method before another to reduce subjects' anxieties and fears or to build sufficient legitimacy and rapport to examine sensitive data sources, such as case files of professional-client interactions. Or, the logic of the problem may require a particular sequence of methods, such as the experiment preceded by a survey in Brannon et al.'s (1973) research.

Another approach to insulation is either to partition the sample to be studied into subsamples or to draw multiple samples, collecting data from each with a different method. This procedure guards against the direct effects of one method upon another, because no single subject is exposed to more than one method. The use of multiple samples also has the added advantage of permitting the researcher to test for these effects by deliberately exposing some subjects to both methods and comparing the results of differential exposure, as Brannon et al. (1973) did. However, the use of multiple samples does not guard against the more indirect effects that may result in tightly knit social groups if members of the different samples hear about one another's research experiences. But here again the sequencing of methods may be useful. If the researcher postpones the use of more obtrusive and likely to be publicized methods, such as surveys, or can complete all the waves of data collecting quickly enough to prevent the spread of rumor, indirect effects may be avoided.

## Interdependence

Although independence is critical for validation, interdependence is equally critical for exploration. In constructing, as in testing theories, certain variables and propositions may be accessible to one method but not to others. If this is the case, then a number of closely linked data-collecting methods are required in order to consider different kinds of variables' possible theoretical significance for one another. However, the intentional linking of data obtained by different methods has at least two rationales besides generating theories. The first rationale, alluded to in the preceding discussion, is the substantive problem of testing theories that contain variables and propositions that can only be tapped empirically by employing multiple methods. The second rationale, alluded to earlier, is the methodological issue of refining ideas and techniques through experience.

Theoretical explanations of relationships between variables often posit the existence of third variables whose measurement requires different methods than those used in collecting the data on the original variables. To simplify data collection, or perhaps because researchers have not considered the multimethod option, these unmeasured variables are often treated on a purely theoretical level. Employing additional methods that would permit these variables' measurement complicates data collecting, but it may have important ramifications for the development of theory. For example, Brewer (1971) has argued that much organizational theory is implicitly multimethod and has demonstrated the theoretical refinements that are possible when multiple data sources are explicitly employed.

Most research progresses from exploration to verification and is interpreted as a sequential sharpening of concepts, propositions, and research methods. Many multimethod studies, therefore, have mixed objectives. Some studies generate a theory with one type of method and test it with another. Other studies are primarily verificational but seek improved single-method verification through the supplementary use of secondary methods to refine the primary method. For example, data from informal interviews and field observations may impart additional face and content validity to surveys by determining how respondents react when given more avenues of response than those provided by a fixed-choice questionnaire. The assumption is that the supplementary research will be conducted discretely so as not to influence the primary test's outcome in any way except by improving the investigator's knowledge. In such instances, the appropriate emphasis is upon flexibility so that secondary methods can be used freely.

## Integration

In studies and phases of research in which verification is not the immediate issue, data collecting may be still more flexible, and fewer precautions may be required. In generating theories, the emphasis is upon a creative and at times even playful meshing of data-collecting methods to encourage serendipity and openness to new ideas. Different data-collecting techniques may be employed simultaneously, as when interviewers measure social status both through questions and by noting the symbols of status in the respondents' living rooms or may intermittently reinforce one another, as when interviewing leads to the discovery of archives or field observations suggest new interview items.

Subjects may also be knowingly drawn into the research and even recruited into more active roles. An individual may first be interviewed as a survey respondent but subsequently become a key informant, assisting in field research by reporting on situations that are inaccessible to the investigator. Or the "debriefing" interview in experiments can serve as a new database, possibly suggesting additional variables and fresh analytic approaches, in addition to aiding in the evaluation of the experimental design. Also, subjects' reactions to preliminary analyses of data may be helpful. Asking subjects if an analysis or an interpretation "makes sense" is a relatively weak form of verification, but it may be useful as a way of eliciting new information and insights.

## Comparability Versus Contrast

Comparability among different data sets is a key requirement when cross-method validation is the prime objective. For example, as Chapter 3 suggested, in validating measures and hypotheses concerning crime, it is essential that the different sets of data obtained by each method of measuring crime actually refer to the same kinds of crimes. Studying comparable samples of individuals and groups is similarly essential. A serious criticism of Walton's (1966) analysis of political scientists' and sociologists' different findings about community power structures (see Chapter 3) is that different kinds of communities may have been studied (Clark, Kornblum, Bloom, & Tobias, 1968). If so, the lack of consensus in these researchers' findings may be attributable to sampling differences rather than, as Walton suggested, to methodological differences between political science and sociology. One would need to apply the different methods of studying community power either to the same or to a sample of the same types of communities to settle this issue. Diverse independently conducted studies can provide suggestive leads and insights, but only more closely coordinated multimethod inquiry can provide the comparability of data needed to answer questions such as those raised by Walton's work.

Multimethod data collecting may also create some comparability problems, however. For instance, one problem is that with each style of research there is some degree of nonresponse among subjects. There are groups and group members who avoid fieldworkers, survey respondents who cannot be found or who refuse to be interviewed, uncooperative experimental subjects, and people who are underrepresented in naturally occurring data sources. These response rates may vary from method to method. For example, survey questionnaires mailed to a population sample typically have a relatively low rate of response, while experiments conducted with college students typically have a relatively high rate. And even applied to the same type of sample, different methods may be expected to elicit different response rates. For instance, rarely are official records equally complete for all the respondents who may be interviewed in an organizational survey. Furthermore, there is no reason to assume that each research style's nonrespondents are identical. Indeed, the opposite assumption (that nonrespondents may differ systematically from method to method and so impair each method's generalizability) is a valid reason to do multimethod research. We have no pat solution to this problem except to suggest that when strict comparability of data is required, and response rates vary, special attention may need to be paid to studying patterns of nonresponse.

In exploratory research, contrast rather than comparability among data may be the keynote. The fact that different types of methods give access to different kinds of phenomena, or to contrasting samples of individuals and groups, makes it possible to explore phenomena and theories more thoroughly. And although multimethod tests of hypotheses require strictly comparable data, hypothesis formation may benefit from contrasting data that describe the wider range of natural variation. As Chapter 2 suggested, the greater the variety of empirical findings to be explained, the fewer the possible hypotheses. Moreover, it may be, as Glaser and Strauss (1967) suggest, that to stimulate the theoretical imagination empirically one must be prepared to collect "a variety of slices of data that would be bewildering if we wished to evaluate them as accurate evidence for verification" (p. 66).

## Cost/Benefit Analyses of Different Methods of Data Collection

We have been discussing analytic considerations in collecting data. Now we turn to two practical matters: (1) the relative costs and benefits of collecting data with each type of research method, and (2) the costs of multimethod research. The primary costs of research are money, time, and effort, whichever method one employs. However, different research styles distribute these costs differently.

Data collection involves two parties: researchers and subjects. This allows us to see its costs in part as a function of the effort assumed by the researcher versus that which is displaced onto the subjects. The four methods vary in this respect. Participant observation and nonreactive research involve few costs to subjects as research participants. The costs of data collection per se, therefore, fall primarily on the researcher. However, in both survey and experimental research, subjects are explicitly asked to become involved in the research, thus calling for a commitment of time and effort by the subjects as well as the researcher. Recruiting survey respondents and experimental subjects is a major expense, but survey and experimental researchers' time and efforts at the point of contact with the data source are thereby greatly reduced. This is indicated by the relative speed of data collection in most survey and experimental studies in contrast to field and nonreactive studies relying on naturally occurring data. The costs to researchers of data for the four methods can, therefore, be grouped into two general categories: the costs of *gathering* data for field and nonreactive studies and the costs of *generating* data for surveys and experiments.

## Fieldwork and Nonreactive Research

For field research, a major cost is the time and effort spent in becoming integrated in and getting to know the field setting. In effect, fieldwork entails the cost of living two lives simultaneously: (1) that of the field setting; and (2) that of the researcher, who late at night or on weekends writes up field notes while the participant/*subjects* are themselves sleeping or recreating for yet another day's or week's activity that means yet more data to be collected by the participant/*observer.* Much of the observational experience and data collected will ultimately be left out of the refined and published piece of research. In the early stages this is inevitable because one is exploring not only the setting but also often searching for a problem on which to focus one's attention and subsequent observation. Once the focus forms in later stages of the fieldwork, much of the earlier observation, though necessary to sift and weed to get to the problem, may appear to have been wasted on tangential matters. But experienced field researchers know through previous payoffs that one must accept these costs of uncertainty, ambiguity, and seemingly undirected behavior.

Some costs remain high in later, more focused stages of field research, but others begin to decline. These shifting costs are often referred to as the *dross rate.* This is the amount of new and useful information per total amount of data being collected (Webb et al., 1966, p. 32). As vague distinctions turn into clearer typologies and hunches turn into hypotheses, the researcher concentrates on collecting very specific data—one more confirming or disconfirming example, one more situation to set the limiting conditions. The acquisition of new data therefore declines over time but with increasingly focused observation. However, there are subsequent costs in the research required to link the data collection to the data analysis: in particular, the costs of sorting and coding an enormous body of rich but unrefined data. Field notes and interviews do not produce a ready set of precoded responses as do surveys, nor do they produce experiments' refined data points for sorting subjects' reactions onto predetermined values of dependent variables.

Nonreactive research similarly involves high costs in the initial search. Like fieldworkers, nonreactive researchers realize that potential data, whether they be smudges on windows or statistics in file drawers, are everywhere. But actual data for specific problems are rarer. Therefore, research costs may be especially high if one has focused attention early on to a specific problem. However, usable data increases as the research progresses. And "finds" are more likely to occur with this method, as one stumbles across some outcropping of observable phenomena (there all the time but never "noticed" before), such as a set of records buried in the basement of some library or city hall. Historians, census analysts, and other archival researchers often tell of discovering such data "mines" (or of having an "outsight," in which they saw something out there in the real world in a new way; namely as "useful data").

Once found or noticed, the nonreactive researcher's data make much the same demands as the field researcher's field notes. That is, enormous time and effort must be spent sifting and sorting to create an analyzable data set. As in field research, making the data useful is the researcher's responsibility. This heavy central cost of both field and nonreactive research stems from the fact that the people providing the data are unaware of participating in the research process and so behave "normally" rather than in the focused manner dictated by survey and experimental research designs.

The primary benefits and costs of these two styles of research are thus similar. First, they make data so ubiquitous that one need never worry about having enough data, although having the right data to address a given problem may involve a costly search. And second, the data collected require neither special efforts on the part of subjects, nor dislocation from their natural social environments, but both fieldwork and nonreactive methods entail high costs to the researcher to transform raw observations into usefully analyzable data.

## Survey and Experimental Research

The costs and benefits of data collection for survey and experimental research are also similar to one another but are decidedly different from field and nonreactive research. We have emphasized that the latter two may be thought of as gathering and transforming data. Survey and experimental research, by contrast, are concerned with generating data. There are two key aspects to this. First, the researcher consciously controls the process of data collection with the goal of producing scientifically useful data. And second, the researcher interacts with subjects to elicit their participation; that is, their knowing expenditure of time and effort—their labor—in producing scientific data.

The ability to control data collection is an obvious benefit in that one gets the kind of data that one wants and no more. Data collection involves little if any dross—new information is, by design, useful information. One seldom hears of survey or experimental researchers complaining of time and effort *wasted* in the data-collection process, although each of these may, in fact, involve high costs. For example, in survey research probably the single largest cost item in a budget is the actual fielding of the questionnaire, including fruitless callbacks. Occasionally, an experimental design will also fail, and the experimenter may think of this failure as a waste of time and effort. However, such failures may result in refined designs. Costs may be high in both cases, but they are not the dross costs of the field or nonreactive researcher.

The costs for gaining control of data collection for survey and experimental research occur in the initial phases of the research and may be thought of as design costs. Both styles of research, because they are often used to test theory, require time and effort for careful literature review, specification and operationalization of hypotheses, and refined statements of sampling and testing procedures. These are early start-up costs borne solely by the researcher. Once data collection begins, however, the time cost is extremely low, much to the jealousy of field and nonreactive researchers who often see data collection costs as *the* major cost of research. Moreover, the coding and transformation costs of producing readily analyzable data for survey and experimental research are far less in time and effort compared with field and nonreactive research.

The time costs of data collection for both survey and experimental research are relatively low. However, important differences between the two are the labor and money costs associated with each. A major national survey may require hundreds of interviewers and hundreds of thousands of dollars simply in the collection of data. By contrast, experimental research may involve no more than a few evenings when the researcher runs groups of subjects through various settings of the experimental procedure. (These costs are, of course, variable; some more natural social experiments may run for years and involve enormous expenditures in time, money, and effort by many people; while some surveys may be conducted by a single researcher with a few students on a small sample.)

The benefits of the interactive nature of survey and experimental research lie in their success in shifting much of the labor of generating the data to the subjects themselves. Once the research design and data-collection apparatus are in place, cooperative subjects generate data (by answering questions or performing experimental tasks) quickly and cheaply by comparison to the time and effort involved in searching out the data that the same subjects might produce in the normal course of their more natural social lives. The actual data collection costs of such interactive research depend, of course, on subjects' willingness to volunteer their "labor." In the absence of true volunteers, researchers employ various techniques, including payment, repeated callbacks in surveys, and the mild coercion of a grade requirement in introductory psychology courses.

## The Costs of Multimethod Research

For the most part, we have stressed the benefits of multimethod research. But its costs cannot be ignored, for employing multiple methods must obviously also multiply research costs by some factor for both researchers and their subjects. If the various costs involved in research (time, energy, and money) were identical for each research style, and were incurred in the same phase of research in each (search, design and instrumentation, recording observation, and data analysis), and were borne equally in each style by the various participants in a study (researchers and subjects), then multimethod investigation would increase the expense of research by a simple factor equal to the number of methods employed. Two methods would double the expense, three would triple it, and so on.

Fortunately, however, this is not the case. Instead, as the preceding discussion of costs/benefits suggests, research styles vary in the resources they consume (money versus time and energy), the research phases at which the heaviest costs are incurred, and they also distribute costs differently between subjects and researchers. This means that, for instance, although a field or nonreactive study plus a survey or an experiment is obviously more expensive than either is alone, the costs involved are not necessarily borne simultaneously, nor are they doubled for all parties, nor do they entail double consumption of the same resources. Instead, field and nonreactive studies most often chiefly consume researchers' time and energy in the search and analysis phase, while surveys and experiments consume researchers' time and energy more heavily in the design and instrumentation phase and require more money and more of subjects' time and energy in the recording of observations (the actual data collection). This diversity of costs makes multimethod research no cheaper in an absolute sense. However, it does increase its feasibility by spreading the costs among different parties and budgets and throughout the research process.

Furthermore, there are a variety of ways of economizing in multimethod as well as in single-method research. Two of the most effective ways are to exploit opportunities that occur as a by-product of one's everyday life and to recycle one's own and others' data. For example, Butler and Snizek (1976) made use of one author's employment as a waitress as an opportunity both for participant observation to construct an hypothesis and to conduct a field experiment to test the hypothesis. Brewer (1971), however, reanalyzed the data from several of his own observational case studies of organizations in conjunction with findings from others' comparative studies of organizational structure based on organizational records and interviews with informants. In this way, he essentially reconstructed from past research a multimethod study that might have been done had the ideas and research capabilities been available to the original researchers. This is an example of exploiting what might be called *unintended multimethod research* (a phrase suggested by Harrison Trice in a conversation with the first author), the situation in which the multimethod nature of the discipline spontaneously produces but fails to coordinate the data necessary to reach a multimethod solution to a research problem. Hunter (1975) employed both of these strategies. He recycled the information from a survey of a Rochester, New York neighborhood done in the early 1950s by Donald Foley, used Foley's study as a base for comparison with a replication that he conducted with the aid of students in the mid-1970s, and interpreted the findings theoretically in the light of his own participant observation as a resident in that neighborhood.

In summary, selecting among the four major styles of research and combining them with an effective cost/benefit outcome for multimethod research require an understanding of the various costs and the benefits involved—especially the costs of time that are highly variable among the four methods and the costs implied by the dross ratio of usable new data to "wasted" time and effort. Issues of validity and reliability of data are, of course, the ultimate *scientific* criteria of cost/benefit analysis—and our preceding explorations, with respect to the costs and benefits of data collection, should be seen as a necessary but small play within the much larger and ultimately more meaningful drama of science.

# Five

# Finding the Objects to Study

Theorizing demands that we think about the real social world abstractly and in general terms. But to do the empirical research upon which theories rest, one must answer the mundane but essential questions: "Where do I go?" and "What do I look at?" Answering these questions requires both a clear definition of the actual social units about which data will be collected and a strategy for sampling from the universe, or population, composed of all such units. Defining these units of study is in part a matter of deciding what types of objects are theoretically relevant to the problem, and the choice of a sampling strategy is in part determined by the kinds of theoretical and empirical generalizations required to solve the research problem. However, research involves a variety of practical constraints as well as theoretical demands, and these must also be considered.

The studies that are feasible at any given moment are confined to particular places, times, persons, and variables. Each study is only a sample of the much larger universe of studies that might logically follow from a research problem's theoretical formulation. This chapter addresses the ways in which researchers employ different definitions of the objects of study and different sampling strategies to cope with empirical inquiry's varied demands for—and constraints upon—generalization from data and how a multimethod approach may improve our ability to generalize.

## The Dilemma of the Few and the Many

The research process requires trade-offs between researchers' ultimate theoretical objectives and the various constraints that determine the feasibility of particular types of studies. Because of this, research inevitably focuses social scientists' immediate attention more narrowly than their broader theoretical interests imply. However, few social psychologists are really curious only about the 20 undergraduates recruited to participate in an experiment, just as few urban sociologists are chiefly concerned about the particular neighborhood of a middle-sized city selected for a case study, and few network analysts are interested solely in the 1500 people selected in a sample survey for the study of their friendship choices. Instead, they are mostly interested in what the findings about those 20 undergraduates, that single neighborhood, or those 1500 individuals might tell us, respectively, about other young adults or even people in general; about this type of neighborhood, or even all neighborhoods; or about the friendship patterns of the eight million people in the metropolitan area from which these 1500 were selected, or even of people in the entire country.

The objects we study are interesting primarily because our findings may apply more generally to a larger class of similar objects. The objects of study and the objects of interest correspond, respectively, to the sample and the universe. Whether the findings from the objects studied will hold true for the objects of interest is a question of the *representativeness* of the sample: How well do these few represent the many? The answer to this question will depend upon how the units and the universe were defined and the way in which the sample was selected. We will see that different styles of research characteristically treat these issues in different ways.

### Sampling and the Costs of Precision

Research, like all human activity, involves costs. Sampling is one way of reducing those costs. The precision of our knowledge is directly related to its cost; that is, greater precision requires greater outlay. The degree of precision sought is, therefore, never absolute but instead relative to the needs and purposes of the research, and utility criteria often determine our information's precision. In everyday life, the degree of precision required is similarly determined. For instance, to decide whether or not to carry an umbrella we usually look out the window rather than conduct a meteorological study. In science, however, the degree of precision is in principle determined by the demands of knowledge rather than by practicality. This is perhaps the source of the popular image of the mad scientist ignoring all costs, moral as well as material, in the "irrational" pursuit of truth. It may also be why such scientists are often depicted as independently wealthy. Actual scientists are neither rich nor crazy and are acutely aware of the costs of their research. Consequently, they are willing, in a rational trade-off, to accept approximations to knowledge.

Sampling, furthermore, facilitates other kinds of precision. By studying a few selected units rather than the whole universe, one may put additional resources into sharpening measurement by acquiring more and also more accurate data about fewer units. However, reducing measurement error may increase sampling error. This dilemma is similar to the Heisenburg "uncertainty principle" in subatomic physics, wherein one may know with great precision the momentum of a subatomic particle but not simultaneously its position or, conversely, its position but not its momentum. Thus, one may spend years getting to know a single case in great detail, as with an individual in psychoanalysis or a community or organization in fieldwork ethnographies. But one may end up with a less convincing argument for generalizing one's findings than other researchers who may ask the same individual only a few questions in a survey or look up a few published census statistics on a neighborhood.

## Units and Universes

If, as the poet Pope said, "The proper study of mankind, is man," then social scientists should study people. However, we must further ask "What is it about people we wish to study?" Rather than looking only at individuals as the units of study, we may be interested in the *groups* in which people live and work, the *interactions* they engage in ranging from murder to love, or the *settings* in which they are born and die. All are, of course, related in varying ways to people and their social behavior, but groups, interactions, and settings are the units, respectively, not persons.

Only by clearly defining our units of study can we select appropriate styles or methods to collect data about those units. If we have defined our units of analysis as eighteenth-century revolutions, for example, then participant observation is obviously of limited use compared with content analysis of archives and written accounts. If we are interested in the current problems of rape, defining the unit of analysis may present more problems. Will our units of analysis be the individual rapists or the victims, will it be the rape itself as an interaction, or will it be communities' varying rates of rape? The unit of study is intrinsically linked to the definition of the problem and the specific propositions and hypotheses that one wishes to develop or test.

A clear statement of the problem and a clear definition of units of study would seem to imply distinct methods appropriate to gathering data about those problems from those units. However, the constraints and limits of research often restrict one to certain feasible data sets that may in fact require a redefinition of units and a recasting of the theoretical problem. The link between how a problem is formulated, the definition of units, and the nature of one's data cannot be logically broken. But, it can be extended by recognizing that multiple data sets and different units of analysis may permit different theoretical formulations of the problem being investigated, and vice versa.

## Units and Variables

In defining units of analysis, care must be taken to distinguish between the units of study and a study's variables. Variables are characteristics of the units of study, which may vary from unit to unit. This may seem to be an easy distinction, but if we return to the example of rape, certain complexities can be demonstrated to sensitize the researcher to confusions that might exist on this point in other research. Suppose that one is interested in studying something about the settings in which rapes occur. Should settings be taken as the unit of study and rape treated as a variable, or should rapes be treated as the units of analysis and characteristics of the settings taken as variables? The answer depends both upon the specific questions one hopes to answer and upon the nature of the data one can collect. If one wants to know where rapes do and do not occur, then settings should be defined as the unit of analysis, and rapes should be treated as a variable across settings. If instead one is interested in differences in settings that may be related to other characteristics of rapes, such as when or to whom they are most likely to occur, then rapes would be defined as the units of study, and characteristics of the settings would become variables.

One way to keep these issues clear is to construct a data matrix in which units and variables are the two dimensions. See Figure 5.1.

In a field study of a community or an organization, there might be only a single unit about which to collect data, but in a sample survey the

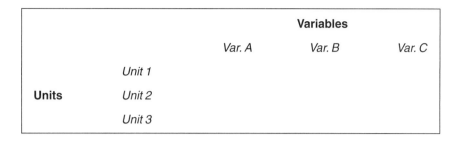

**Figure 5.1**     A Data Matrix of Units and Variables

number of units may be in the thousands. Furthermore, in any given piece of research one might collect data on different types of units simultaneously, as when a fieldworker or an experimenter studies the group as a whole as well as the individuals, subgroups, or dyads that comprise the group. As units of study shift, so too does the nature of the data collected and the types of problems that can be explored.

The data matrix is a heuristic tool that describes a range of trade-offs between the number of units studied and the number of variables studied for each unit. For example, the case study may be thought of as focusing on only a single row but on many columns of the data matrix; that is, collecting many variables (the "rich data" for which case studies are valued) on a single case. By contrast, large-scale sample surveys (national opinion polls, for example) collect data on one or a few variables (one or a few columns) across many different units (rows). The trade-off between the number of cases studied (rows) and the number of variables studied for each case (columns) represents a real-world constraint on research design. In short, though one might ideally prefer to study many variables about many units, theoretical demands and limited resources (time, money, and personnel) may narrow the choices.

However, the data matrix also suggests the possibility that a single piece of research may fall at a variety of points within "the attribute space of research design" defined by the matrix. For example, the *comparative* case study begins to expand the number of columns to two, three, or more cases moving in the direction of styles relying on larger samples. Alternatively, surveys or other large sample designs may select not one universe to sample from but several, which then become different cases to be compared. Multimethod research designs clearly offer many possibilities here. For example, longer in-depth interviews may shrink sample size (the columns) but expand the rows (the number of variables studied), compared with telephone or mail surveys having a larger number of sampled units but fewer questions and fewer variables.

## Types of Units

It is useful to list briefly the more common types of units and the corresponding styles or methods of research commonly used to study each.

*Individuals.* Individuals, considered as units, have doubtless been studied with the widest range of methods, from direct observation and interviewing, to analyses of archives, and experiments. The application of so many different methods to the study of individuals suggests that the linkage between the way in which problems are stated and the methods selected to study them may be attributable more to convention than to intrinsic properties of methods or the nature of the units studied.

*Attributes of Individuals.* Characteristics of individuals are more often treated as variables than as units of study. However, just as medical researchers may focus on individual's specific organs as the unit of investigation (e.g., kidneys, of which most *individuals* have *two*), so social scientists may focus on individual's specific characteristics. For example, in attitude research social psychologists are often interested in different attitudes as the units of analysis, recognizing that attitudes themselves may have variable properties such as saliency, intensity, and direction. Experimental and survey research have been commonly used to study these properties. However, field observation of behavioral expressions of attitudes as well as content analyses of documents and artifacts may also be employed.

*Actions and Interactions.* The units of analysis are often defined as specific actions or interactions. Take the foregoing example of rape. Rather than focusing on the criminal or his victim as individual units of analysis, we may focus instead on the rape as an action or behavior, considering either the rapist's acts, as in many criminological studies, or the victim's response, as in many victimization studies. However, we may also define rape as an interaction, and by so doing define yet another class of variables for investigation (degrees of force used and resistance encountered or mutual prior acquaintance).

Observation, in either field or laboratory settings, is the method that most directly measures behavior. Interviews may provide self-reports of behavior, or written records may contain accounts of specific actions, but they are only behaviors in themselves if one focuses on the activities of self-reporting and record keeping. By being aware of these nuances in the definition of units of analysis with respect to behaviors, one may avoid numerous problems of inference in later stages of analysis. Furthermore, it may alert one early on to select methods that will more directly measure behaviors.

*Residues and Artifacts of Behavior.* When we are unable to observe individuals or their behaviors directly, we may instead exploit the fact that much behavior leaves residues. Residues are physical products or artifacts that may be selected as units of study and from which we may make inferences about the behavior itself. Webb, Campbell, Schwartz, and Sechrest (1966) discuss at length the creative use of "erosions" and "accretions" in the physical environment as indicators of past human actions. For example, defining smudges on the glass surrounding exhibits at a museum as units may enable one to make inferences from the smudges' frequency and height about the popularity of different exhibits among different age groups. Similarly, records in the files of an organization may be defined as units of study as indicators of the behavior of the individuals whose behavior is being recorded (say, a worker's production record), and also the individual doing the recording (a foreman or a manager).

The method of content analysis is specifically geared to dealing with physical residues of symbolic behaviors as in newspapers, novels, or popular songs. In such research, great care must be taken to define the unit of analysis and the sampling strategy because the unit may be either the content of the material (e.g., the crimes reported in newspapers) or different physical forms of the media (e.g., the entire issue of a newspaper, the front page, or the story or article). For example, in the 1960s, a number of studies of urban riots used newspaper accounts as the source of data while defining the riots themselves as the unit of analysis. Later researchers questioned the validity of this research by shifting the definition of the unit of analysis from the riots to the newspaper accounts or articles themselves (Danzger, 1975). Where the former raised substantive issues about riots and riot cities, the latter raised issues about the operation of the press and the role of the media in depicting civil disorders. Such simple questions as the physical proximity of the newspaper to where the event occurred may produce a distortion in the data, as recent research has shown (Myers & Caniglia, 2004). Again, how one defines the unit of analysis may raise different theoretical issues even when, as in the preceding example, the data set itself remains the same.

*Settings, Incidents, and Events.* In addition to individuals and their behaviors, there are settings, incidents, and events. All definitions of units and of samples imply space and time. However, this class of phenomena is explicitly defined using space and time coordinates. Settings may range from private rooms to expansive public places. Often the analysis of settings is accomplished through observation or the recording of observations with the use of cameras and video equipment. This unit also has been widely used in multimethod research, in which observation may be paired with the analysis of archives about events or incidents that may have occurred in different settings, or with interviews and surveys to tap people's attitudes and feelings in the settings.

When defined as the units of analysis, and not just as a convenient sampling frame for getting at other units, characteristics of social settings have proven to be important variables in their own right. Interest in the physical settings of behavior, or "situated action," is seen in the development of several subfields, such as "environmental psychology." Newman's (1972) work on "defensible space" is an excellent example of multimethod research using settings as the units of study. Newman was interested in the design and settings of buildings (specifically, high-rise public housing) and their relationship to crime and residents' fear of victimization. Settings were observed, crimes were analyzed through records, and residents were interviewed about their reactions. By combining these methods, Newman could explore a wide range of variables in the most efficient manner, systematically exploring propositions that had been hinted at but left unexplored in previous research.

In contrast with settings, which are spatially defined, incidents and events are temporally defined units of analysis. They have a definite beginning and an end, have a known and perhaps significant place in historical time, and are recurrent. Public ceremonies, elections, city council meetings, and urban riots are all examples of this type of unit. Of course, each of these phenomena can also be studied by defining other characteristics as the units of analysis. For example, one might define rituals, electoral candidates, council members' voting records, or the cities in which riots may occur as the relevant units. However, focusing upon incidents and events temporally, as historians do, for instance, orients the researcher to variables in data that highlight the ordering and sequencing of behavior, the causes of beginnings and endings, and the conditions under which phenomena recur.

Studying incidents and events, especially in their recurrence, leads the researcher to state dynamic propositions (or theories of process) and to search for data that will correspondingly capture the phenomena at several points in time. One immediately thinks of historical archives, census data over the years, or successive waves of interviewing in panel surveys as appropriate methods. Even the classical experimental design measures phenomena at two points: before and after the experimental intervention. Cross-sectional, one-shot surveys also often include retrospective data about the respondents and their experiences. Moreover, a combination of methods may be employed, and multiple methods may be especially useful in studying past incidents and events in comparison with the present. For example, Erikson (1976), in his postanalysis of a flood disaster, uses both interviewing and archival research to recapture the flow of events and to determine their impact on the community at the time of his study.

*Collectivities.* The final general class of units to be considered deals with human beings in the aggregate. Such analyses begin from the recognition that the whole is greater than the sum of its parts. Collective units—such as families, organizations, communities, professions, or nations—have unique characteristics or properties that cannot be arrived at simply by adding up the traits of the individual members. For example, individuals do not have power structures, only collectivities do.

Defining collective units often involves "boundary problems" of deciding where the organization or community ends, of deciding who is in it and who is not. One may take participants' definitions; for example, the list of an organization's members. But often, the members of a unit of social structure may be unaware of the collective unit itself or of its constituent members. As Kadushin (1966) has shown in his study of social circles, or as Fischer (1982) and Wellman and Leighton (1979) have shown in their studies of urban networks, circles and networks may have distinct and varying properties and be studied as units of analysis even when only the researcher (but not the participants) is able to objectively define them.

The problem of defining the boundaries of collective units of study is very similar to the problem of defining the universe from which to draw a sample. In both cases, care must be taken to establish logical and measurable criteria for membership. In the former case, the purpose is to define units for study; and in the latter, to define the appropriate universe from which to sample.

Furthermore, there are numerous ways to define most collective units of analysis. For example, the debate on how one should identify communities has occupied the literature of urban sociology for over half a century. The way in which a unit is defined is closely linked to the nature of the data one collects and the propositions one explores. However, different definitions of units can be used in the same research, with appropriate but different data sets being collected, and either different or the same propositions being tested. For example, Hunter (1974), in a study of urban neighborhoods in Chicago, defines community in three different ways and collects different data to test *different* propositions that relate to these different definitions of the units of study. In contrast with Hunter's work, Kasarda (1974) demonstrates how the *same* proposition may be explored across shifting definitions of the units of analysis. He tests the relationship between the size of social units and their administrative ratio for different types of units ranging from organizations to communities to nation-states.

The preceding discussion of types of units and corresponding research styles is presented not as a codified system matching one type of unit to a given type of problem and then to a corresponding "best method." We do stress that care must be taken to define units of study so that logical consistency will exist among types of units, the nature of the data, and the form of one's propositions. But our underlying theme is that a multimethod approach, because it gives access to different types of units and appropriate data, may increase the logical consistency of our work as well as suggesting new and important avenues for both research and theory.

## Units of Observation and Units of Analysis

We can define units of analysis as those entities *about* which we collect data and about which we want to generalize or make inferences. Observational units may be defined as those units *from* which data are collected. Following common practice, however, a study's units of analysis may be different from its units of observation. For example, one may collect data from a housewife (unit of observation) about the size of her family (the family being the unit of analysis). Sometimes there is confusion at both data-collection and data-analysis phases about the unit of analysis, and it usually centers upon ambiguity as to whether one is making inferences about individuals or groups (collectivities), and this in turn is often related to the failure to distinguish between units of observation and units of analysis.

## Ecological Fallacies, Structural Effects, and Hierarchical Embeddedness

Two methodological and analytical issues in the social sciences relate to this distinction between units of observation and units of analysis. The first is the often noted "ecological fallacy," or the inappropriate drawing of analytic inferences about *individual-level* correlations or relationships from aggregate data on *collective-level* units of observation. For example, if one finds that cities with a greater proportion of their population between ages 13 and 18 have higher crime rates than cities with a lower proportion of teenagers, one cannot conclude from this that teenagers are more likely to commit crimes than other age groups. This involves shifting from collective-level units of observation (cities' age distributions and cities' crime rates) to individual-level units of analysis (individuals' ages and individuals committing crimes). Recent statistical procedures have been developed to provide some "range" of estimates of individual level relationships from collective-level data (see Hammond, 1973).

A more direct way to deal with the problem is to use multiple methods to gather data at both individual and collective levels in order to permit analysis at both levels. This is not to suggest that the object of such research is always to obtain individual-level correlations. Sometimes the aggregate level may be sufficient and appropriate for the problem at hand (for example, selecting cities and using indicators such as age distribution in deciding where to target money for anticrime activity). However, selecting multiple units of analysis and using multiple methods of data collection is a direct way to deal with the problem. In addition, it may raise intriguing theoretical issues in explaining the similarity or differences in the relationships that are found between the two levels.

A second issue related to the distinction between units of observation and units of analysis is that of structural effects (Blau, 1960; Davis, Spaeth, & Huson, 1961). The same data may be collected on individuals and aggregated to a group level (e.g., age of individuals and *average* age for the group), and these may interact with one another in predicting to some individual-level dependent variable (e.g., committing a crime). The question of structural effects is often posed as whether individual characteristics or group characteristics predict behavior better. Structural effects may likewise be analyzed when data are collected on unique properties of the groups themselves that are not reducible to individuals and not simply aggregated from individual-level data (e.g., duration of the group versus an individual's duration as a member). As with ecological fallacies, multiple methods can be usefully applied to gather both the individual- and group-level data required to address this complex class of theoretical questions.

Third, the idea of ecological effects has recently been extended both statistically and methodologically by combining a number of different embedded levels of analysis and different and distinct data sets. Much of the current research on "neighborhood effects" in education, for example, is an attempt to disentangle personal and family variables (such as age or number of sibs) from school effects (such as average class size) and from local community variables (such as crime rate). Distinct data sets and distinct variables appropriate to each level of analysis are combined in estimating the unique contribution of each factor and also their joint effects or interaction effects on a student's educational outcome (Duncan & Raudenbush, 2001). Research by Sampson and Raudenbusch (1999) on systematic observation of street activity related to crime similarly uses an embedded approach in which the units of observation ranged from individual behaviors to physical characteristics of face blocks to whole neighborhoods and local communities. Data sources on the different levels or embedded units of analysis included videotaping of street behavior, coding of physical characteristics of the street block, and gathering of archival crime data and census data on the neighborhoods and local communities. Again, a multimethod strategy of combining different units of analysis and different data sources proved invaluable for capturing the complexity of the phenomenon being studied.

## Types of Sampling

Social scientists employ two major types of sampling, each of which includes several subtypes. First, there is probability sampling, which includes simple random samples, systematic samples, stratified random samples, and multistage cluster samples. Second, there is nonprobability sampling, which includes quota samples, purposive samples, and convenience samples.

## Probability Sampling

The key to probability sampling lies in our ability to assess the probability that a given set of units that make up the sample would be drawn from the universe of such units by chance. In making this assessment, we rely upon "sampling theory." This theory is based upon the *idea* that one could take repeated samples of the same population and compare the samples. For example, if you were to select different samples of 10 students from a population of 100 students, 50 of whom were males and 50 of whom were females, most of the time the randomly selected samples would have 5 males and 5 females. But sometimes there might be 6 males and 4 females, or vice versa. And rarely, though possibly, you might by chance select a sample in which all 10 were males. These repeated hypothetical samples from the same population are called the *sampling distribution.* In practice, we usually select only one sample. But given the hypothetical sampling distribution, we can assert that most of the time our sample will reflect the "true" characteristic of the population as a whole (in the preceding example, the percentage of males and females).

Probability sampling does not ensure that one truly knows what is going on in the population, but it provides a known probability of error. It allows one to say, in effect, I'm not absolutely sure that this is true, but I'm 95 percent confident that it is. With nonprobability sampling, there is also a possibility of error, but here we are left in the dark as to how much confidence to place in generalizing from what we have studied to what we have not. However, there are off-setting advantages, as we will see, to using certain types of nonprobability samples.

Simple random sampling, though heralded because of its seeming simplicity and because of its closeness to fitting the major assumptions of "probability sampling theory," is nonetheless one of the least used strategies. The primary reason is that often we have no way of identifying beforehand all the units that make up the universe, or population, from which the sample is to be drawn. If one can identify all the units, then the procedure is indeed simple. Merely assign a number in sequence to each unit, and then, by using a random number table, select those units whose numbers come up until one has the sample size desired.

Systematic sampling is a widely used probability sampling strategy that relies upon a list of units from the population, usually a list generated for other purposes, such as a roster of members of an organization or a list of registered voters. Rather than assigning a number to each member on the list and selecting the sample by using a random number table, one merely picks a random place to start on the list and then selects every Nth unit (every fourth, fifth, or twenty-first name, depending both upon the size of the list and the proportion of the population one wishes to draw into the sample). One must be careful that the list does not display a pattern that matches the interval of selection such that a biased sample would result. Furthermore, one must be especially careful to understand how and why the lists were generated, who from the population might be systematically excluded from the list, and who might be selectively included. To justify the use of a given list and to understand the origin of the list often requires research by other methods, such as observation and interviewing of those who have generated the list.

Stratified random sampling can provide even greater representativeness of a population than simple random sampling. However, stratified random sampling presupposes another data source because it requires some prior empirical knowledge of the population. If one knows the proportion of certain categories (or strata) within the population (such as the proportion of white or black), then, by randomly selecting units within each category in the same proportion as in the population, one may actually ensure a more representative sample than might by chance be generated by a simple random sample. For example, it would not be possible, by chance, to end up with an all white sample as might happen with simple random sampling.

Multistage cluster sampling is a hybridized sampling strategy that relies on at least two different scales of "units" in which the smaller scale units (e.g., people) are distributed in a number of large scale units (e.g., neighborhoods or organizations). One first randomly selects a number of larger scale units as a first stage sample (e.g., a sample of neighborhoods or organizations). Then, from each of these larger scale units one selects a random sample of the smaller scale units. Often this sampling strategy is used to reduce the cost of data collection so that one does not need to go to every organization or every neighborhood to collect data on a sample that is statistically representative of the population. In effect, this is a multimethod strategy, in that different scales and different units of observation have been identified. However, too frequently these different scales of units are not fully included as such in the analysis. We have seen that certain significant empirical and theoretical issues such as "ecological fallacies" and "structural effects" might be explored by means of this sampling strategy.

## Nonprobability Sampling

Quota sampling is a nonprobability sampling strategy that is a precursor to more fully developed forms of probability sampling and is explicitly concerned with trying to select a representative sample. Quota sampling assumes a known distribution of certain important characteristics of the universe or population, such as the proportion of male and female, white or black, in different age categories. One then selects people who have those characteristics until the sample proportions match the proportions of those characteristics found in the universe or population as a whole. Ideally, for example, one would end up with the same proportion of black men in their forties as there are in the population.

One of the major problems with quota sampling is determining which specific population characteristics should be taken into consideration in developing quotas. Often these are characteristics that prior research has shown to be significant in relation to the variables presently being studied. For this reason, quota sampling is very dependent upon prior research findings in the field. Another problem is that one cannot assume that the sample is representative of the population for the characteristics not explicitly taken into consideration. In the preceding example, one might have sampled those black men in their forties near a military base, and so they might overrepresent one particular occupation in the sample. However, if the sampled characteristics are theoretically significant, this may be presented as a concern overriding the statistical concern of representativeness. But if so, one is never sure that these associated but unsampled characteristics are not, in fact, the determining variables in one's analysis.

Like quota sampling, purposive sampling relies on the researcher's prior theoretical and empirical understanding of the universe with respect to the issue under study. Also, like stratified sampling, purposive sampling often attempts to include particular categories or subgroups of the population, but it differs in that rather than trying necessarily to select subgroups that are fully representative, purposive sampling may select only certain subgroups that represent theoretically meaningful variation. We will see, for example, that the testing of grounded theory relies on a form of purposive sampling in which the units selected are theoretically defined as important and not statistically determined to be representative. Purposive sampling, in short, is a claim on the part of the researcher that theoretically significant, not necessarily statistically significant, units have been selected for study. It is, therefore, incumbent upon the researcher to justify the selection process with a qualitatively different, but an equally rigorous, rationale as that used by those arguing for statistical representativeness.

Convenience sampling is perhaps the most widely used, but the least statistically or theoretically justified, sampling strategy in the social sciences. Convenience sampling, as its name implies, means that the researcher has studied a particular unit or set of units because it is readily at hand. For this reason, it is a relatively low-cost technique. Usually, convenience sampling is associated chiefly with participant observation and experimentation in which researchers frequently study easily accessible settings and subjects who are close to home.

However, convenience sampling may be defined more broadly to include any research in which the composition of the sample is determined primarily by consideration of the costs of access to the data rather than by one of the more rigorous sampling techniques discussed previously. It can even be extended to include a convenient definition of the universe from which a sample is drawn rather than a theoretical definition of the appropriate universe. So defined, a study based upon readily accessible organizational records, or easily available public data such as the census, or media reports of conflict may also be thought of as employing a convenience sample.

If convenience samples are employed for exploratory purposes or with the appropriate statistical or experimental controls for testing hypotheses, they may be quite valid within certain limits. However, a problem arises in that because they are convenient, the same types of samples tend to be overused. This limits both their potential for discovery in exploratory work and also their external validity in verificational studies. To remedy this, as Webb et al. (1966) have suggested, such studies may be augmented by using perhaps equally convenient but less stereotypic samples. With extensive data sources such as the census, this supplementation might seem to be unnecessary. However, as demographers know, even the census underrepresents certain segments of the population (e.g., the homeless) who may be of equal research interest and who may, therefore, need to be studied with other methods.

At yet another level, any sample may be considered to be a convenience sample to the extent that the researcher fails to sample from a theoretically defined, as opposed to a statistically defined, universe. A universe may be casually defined by convenience, while a sample of that universe may be rigorously drawn and defended statistically. From the viewpoint of testing theories and of accumulating theoretical knowledge, this is clearly an instance of misplaced concreteness. For example, researchers who have used the very rigorous sampling strategy employed in selecting individuals to be interviewed in the Detroit Area Studies of the University of Michigan would be hard-pressed to justify the selection of Detroit over any other American city on any other grounds but its proximity to Ann Arbor. Is this any less convenience sampling than the field researcher's decision to study the neighborhood surrounding her home or the experimenter's to study his students?

The multimethod strategy suggests that convenience must be addressed forthrightly as one among many rationales for choosing a particular sample of units for study and that its limitations must be recognized and compensated for. Heirich's (1977) research on religious conversion provides a good example of convenience combined with statistical and theoretical rigor. Over a period of seven years, he observed firsthand the growth of Catholic Pentecostalism near his university. Reviewing earlier research on conversion, Heirich (1977) notes that "Most were descriptive studies of odd clusters of converts, with little sense of how generalizable the description might be" (p. 657), and with no control group of unconverted persons to determine whether they too might be influenced by the same factors as the converts. To improve upon this earlier work, Heirich (1977) first drew a purposive snowball sample of local converts to Pentecostalism, attempting to interview the entire universe of members within his limited geographic area, by asking each respondent to name other converts. Then, to provide a control group, he drew a systematic probability sample of Catholic students (most converts were also students) from lists provided by the university and the Catholic students' organization. In this way, he was able to test hypotheses requiring comparisons between converts and a sample representing the pertinent population of nonconverts. He found that several hypotheses from earlier research on conversion were strongly supported by data from the converts alone but were then disconfirmed when tested with data from the control group as well.

## Sampling and Generalization

In sampling, the central question is how generalizable, or representative, are the research results? Even if all other questions are adequately answered, a skeptic may still ask if one's findings hold true beyond the particular objects investigated in a given piece of research. An experiment may be valid for this class of introductory psychology students, but is it valid for other people? A field researcher's ethnographic account of family life in a slum community may be valid for that community, but is it valid for other slum communities? Or, a survey may be valid for a randomly selected sample of adults within a metropolitan area in a given year, but is it true of people in other metropolitan areas and at other times?

The multimethod perspective suggests new ways of thinking about these issues. First, both statistical and theoretical representation must be considered and counterbalanced in the sampling of subjects for study (neither purely statistical adequacy nor purely theoretical relevance is sufficient in itself). And second, the conventional dichotomy between probability sampling procedures usually associated with survey research and the nonprobability strategies associated with other research styles needs to be reconsidered.

These issues of different sampling strategies have recently come to the fore in discussions about survey research using the Internet. The fact that the Internet can be used to generate huge (20,000+) "convenience samples" relatively inexpensively when compared with traditional survey research samples forces one to confront the issues of bias and generalizability without denying the utility of such large data sets. James Witte (2004), a pioneer of Internet surveys, has explicitly called for a "multimethod strategy"—one that would systematically compare results from the convenience sampling of large Internet surveys with results from more controlled statistically representative random samples. Such multimethod sampling comparisons would allow one to simultaneously assess the generalizability and biases of the survey while still retaining the analytical power generated by its sheer size. Witte (2004) notes that "Methodologically, the goal of survey research is to collect data on a sample that represents a population. Randomness does not guarantee representativness; rather, it provides the means to quantify the level of confidence with which one can say that the sample does not represent the population. Survey 2001 [his large Internet survey] did not yield a random sample, and we do not 'know' the selection probabilities for sample members. However, this *does not mean that the survey cannot yield representative social science data.* (italics in original). Although we do not 'know' the selection probabilities, our data allow us to 'estimate' these probabilities. The survey collected data on standard demographic characteristics (e.g., gender, age, race, education), and combinations of these attributes can be compared with other data sources" (pp. xviii-xix).

## Theoretical and Statistical Representativeness

In atheoretical research, questions of representativeness are almost wholly statistical. For instance, with a public opinion poll, we would be interested solely in determining the probability of error in generalizing from the poll's sample to the larger population. But in theoretically oriented research, there is an additional consideration: How well does the population from which the sample was drawn satisfy the conditions under which the theory being investigated is thought to hold true? As Haas (1982) has observed, much social research presently fails to address this second type of question.

Under the hypothetico-deductive model [of knowledge], a research report would describe the population studied in terms of the general, analytic variables of the theory being tested. The description would establish the fact that the population satisfied the conditions under which a specific relationship was predicted to hold. Sociologists, however, almost never describe the populations they study in any such way. Instead, they are described in ways that permit a reader to judge whether and to what degree they are representative of historically specific societies of interest, an approach that makes sense only under the survey sampling model (Haas, 1982, pp. 108–109).

In short, statistical rationales for sampling are limited by the failure to identify and define universes theoretically. To the extent that the pertinent theoretical universe differs from the population actually studied, there is likely to be analytical and predictive slippage between whatever generalizations are advanced or tested in the research and the data upon which those generalizations are claimed to rest. We do not mean to suggest here either that statistically rigorous sampling techniques should be abandoned or that a survey sampling model of knowledge should replace the hypothetico-deductive model (Haas, 1982). Rather, we suggest that a multimethod perspective on research must recognize the degree to which even the most rigorous techniques may be embedded in a less rigorous selection process, and must be as skeptical about the significance of statistically proper but atheoretical samples as about theoretically relevant but empirically unrepresentative ones.

## Methodological Restrictions on Universes

One of the major advantages of survey research is its capability to generalize to the population from which the survey sample was drawn. A major drawback of fieldwork and experimentation has often been their inability to do this because the persons or groups studied were chosen by nonprobability techniques. In nonreactive research that employs archives and records, the difficulty is often in defining the actual population from which the information was assembled.

By adapting the sampling techniques of survey research to the particular needs of the other styles of research, these limitations can sometimes be overcome. For example, probability samples of experimental subjects can sometimes be drawn from the population to which one wishes to generalize the experiment's findings. And greater care can be taken to sample natural groups and settings or the individuals or events in them, as Heirich's (1977) research illustrates. However, while borrowing the sampling techniques of survey research may help to solve some problems of generalization in social research, there are other problems that it may not solve. As Webb et al. (1966) have pointed out, the model of survey research pays little attention to the fact that "only certain universes are possible for any given method. A method-respondent interaction exists— one that gives each method a different set of defining boundaries for its universe" (pp. 23–24). What this implies is that the special demands of each research style's data-gathering techniques, including the techniques of survey research, lead their practitioners to study selectively certain universes of persons and groups while putting others beyond their reach.

For example, fieldwork tends to be conducted principally among relatively peaceable people in lower- to middle-level social positions, because they are people who are both less able and less likely to defend the perimeters of their groups than others who are either more prone to conflict or more elite. The interviews and questionnaires characteristic of survey research presuppose, among other things, relatively high levels of articulateness and literacy. Laboratory experiments and even many unobtrusive field experiments require relatively cooperative and compliant subjects for their successful completion. And the use of official statistics and archives may lead to study those who have attracted, or at least failed to avoid, official attention, but may direct study away from either less prominent or more elusive people.

An important implication of these methodologically related population restrictions is that even if a method's sampling procedures are improved, the generalizability of its results may yet be questionable, because the *universes* from which the data are obtained may be systematically biased by the constraints of the characteristic data-collecting techniques. An unbiased sample of such a biased universe can be as misleading as a poor sample, especially if the nature or existence of the population bias is unknown. Fortunately, however, the different data-collection techniques associated with each style of research provide the opportunity to over-come these methodological restrictions on universes.

## Dimensional Sampling

Sampling from a population to collect data and generalizing from a sample to a population are distinct but obviously interrelated sides of the same coin. However, there are stylistic differences among social science methods that emphasize varying degrees of precision and timing with respect to these issues. Field researchers often select a group because it is of interest or is accessible, and consider it sufficient to generalize from this group with decreasing confidence from a small number of similar groups to a larger number of different groups. Survey researchers, by contrast, are more interested in the precision of the sampling and in generalizing with greater confidence to a known population. Field researchers justify their lack of precision in sampling and generalization by pointing to the richness of data collected on a small number of units or even a single unit (the case study). They emphasize the synergistic "gestalt" and their more complete understanding of the structure and processes of the single case. Survey researchers justify the limited data they collect on their units (often data on individuals are reduced to a limited number of question-naire items) by pointing to their confidence in the representativeness of what they have found. The field researchers are "hedgehogs" (they know a lot about a little), while the survey researchers are "foxes"—they know a little about a lot.

Several attempts at accommodation between the hedgehogs and the foxes have been proposed. Glaser and Strauss (1967), for example, pro-posed the "constant comparative method" as a strategy of sampling units in field research—a strategy that directly addresses the sampling question of what group or situation should I next study—or where do I go from here? Depending upon one's varying analytic goals, one selects either a similar group or a greatly different group. The strategy can be repeated ad infinitum until one has exhausted cases for all the theoretical dimensions that have emerged as significant in the research.

Arnold (1970) has suggested a somewhat different approach, which he calls *dimensional sampling*. This approach combines the survey researcher's concern about precision in defining units and selecting samples prior to data collection with the field researcher's concern about gathering "rich" data on a few selected, comparative cases. In dimensional sampling, one first selects the salient theoretical dimensions that have emerged in the literature and then uses these to construct an "attribute space" that defines a theoretical sampling frame or universe. This process is much like the survey researcher's attempt to define a population or a sampling frame in order to select a probability sample that will ensure unbiased representativeness prior to actually collecting data. In dimensional sampling, Arnold argues, one is much more likely to get an exhaustive, theoretically representative sample than the traditional comparative case study approach used in most fieldwork.

An example of the use of dimensional sampling is Hunter and Fritz's (1985) research on the power structures of community elites. Most studies of community power structures have taken one of two sampling strategies: the case study approach—as in the work of Floyd Hunter (1953) and Dahl (1961)—or a much larger sample of cities with fewer survey type variables—as in the work of Clark (1968). Hunter and Fritz (1985) combined these approaches by selecting four communities from a theoretical sampling space defined by two cross-cutting dimensions shown in previous research to be related to variations in community power structures, community size and complexity versus the social class composition of the community. The four communities they selected consisted of one which was small and poor, another large and poor, a third small and rich, and the final one large and rich. They then conducted a systematic survey of elites in each of the four communities and explored variations in power structures related to these two critical dimensions.

## Sampling and Synecdoche

Sampling is generally viewed as a process of selecting one or more cases for investigation for the purpose of generalizing to a larger universe of such cases. That is, one selects a few individuals, neighborhoods, or organizations in order to say something about a larger class of similar individuals, neighborhoods, or organizations. However, sometimes one selects cases in order to say something about a larger whole of which the sampled units are seen to be a functioning part, a microcosm. For example, one may study a number of groups, organizations, or institutions, as William Foote Whyte did in *Street Corner Society* (1955), in order to say something about a larger social unit of which they are a part. Whyte, for example, was not interested in simply generalizing to a universe of other small groups in Boston, or even small groups in American cities in the mid-twentieth century, but rather he was interested in saying something about an Italian slum community. In such a case, the groups are not just part of a statistical aggregate consisting of some universe of similar small groups, but instead they are seen as functioning parts of a larger whole, be it a neighborhood, a city, or an entire society. Similarly, Robert and Helen Lynd (1929) were not interested in studying *Middletown* (Muncie, Indiana) simply to generalize to a large universe of middle-sized cities in the United States; rather they had selected Middletown as prototypical, a functioning part or microcosm of American society, which, if they could understand it, would enable them to make generalizations about American civilization as a whole.

The use of such microcosms is not uncommon in social science research. Even if a large-scale sample survey is done throughout a single metropolitan area, analysts will often generalize their findings not only to other metropolitan areas (a larger universe of similar units) but to American society as a whole. We can refer to this type of sampling as a type of metaphor, namely *synecdoche,* in which the part is used to stand for the whole. For example, when a ship's captain shouts, "All hands on deck!" he does not expect to see a science fiction scene of disembodied hands scurrying about, but the sailors themselves fully connected to their functioning hands.

Generalizing by synecdoche is not, however, simply metaphor. It is a claim that the essential features of the larger social unit are reproduced in microcosm within the smaller social unit, and that by studying them in micro we might make inferences about the macrostructure of which they are a part. In this, it is not unlike the older theory of human reproduction, the homunculus, wherein human beings were completely formed but on a vastly smaller scale within the germ cells of their parents. In social science research, we might refer to this as socioculus.

Claims of generalizibility made by synecodoche stress not simply a statistical representativeness but most importantly a functioning parallelism, and such claims often include an explicit set of functioning linkages between the larger whole and the smaller part. This is the point at which sampling crosses into the realm of what we may call *contexted* sampling.

Claims for representativeness and generalizability stress that such and such is true in this given context or under this set of limiting and specified conditions. The argument is that, of course, one might expect to get different findings by focusing on a different part, by taking into consideration a different context, or a different set of conditions. These posited or asserted—but often unexplored—contexts and conditions are the constants, not the variables, in most analyses. However, these contexts and conditions can be turned into variables; all that is required is a selection and sampling strategy at a larger scale of analysis.

These observations on synecdoche and contexted sampling are themselves not unlike recent developments in the *fractal geometry* of Mandelbrot sets. The same question is seen to generate a pattern comprised of smaller units that reproduce the pattern of the larger unit, and the larger unit itself is seen to be a part of a still larger unit that has a similar pattern. Though the patterns are similar, they do show local variations at different scales. The fact that there is a similarity to the patterns across the different sizes of the units is called *scaling*. Furthermore, a most intriguing aspect of fractals across these different scales is that they are, throughout the scales, functionally connected. Perhaps there is a parallel "fractal geometry" to social structure.

## Sampling Throughout the Stages of Research

A central thesis of this book is that multimethod research means more than simply triangulation or multiple methods of measurement. It is a perspective that permeates all stages of the research process from initial theoretical hunches to final publication. The same may be said of sampling. If sampling is seen as a rational selection process that has implications for the truth claims of one's research, then sampling is going on all the time. It is not restricted to the process of selecting units for observation, although this is its more technical and limited meaning. Sampling also enters into theory, in the selection of one or more general paradigms from among a universe of such paradigms; in the initial selection of concepts from a universe of concepts within a paradigm; and in the selection of a few key testable operationalized hypotheses from among the many that might be delivered from a single more abstract proposition. Furthermore, not only do we select units within universes, the more limited domain of sampling, we also select universes themselves. Multistage cluster sampling may be thought of as the social scientist's analogue to both the poet's and the physicist's recognition that there may be multiple universes out there. We could continue this logic to include selection of measuring instruments, items on a questionnaire, and ultimately the selection of the forms and outlets for publication (few researchers randomly distribute their findings). We are indebted to Allan Schnaiberg, who shared his ideas on this broadened meaning of sampling that he has developed in his course "The Logic of Social Inquiry" at Northwestern University.

Perhaps we have overextended the idea of sampling here to the point where it is equated with mere selection and choice. However, we have done so purposefully. The rigor and precision with which people continue to debate various sampling strategies for selecting their units of observation should apply equally to the sampling that goes on throughout the research process. Viewing choices and selections at all stages, those critical decisions that have implications for the validity of one's research, as sampling questions to be considered in relation to a universe of options, may promote both a broader search and a more rigorous justification for the choices we finally make.

# Six

# Measuring Concepts and Assessing Measurement Validity

W e construct social science concepts in the hope of capturing social reality with ideas and thereby making that reality easier to comprehend. With some of our concepts, we try to identify phenomena that need explaining and to see these puzzling events more clearly by distinguishing them as sharply as possible from other phenomena with which they might be confused. With other concepts, we lay the groundwork for discovering explanations by naming each problematic phenomenon's possible causes, consequences, and correlates. To build a theory (or possible explanation), the most likely cause-and-effect relationships between these various conceptually defined phenomena are summarized in a set of complementary hypotheses (or propositions) in the manner we illustrated in Chapter 2.

One approach to conceptualizing problems and building theories is to think the research problem through in the light of past theory and research, which usually suggests a variety of pertinent concepts and promising hypotheses. Another approach is to conduct exploratory research aimed at locating the problem's major dimensions and possible solutions afresh by examining the "shape and trend" of new bodies of data. As we have shown in Chapter 3, there has been considerable dispute over these two different modes of conceptualization and theory building. But no matter which mode is employed or whether one employs both (as might well be done in a multimethod project), once concepts are clearly defined (including, as Chapter 5 said, definitions of the various units to which the concepts may apply), the next stage in social research must be measurement if the hypotheses are to be tested.

## Defining Social Scientific Measurement

Social scientific measurement is the process of making and organizing research observations so that the resulting set of data reflects as precisely and accurately as possible the degree to which a particular social characteristic is present in a sample of persons, groups, or events. Qualitative (or nominal) measurement sorts the sample into two categories: those units that possess the given characteristic (or quality) and those that do not. Quantitative measurement makes finer distinctions: either rank orderings of the individual units or numerical arrays in which individuals are assigned a value on a scale whose steps represent different degrees (or quantities) of the characteristics being measured.

To make either qualitative or quantitative measurements, one of course needs measures (or measuring instruments). And for measurements to be useful in building and testing theories, the measures must provide good empirical estimates of the social phenomena about which we theorize. The measurement stage of research therefore has two principal phases: instrumentation and validation. The instrumentation phase consists of either constructing or (if others have studied the problem before) borrowing measures appropriate to our concepts. The validation phase determines just how precisely and accurately those measures represent the theory's concepts, and accordingly determines just how fair a test those particular measures give that theory's hypotheses.

The multimethod approach to instrumentation (as previous chapters have illustrated) is to seek not one measure for each concept but rather a set of measures (two or more) whose indicators point to the same social phenomenon, but whose quite different data-collection techniques minimize the risk of overlapping methodological biases. The purpose of triangulation (as this multimethod approach is often called) is to ease validation which, as we shall see shortly, involves comparing various measures' readings of the same or nearly identical social situations. From these comparisons we infer the level of measurement validity that the measures have attained.

The general rule in validation is that if two measures really do point to the same phenomenon, then their readings should agree. However, because consistency between measures that employ quite similar research methods might be attributable to a shared source of methodological bias rather than to a shared substantive focus, a clear inference can only be made from a comparison if the measures compared are unlikely to suffer from a common source of error. For that reason, multimethod research stresses the need to analyze different measures' weaknesses as well as their strengths in relation to the particular measurements that the measures will be called upon to perform. In designing new studies, the multimethod strategy involves selecting measures that have a low probability of common error. And in the equally important matter of assessing earlier research, the multimethod approach involves asking how closely the measures that were employed in past studies approximate the ideal, or model, of triangulated measurement.

As we have seen in earlier chapters, various measures of any given concept may employ quite different data-collection techniques. Perhaps the most marked, but by no means the only significant, difference is between reactive and nonreactive measures. Reactive measures either call upon the research subjects to respond to a stimulus presented by the researchers (for instance, a survey question or an experimental task) or (as in fieldwork) to cooperate with the researcher by carrying on "as usual" while their "natural" behavior is being observed. In contrast, nonreactive measures call upon the researcher either to find naturally occurring data, to observe unobtrusively, or to create situations in which the subjects are unaware of being parties to research. However, there is also a great deal of variety among, as well as between, reactive and nonreactive measures. For example, interviews may consist of closed or open-ended questions and answers, observation may be participant or nonparticipant, and experiments may be conducted in the laboratory or in the field, to name only a few possible variations. And Webb, Campbell, Schwartz, and Sechrest (1966) distinguish several different types of nonreactive measures: physical traces (erosions and accretions), archives (running public records and episodic private records), simple observations of easily accessible public behavior, and contrived observations of more private acts.

Knowing which measurement procedures are available and knowing how to develop new measures when the existing ones are too similar to permit triangulation is obviously a prerequisite for multimethod research. However, cataloging available measures and introducing the logic and technique for constructing new measures are beyond this chapter's scope. Rather, our aim here is to show why it is essential to make use of a variety of measures to judge any one measure's validity and how multimethod researchers do so.

## Judging Measurement's Success From Facts Rather Than Fiction

The idea of measurement validity can be stated briefly and simply. Here, for instance, are two representative definitions. "In scientific usage a measurement of a given phenomenon (as designated by a given concept) is viewed as a valid measure if it successfully measures the phenomenon" (Phillips, 1971, p.197). And, "The *validity* of a measuring instrument may be defined as the extent to which differences in scores on it reflect true differences among individuals on the characteristics that we seek to measure, rather than constant or random error" (Selltiz, Wrightsman, & Cook, 1976, p. 169). Unfortunately, the procedures for judging measures' "success" or freedom from "constant and random error" are both more complicated than our usual definitions of validity imply and (even more unfortunately) do not follow obviously from most definitions.

Indeed, our usual ways of speaking about measurement validity may inadvertently foster a mistaken view of validation, a misconception that Kaplan calls the *fiction of the true measure*. For example, defining a valid measure as one that reflects "true differences" in the characteristic being measured (as in the second definition by Selltiz et al.) implies the possibility of a comparison between the measure in question and some other entirely error-free measure that will reveal those differences with perfect accuracy and so set the standard against which the validity of more fallible measures can be judged. However, as Kaplan (1964, p. 202) points out, there are no such true measures, and so the implied comparison is an impossibility. What we can do, however, is take multiple measurements, employing different types of measures, and make comparisons between them. And, of course, it is by comparing imperfect but very real measures and measurements to one another (not to the fictional standard of a "true measure") that we actually do proceed with validation.

In this chapter we will see the comparisons between measures and measurements that constitute the various steps in the validation process are of several different kinds. Each kind supplies a different type of information about a measure's performance, and all are necessary to reach a verdict on measurement's success. First, we compare measures to determine their relative *face validity* and *content validity* with respect to the concept to be measured (which from here on we will call the *focal concept*). Second, we compare multiple measurements of the focal concept to test the measures' *reliability* and *convergent validity*. And finally, we compare multiple measurements of one focal concept to multiple measurements of other focal concepts to test the measures' *discriminant* and *predictive validity*. Measures that are found to have high convergent, discriminant, and predictive validity are said to be *construct valid*. We will now examine each of these aspects of validity and validation in turn.

## Face and Content Validation

A measure is said to be *face valid* if it is obviously more pertinent to the meaning of the focal concept than it is to the meaning of other concepts. (For instance, on the face of the matter, data from the police blotter give a better indication of a community's crime rate than do data on citizens' contributions to charity.) A measure is *content valid* to the extent that its data provide an adequate sampling of the various social behaviors subsumed by the focal concept. (Thus, although the local newspapers' front page crime stories and police statistics are both face valid measures of crime, the newspaper reports are less content valid because they generally ignore the bulk of ordinary offenses in favor of the more sensational.)

We pave the way for convergent, discriminant, predictive validation by determining how clearly and fully each of the several different measures that will be compared in those later tests renders a given focal concept's meaning. Careful face and content validation serve to eliminate the measurement errors that would result from using either irrelevant or skimpy measures. Of course, no matter how obviously relevant a measure's indicators are to the property one is trying to measure or how fully those indicators represent that property's various facets, actual measurements may still prove to be mistaken (owing to other factors such as methodological bias). But while high face and content validity are no guarantee of high convergent, discriminant, and predictive validity, they are nonetheless prerequisites. No one, for instance, has ever successfully measured air temperature with a ruler or the area of a nonequilateral triangle by taking the length of only one of the triangle's sides.

## Reliability Tests and Convergent Validation

Once we have two or more measures that appear to render a focal concept's meaning reasonably well, the next step in the validation process is to compare actual measurements to determine the measures' reliability or—if the measures employ different enough research techniques—their convergent validity. A reliable measure reports consistent readings of unchanging social situations—no matter who uses the measure and irrespective of either minor variations in technique or chance fluctuations in the circumstances of measurement. In other words, a reliable measure is free from the influence of random errors. Hence, reliability may be tested either by comparing the findings from repeated applications of precisely the same measure in slightly different circumstances or by comparing the results obtained in the same circumstances using measures that are highly similar in their techniques.

However, while a reliable measure's readings may be depended upon not to vary unless there are actual variations in the phenomenon measured, reliability does not guarantee that a measured phenomenon is the same one defined by the focal concept. Instead, consistency between measurements may be attributable to a constant or systematic error. Convergent validation's purpose is to establish confidence that agreement between different sets of measurements is in fact attributable to the parent measures' common focus on the focal phenomenon, not to a shared bias stemming from research procedures. Hence, convergent validity is determined by comparing measurements made with methodologically dissimilar measures.

## Predictive and Discriminant Validation

Finally, we compare measures of different focal concepts. These comparisons are of two kinds: (1) comparisons between measures of concepts naming phenomena thought to be causally linked and (2) comparisons between measures of supposedly unrelated phenomena. The former type of comparison (between measures of theoretically interrelated concepts) is made to test a measure's predictive validity, which is the measure's ability to confirm hypotheses that are thought to be true. On the other hand, comparisons between measures of unrelated ideas test the measure's discriminant validity, which is its ability to distinguish the phenomenon it claims to measure from other phenomena to which it is supposedly irrelevant.

For example, if there were evidence from past research that juvenile delinquency and adult crime are either related as cause and effect in some fashion or spring from the same sources, then we would expect to find a high correlation between measures of these two different types of deviance. And we would take that correlation as evidence both that the past work was probably correct and that our own measures were probably valid. On the other hand, if juvenile delinquency and adult crime bear no causal relationship to one another, we would expect instead to find that measures of the two phenomena would be largely unassociated empirically. And if contrary to our expectations we found measures of delinquency and adult crime to be correlated, then we would suspect either that our theoretical understanding was wrong or that one or both of our measures was in error.

Predictive validity is important because measurement's chief purpose is to investigate theories built from the measured concepts. A successful measure is expected not only to converge with other measures of the same focal concept but also to correlate highly with measures of whatever other concepts a theory links to the focal concept (unless, of course, the theory is false). But while high convergent and predictive validity are necessary for successful measurement, they are not sufficient. Discriminant validity is required as well. This is because measures may converge not because they accurately measure the same or causally interconnected events but because the measures compared are too insensitive to discriminate between unrelated phenomena or because the concept or concepts measured are too broad or perhaps too vague.

Of course, convergence between measures of different concepts (either predicted convergencies or unexpected failures to discriminate) may be attributable to the influence of a common source of constant error, just as convergence between measures of the same concept may be. (For instance, if we observe that rates of juvenile delinquency and adult crime, as measured by police statistics, rise and fall together in a community, this might be because changes in official detection, record keeping, or crime reporting practices affect the reported occurrence of each type of offense equally and so create a spurious correlation between them.) For that reason, it is important to test predictive and discriminant validity, as well as convergent validity, with different methods of measurement.

## Construct Validation: Redefining Measurement Validity

Measurement validity may now be redefined in terms of the comparisons among actual measures and measurements, which we have just described. This new definition will be somewhat longer and may seem more complex than the definitions that we offered earlier in the chapter, but it has the virtue of defining validity in terms of the actual process of validation. This places the burden of proof where it belongs, which is on the facts that we obtain by comparing real measures and measurements. Thus, a valid measure is one that correlates highly both with other equally face- and content-valid measures of its focal concept and also with measures of that concept's known or supposed correlates, while showing little or no empirical association with measures of concepts unrelated to the focal concept. Furthermore, to be judged valid, a measure must yield this pattern of correlations with other measures regardless of whether those measures employ research techniques similar to or dissimilar from its own. Measures that correlate highly only with methodologically similar measures may be reliable, but their validity is doubtful because of the strong possibility of methodological bias.

Because measurement validity, as we have just defined it, has several different aspects, one might well wonder how it is logically possible to reach a single meaningful verdict on measurement's success. But if you keep in mind that measurement's chief purpose is to test theories containing the measured concepts and that validation's purpose is to determine how free of measurement error our tests are, then the logic involved in judging measurement's success becomes clearer.

If we find that quite different measures of the same focal concept correlate highly with one another and also with measures of that concept's theoretical correlates, while at the same time showing little or no empirical association with measures of unrelated concepts, then we have evidence of construct validity. Construct validity signifies confidence that the concepts we have constructed in building our theory indeed define measurable traits of the people or groups sampled, and also confidence that our measures in fact measure those conceptually defined (or constructed) traits. And as Selltiz et al. point out, construct validity carries the added benefit of "... reducing the need for evidence about reliability per se"

(1976, p. 197). Because "If a measure can be shown to be reasonably valid—that is, if several measures of the same characteristic using quite different methods show considerable agreement, or if scores on the measure show reasonably high correlations with other variables that it would be predicted to relate to, it must ipso facto be reasonably reliable, since a measure with a large error component could not show such consistent results" (1976, p. 197).

There are essentially two different but complementary multimethod approaches to construct validation: verificational studies that do multimethod tests of hypotheses involving the construct in question, and validation studies that focus more on measures' convergent and discriminant validity than on prediction (or hypothesis testing). The verificational approach skips the steps of convergent and discriminant validation on the plausible assumption that if the measures employed in the different tests are erroneous, then the test results will fail to corroborate one another, and if the measures are undiscriminating, then null hypotheses (hypotheses predicting no relationship between certain of the variables) will fail to be confirmed. If the different tests do in fact support one another's conclusions, a major benefit of this approach is that measurement validation is achieved as a byproduct of the central research effort to test theories and hypotheses. (And the approach may be especially economical if it is possible to simulate a multimethod project by comparing the results of existing studies, as illustrated in Chapter 3.) However, if as is often the case, the various tests do not corroborate one another, then one must decide whether the failure indicates invalid hypotheses or instead is attributable to unreliable, biased, or undiscriminating measures. Which is to say, a measurement validation study must be undertaken.

## Designing Validation Studies

The idea of construct validity serves to link validity's various aspects logically, but to do a validation study there remains the logistical problem of arranging for the actual measurement comparisons required to test each aspect. And unfortunately, no single comparison will do the entire job because the various steps in the validation process call for different degrees and kinds of contrast between measures. Comparisons intended to test reliability need only small differences in technique or mode of application to judge the magnitude of random error. But convergent, predictive, and discriminant validation require measures whose techniques are so different that any convergence found in the measures' results could not possibly be attributable to overlapping sources of constant error. And to distinguish different focal concepts (discriminant validation) and to determine if concepts are related in theoretically predicted ways, measures must differ not only in their methods but also with respect to the concepts for which they are face and content valid. (And if two measures are different *enough* to be face- and content-valid measures of different focal concepts, then they are clearly *too* different to test one another's convergent validity.) How then are all the necessary comparisons to be obtained and brought together in a single analysis?

Because every step in the validation process involves at least two sets of measurements, and because each step requires a different type of contrast between the measures compared, research designs for validation studies are usually rather complex. And if the number of measures in question for each focal concept is greater than two, then the logistics of obtaining comparable measurements from the same sample of individuals or groups of comparing the measurements may become truly formidable. Partly for that reason, and partly because most social scientists prefer building and testing theories to the more mundane job of checking their measuring instruments' accuracy, studies aimed at assessing the validity of commonly used measures are relatively rare. Often, validation studies are undertaken only when the disagreements between different studies of the same problem become so marked that investigating the possible sources of measurement error seems the only alternative to scrapping the concepts and theories involved. We turn now to some examples of this complex (and perhaps rather thankless, but necessary) task.

## Distinguishing Reliability From Convergent Validity

Turk and Bell (1972) have compared nine commonly used measures of power in families, all applied to each family chosen in a survey style sample. Three of the measures rely on the questionnaire techniques of survey research. Through differently phrased questions, these three measures ask family members to tell the researcher who wields how much power in family decision making. Two other measures rely on the techniques typical of the laboratory experiment. These two present each family with an experimental decision-making task designed by the researcher to show clearly who in the family wins when family members disagree and to observe the actual outcomes of the decisions. The last four measures employ the fieldworker's technique of direct observation of social interaction between family members, although in this case the interaction observed is not "natural" interaction but interaction that occurs during the course of the experimental task. These measures classify family members by the degree to which they act like leaders while talking with one another.

Turk and Bell's (1972) study illustrates the multimethod approach to testing reliability and distinguishing reliability from convergent validity. They began their analysis by replicating each measure more or less exactly and comparing their findings with the results of earlier studies employing the same measures. (At this step of the validation process, they found comfortingly consistent results.) Next, they compared each measure to one or more other measures that use basically the same data-collection technique (that is, questionnaire, observation or outcomes on an experimental task, or observation of interaction). Here, too, they found a fair amount of agreement between measurements. And finally, they compared the three sets of measures with one another. By making these progressively diverse comparisons, they first tested reliability by replication, then tested reliability further by testing the equivalence of similar but not identical measures, and, finally, tested convergent validity by comparing the sets of quite different measures. In the final comparison, they discovered that despite the internal consistency that each single measure showed upon replication, measures using different methods failed to agree. Each set instead yielded a quite different picture of who wielded the power in the families studied. This finding makes the point well that measures may be very reliable without being convergently valid.

Turk and Bell concluded that because the various measures of power are not very highly related to one another, although each is apparently fairly reliable, "Continued use of these measures is not justified without further specification of what aspect of the general phenomenon is being measured by any given index." And they suggest the additional possibility "that there is no one meaning of power, or, if there is, that such measures as these are not measuring the phenomenon with enough precision to be useful" (1972, p. 222).

## The Multitrait-Multimethod Approach to Construct Validation

Once research like Turk and Bell's (or the studies of crime which we reviewed in Chapter 1) suggests that a concept may subsume several uncorrelated or perhaps negatively correlated phenomena (rather than representing a unified phenomenon whose components are closely and positively interrelated), then the problem is to determine which—if any—of the concept's subphenomena are related to which others—and in what ways. And just as in building and testing any other hypotheses linking social phenomena, we must ask how well various measures measure each phenomenon (the question of convergent validity) and also how well various measures discriminate and predict. Solving this problem of construct validity requires a still more complicated research design and data analysis than Turk and Bell (1972) employed to test only reliability and convergent validity. Specifically, it requires a set of procedures called multitrait-multimethod validation developed by Campbell and Fiske (1959).

The multitrait-multimethod approach involves precise identification of a focal concept's constituent traits (or component phenomena) and the application of at least two different methods to develop multiple measures of each trait. These measures are then applied to the same sample of individuals or groups. The resulting measurements yield a matrix of information showing the strength of the empirical associations between different measures of the same trait, between similar measures of different traits, and also between different measures of different traits. The simplest possible matrix is illustrated in Figure 6.1. It assumes two traits (A and B) and two measures (1 and 2), and uses the symbol $r$ to represent a statistical measure of correlation between measurements. If the measures adequately measure their focal traits, while discriminating between different traits (assuming the traits A and B to be unrelated), then one would expect the correlations between measures of a given trait ($r_{A1, A2}$ and $r_{B1, B2}$) to be stronger than those between measures of different traits ($r_{A1, B1}$, $r_{A2, B1}$, etc.).

Pennings (1973) applied the multitrait-multimethod approach to the problem of measuring the concept of bureaucracy. Many social scientists have concluded that the concept of bureaucracy refers not to a unitary phenomenon but rather to a set of organizational traits or structural features, which all seem to be characteristic of many contemporary business, government, and other administrative organizations. However, in samples of particular organizations, these traits have only sometimes been found to be positively related; other times showing low or negative correlations. Centralization of authority and formalization of organizational activities are two important traits of bureaucratic administration for which such an inconsistent pattern of correlational findings has been found in past research. Pennings investigates the possibility that the past studies' disagreements may be attributable to variations in measurement

| Trait | A | | B | |
|---|---|---|---|---|
| Method | 1 | 2 | 1 | 2 |
| A    1 | | | | |
|       2 | $r_{A1,A2}$ | | | |
| B    1 | $r_{A1,B1}$ | $r_{A2,B1}$ | | |
|       2 | $r_{A1,B2}$ | $r_{A2,B2}$ | $r_{B1,B2}$ | |

**Figure 6.1**     A Simple Multitrait-Multimethod Matrix

techniques rather than to variations in the actual structure that the previous studies were trying to measure. He does so by simultaneously applying two sets of measuring instruments (instruments used separately in earlier work) to the same sample of manufacturing firms, measuring both centralization and formalization with each of the different types of instruments. One type, which Pennings calls *the institutional approach,* measures an organization's structure with data from organizational records and from descriptions obtained in interviews with top executives. The other type, *the questionnaire approach,* surveys rank-and-file members about the characteristics of their work environment and aggregates their individual responses to build a composite picture of each organization's degree of centralization and formalization.

Pennings' (1973) research design and subsequent data analysis are somewhat more complex than our illustrative matrix shown in Figure 6.1 because each of his measurement approaches yielded two or more face-valid measures of each trait. And he intercorrelates each of these submeasures with one another as well as with its "different measure" counterpart to determine how closely methodologically similar measures of the same trait converge. These comparisons are analogous to Turk and Bell's (1972) internal comparisons among questionnaire, task, and interaction-based measures of power in families. However, the logic of his study remains the same, although complicated by the multiplicity of "same-method" measures.

Pennings' (1973) assessment of the construct validity of "bureaucracy," of its components of centralization and formalization, and of the measures employed are far from either simple or encouraging. He suggests that for the most part neither same-method measures of centralization and formalization, nor different-method measures of the two, intercorrelate highly enough either to conclude with much confidence that bureaucracy (as measured by the two approaches considered) is a unitary phenomenon, or that the two components of bureaucracy (centralization and formalization) are unitary. He concludes with the caution that in the study of bureaucracy "forward steps cannot even be considered until researchers have developed concepts and corresponding operations that can describe similarities and differences among organizations along meaningful and differentiated dimensions, using methods that fit the concepts. Even this primitive stage of development has not been achieved" (1973, p. 702).

Perhaps studies evaluating commonly used measures of social science concepts are relatively rare because they so often seem to end on a depressing note. Or it may simply be—as Bollen and Paxton (1998) suggest—that the data requirements for the classic multitrait-multimethod design are too stringent for many researchers, particularly those using subjective measures based on secondary data. To remedy this, they explore several less-demanding approximations, carried out "under more relaxed conditions," and illustrate the possibilities with studies measuring liberal democracy, the reputational quality of graduate programs, and the comparable-worth of jobs to investigate gender differences in pay. They also urge researchers who detect systematic method-related errors not to abandon their efforts but rather to continue their analyses to discover the possible determinants of these errors. These determinants may then be factored into their investigations. We will provide an example of this procedure in the next chapter with the work of Danzger (1975) and others on the use of newspaper accounts of protest events.

## What to Do if Measurement Fails (and How to Guard Against Failure)

When measures fail to intercorrelate in the expected ways, it is generally taken as discouraging evidence. But what should one be discouraged about: the validity of the measures, or rather the viability of the concept, or (in the case of predictive validation) the truth of the hypothesis in question? Measurement may fail because of poor measures but also because of poor ideas. Measures may not represent a concept well empirically because the concept is, so to speak, unrepresentable. The concept may have named and defined a nonexistent phenomenon in the sense of grouping together under one conceptual heading a number of behaviors that occur in such disparate circumstances that they do not hold together empirically, even though a theorist has seen important logical or semantic interconnections between them. Or the concept may simply have been too vaguely or too loosely defined to permit accurate measurement.

When measures have been found to be reliable, there is a presumption that they are measuring "something," because otherwise their measurements would vary randomly. But if reliable measures do not intercorrelate in the expected ways, then it is doubtful that they are measuring the same "something." Hence, when many reliable measures fail to converge (as in the study conducted by Turk and Bell [1972]), it is generally assumed that the focal concept is at fault; that there is no single phenomenon of, for instance, power in families (or, as we saw in Chapter 1, crime), and that the original concept needs to be revised to define a number of independent, more narrowly specified elements. Because, as Blalock (1979) points out, social scientists tend to work with complex concepts encompassing many diverse behaviors, this conclusion is often warranted. And, indeed, an important contribution of negative validation results is pointing out needed reconceptualizations. However, carried to an extreme, this procedure would lead to as many concepts as we have reliable but empirically unrelated measures; each measure seen as indicating a completely different phenomenon. We need, therefore, to consider further precautions against measurement failure and ways of salvaging potentially valuable ideas that apparently have not stood up to measurement.

## Measurement and Meaning

Face and content validation are usually said chiefly to involve the exercise of common sense and care in defining concepts and constructing appropriate measures. For instance, Bailey writes that "face validity is simply assessed by the evaluator studying the concept to be measured and determining, in his or her best judgment, whether the instrument arrives at the concept adequately" (1978, p. 58). However, as Blalock (1979) makes clear, determining which observable behaviors indicate which concepts (or conversely, which concepts correctly subsume which observable behaviors) is usually a far more complicated analytic task than our conventional treatments of face- and content-validation acknowledge.

If social scientists employed concepts that each designated only one form of readily recognizable behavior, then conceptualization and measurement might pose few problems beyond the difficulties of initial definition and observation. However, that approach would create other problems. As Blalock points out: "Human behaviors are extremely diverse, so much so that if we were to try to explain each one separately the situation would become hopeless" (1979, p. 883). Therefore, instead of treating each sort of observable behavior separately, we generally work with "theoretical constructs": broad categories that group together "conceptually similar" behaviors, which may bear little similarity to one another in their overt, or directly observable, characteristics. For instance, "one may *achieve status* in a variety of ways, such as killing enemies, saving lives on the operating table, tackling opponents on a football field, or making vague political promises" (Blalock, 1979, our italics). These constructs are not "real" in the sense that a killing, an operation, a tackle, or a political speech is "real." Instead, "all that the use of these concepts implies is that they are convenient things to talk about and to use for explaining phenomena" (Willer & Webster, 1970, p. 751). And as we have seen earlier in this chapter, the validity of a construct's measures is ultimately judged by their capability to allow the construct to perform its explanatory role.

Although the use of constructs may solve some problems of explanation, it creates other problems of conceptualization and measurement because there are generally a great many different forms that the phenomena defined by constructs may take. (Consider only, for instance, the diverse behaviors that we have seen in even such an apparently straightforward idea as "criminal deviance" implies, never mind less intuitively "real" phenomena such as "status attainment," "alienation," or "anomie.") A key problem is that in developing their measures, researchers must choose a few from among the many possible behaviors in order to devise a given measure. No given measure can include all the behaviors that a theoretical construct implies. And even if the "few" behaviors that a complex and ambitious measure might encompass may be absolutely large in number, it remains small when compared with the nearly infinite number of behaviors that many constructs imply. To cope with this problem, we (often implicitly, Blalock [1979] suggests) adopt definitional strategies, or models, for measuring the complex phenomena named by our constructs.

## Making Measurement Models Explicit

These definitional strategies, or measurement models, are sets of assumptions adopted by researchers to justify narrowing the field of behavior that they need to consider in selecting indicators for measurement. Blalock (1979) discusses four commonly invoked strategies. The first ("behaviors defined in terms of internal states") distinguishes between conceptually relevant and irrelevant behavior on the basis of the social actors' perceptions, attitudes, and motivations with respect to the behavior in questions. The second ("behaviors defined in terms of consequences") sets aside the actors' subjective definitions of the situation and instead asks only about the objective consequences of behavior. The third ("behaviors defined in terms of standards") takes supposed social norms and values as a reference point. And the fourth ("behaviors defined in terms of replication") looks for an assumed linkage between the behavior and other variables that cause this behavior to be repeated, with replication being an essential component of the definition. (For example, if Pavlov's dog salivates, this behavior may or may not indicate the presence of a "conditioned response." To determine this, one must know if the salivation was preceded by the presentation of food to the dog, food accompanied by a ringing bell, or a ringing bell alone. Only in the latter case can one say with much certainty that the salivation indicates a conditioned response. And then only if the dog also salivates on later occasions—the replication—when the bell is rung in the absence of food.)

Blalock's (1979) point is not that these definitional strategies and the simplifications they imply should be shunned in favor of efforts to achieve total realism by attempting to observe everything. That would be impossible. Rather, his point is that researchers should make their measurement strategies as explicit as possible so that whatever biases each strategy may entail can be systematically accounted for when interpreting different measurement results.

Careful analysis of measurement strategies is especially important in multimethod research. In following the multimethod strategy's injunction to choose measures sufficiently different that their possible methodological errors will not overlap, there is a very good chance that one will choose methods that will employ quite different measurement models as well. If so, a major issue in interpreting the results of these different measures will be deciding whether differences between their measurements are attributable to the different techniques employed or instead to the different model upon which each measure was founded. Criminal victimization surveys, for instance, equate crime with survey respondents' perceptions of offenses; while police statistics equate crime with official reactions to alleged offenses. It is reasonable, therefore, to ask whether different measures of crime yield different results because their techniques distort findings in different directions or instead because each measure names a different set of behaviors as indicative of crime?

In Chapter 1 we suggested that if two measures, despite using different techniques, really do measure the same conceptually defined phenomenon, then their measurements should converge as each measure's methodological errors are corrected. And furthermore, we suggested that if the measurements continue to diverge as errors are corrected, then one is justified in assuming that each measures a different phenomenon (or perhaps independently varying aspects of the same phenomenon). Blalock's (1979) analysis allows us to refine these interpretive criteria further by offering a third possibility. Measures may fail to converge with the correction of methodological errors not because they measure different concepts, but instead because the measures derive from different measurement models of the same concept.

This is an important refinement. Without the idea of measurement models that translate abstract conceptual meanings into concrete measurements (and vice versa), we would be forced to conclude that whenever two measures diverge sharply in their readings, they in fact measure something quite different, no matter how apparent it may be that the measured events are closely related analytically. (Reported and unreported crime are obviously both "crime" in an analytic sense, even if estimates of the crime rate may vary greatly depending upon which kind one studies.) Given the relatively low correlations between different measures of the "same" social phenomena, this procedure might quickly trivialize social theory. The current core of social science concepts that define major social phenomena would be reduced to a much larger set of minuscule ideas, each operationally defined by a unique set of measurement procedures, and the advantage that theoretical constructs afford would be lost.

There is, of course, a contrasting approach to measurement, called operationism, which argues that each different set of measurement procedures must be regarded as measuring a different concept. Multimethod research rejects this argument because the argument disallows the possibility of the same concept being measured by completely different operations; and the argument also denies that different measures may converge because they, in fact, measure the same thing. However, multimethod research accepts the operationists' insight that measurement and meaning are interdependent.

In conclusion, we draw two inferences from this insight. The first inference is that multiple operationism is required to learn what a concept means. And the second inference is that comparisons between measures are needed to determine which of a concept's various implications, as revealed by the use of different models and modes of measurement, are in fact sufficiently related empirically, as well as analytically, to be usefully included within a single construct.

# Seven

# Explaining Social Phenomena Causally

R esearch problems refer to events that require explanation either for practical purposes, to advance theoretical knowledge, or both. "All explanations," Brown (1963) writes, "are attempts to explain away impediments of some kind. They are efforts to deprive puzzles, mysteries, and blockages of their force, and hence, existence" (p. 41). In this broad sense of the word, even methodological skepticism (the position that all research findings are questionable because all research methods are flawed) offers an explanation of sorts for problematic phenomena. It suggests the hypothesis that each method of social research has inherent weaknesses that impede our efforts to learn the true causes of events and so explain their occurrence.

However, methodological skepticism does not solve research problems in any substantial way. Rather, it challenges the validity of research findings on methodological grounds, and in so doing identifies a major obstacle to achieving more substantive solutions. The multimethod approach to research is a strategy for overcoming this obstacle by exploiting the fortunate circumstance that although all methods are imperfect, their weaknesses differ, and their varied strengths provide the opportunity to check and compensate for their varied faults. The preceding chapter addressed the multimethod strategy's application to measurement and the analysis of multimethod data to assess measurement validity. This chapter assesses the strategy's application to causal inference and the analysis of multimethod data to determine the validity of causal explanations.

# Causation and Causal Explanation

Causes are phenomena of a special kind. They are events that either produce or aid in the production of other events, which we then call their effects or consequences. A *sufficient cause* is a factor that inevitably has a particular consequence. A *necessary cause* is a condition that must be present for an effect to occur, although it may be insufficient in itself to produce that effect. A *probable cause* is a factor that only sometimes (or with a certain probability) has the given effect. A *contributing cause* is a condition that although inessential to a phenomenon's occurrence nonetheless increases the probability of its occurring. A *hypothesis* offers a causal explanation if it identifies either a sufficient, necessary, probable, or contributing cause for a phenomenon.

## Criteria Essential for Causation

To establish that one phenomenon causes another, three things must be demonstrated empirically. First, it must be shown that the two phenomena *covary*. Which is to say, changes (or variations) in their values must occur together more often than chance alone would lead you to expect. (If two variables are associated no more often than chance, one variable might, of course, still be a cause of the other. But the influence of a cause so weak as to be indistinguishable from the influence of a large number of small, unorganized causes, or chance, is obviously of little explanatory value.) Second, it must be shown that variations in the supposed cause ($X$, for short) occur before variations in the supposed effect ($Y$, for short), since simple covariation is consistent with either the hypothesis that $X$ caused $Y$ or the reverse hypothesis that $Y$ caused $X$. And third, it must be shown that variation in the supposed cause can bring about variation in the supposed effect even when other possible causes of $Y$ are constant or inoperative. (In other words, to observe the influence of any one cause it is necessary to control in some fashion the influence of other causes.) This last piece of evidence serves to distinguish covariation attributable to causation ("genuine" covariation) from mere correlation (or "spurious" covariation) attributable to a noncausal tie between variables. (For instance, midwives today generally have a better record of delivering babies than other medical personnel. However, the correlation between midwifery and healthy babies is spurious, owing to the fact that expectant mothers for whom trouble is anticipated are more likely to be attended by physicians.)

For convenience, these three criteria of proof for causation are usually referred to simply as *covariation, causal order,* and *nonspuriousness.* Logically, the second criterion (causal order) should perhaps precede the first (covariation), since covariation implies causation only if the phenomena vary in causal order. However, from a research point of view, covariation takes precedence. Because while any event is preceded by an infinite number of past events, any one of which might be among its causes, correlations greater than chance are far more rare and indicate possible causes more precisely than the mere fact of temporal priority.

However, while correlations indicate possible causes, they do not prove causation—even if the variables do vary in causal order. The criterion of nonspuriousness makes that clear. In a spurious correlation, two causally unrelated phenomena covary owing to the influence of one or more "third variables" ($T$, for short). This may happen in either of two ways. First, the two phenomena may have a common source that creates the illusion of a causal relationship between them. Thus, $X$ and $Y$ may covary, not because $X$ causes $Y$ but because $T$ causes both $X$ and $Y$. (For instance, if the anticipation of a difficult birth leads women to seek physicians rather than midwives, and also this selection process causes a higher rate of difficult deliveries attended by physicians, then it may appear that physicians cause difficult deliveries.) Second, during the period of time in which a correlation between the two phenomena was observed some other actual cause of $Y$ may have incidentally varied along with $X$. If $X$ and $T$ are confounded in this way, $T$'s causal influence may be mistaken for $X$'s. (For instance, if in a study to determine the relative effectiveness of midwives and physicians an epidemic of a mysterious new disease swept the physicians' hospitals, but not the community outside where midwives practice, this could lead to the erroneous inference that physicians were the cause of the maladies.)

Although these are different types of spuriousness, in either case the test for nonspuriousness is the same. If covariation persists when one holds constant or eliminates the influence of the suspected third variable, then that covariation is genuine, at least with respect to that variable. If instead the covariation disappears, then the original relationship is spurious. (Thus, if the relationship between healthy babies and midwifery were spurious, it would be predicted that the relationship would disappear if midwives' and physicians' records were compared only for women whose deliveries were expected to be normal.) However, because there are always more possible sources of spuriousness at any given moment than a researcher can check—or perhaps even conceive of—a finding of nonspuriousness is to be read cautiously as "lack of demonstrated spuriousness" rather than to mean "definite causation."

## Interpreting Causal Relationships

Attributing a phenomenon's occurrence to a cause tells "how" that phenomenon occurs. But it does not tell "why" the cause has its effect. *Interpreting* a causal relationship means explicating the process, or sequence of events, through which one phenomenon causes another. Interpretation involves identifying variables that behave as if they were both effects of $X$ and causes of $Y$. These are intervening third variables ($I$, for short): variables that covary with $X$ and $Y$, intervene between them in time, and cause the relationships between $X$ and $Y$ to disappear when their influence is eliminated.

This point may be illustrated with our midwives and physicians example. If midwives' record of healthy deliveries may be explained away by the fact that women who choose midwives preselect themselves or are preselected by medical personnel, then midwives' record of effectiveness is spurious in that the midwives themselves did nothing to produce the differential between their performance and that of the physicians. However, if one were to find that midwives were responsible for referring trouble-prone women to physicians, then one might say instead that the midwives had indeed caused the differential between themselves and physicians, although not in the way it might first appear (that is, not by their superior practice of medicine). In other words, one has reinterpreted rather than discredited the relationship between $X$ (type of medical care) and $Y$ (healthy deliveries) by suggesting the theory that it is the social process of referral rather than the medical process of treatment that may explain the differential success of different types of medical practitioners.

This may sound simply like another form of spuriousness. And, in fact, some researchers treat it as such. For example, Cook and Campbell (1979) suggest: "To conclude that A causes B when in fact the model A - C - B is true would be to draw a false positive conclusion about cause" (p. 50). However, there is another view as well. Blalock (1964) writes that "through interpretation one is putting frosting on the cake, so to speak. He is not discovering anything radically wrong with the notion that X [or A] causes Y [or B]. He is merely making it seem more plausible by finding the intermediate links" (p. 85). And earlier, Hyman (1955) urged that finding one or more intermediate links might serve as a fourth criterion for causality, demonstrating a substantial link between the supposed cause and effect and thereby making their relationship more plausible yet.

At issue here is the type of hypothesis being tested. If X is supposed to be the ultimate cause of Y (a cause that brings about this effect directly), then indeed finding an intermediate link disconfirms that hypothesis. If to the contrary, X and Y are thought to be merely the end links in a longer causal chain, then investigating the various possible causal linkages by testing for the effects of various intervening variables is essential. For, as Hirschi and Selvin (1967) suggest, "two-variable relations offer as much support to one interpretation as another." And "it is the kind of intervening variable that a theory stresses that is crucial in differentiating one theory from another" (p. 95). Thus, while interpretation is perhaps unnecessary to establish causality, it is essential for determining how causes bring about effects, and therefore it is important for building a set of causal hypotheses into a theory.

## Causal Laws and Lawlike Statements

A causal law is an empirically confirmed causal hypothesis that is derivable from a theory. It sets forth a generally accepted account of the conditions that govern a phenomenon's occurrence. A *lawlike* statement is a proposition similar to a law in all respects but proof. A very famous example of a causal law is Durkheim's (1897/1951) hypothesis that reduced social integration leads to increased rates of suicide. It follows logically from Durkheim's theory (the so-called theory of egoistic suicide) that low social integration creates a social climate of individualism in which each person's behavior is guided more by his or her own sense of appropriate morality than by strictly defined and enforced social norms, including norms prohibiting suicide.

Causal laws and lawlike statements have several advantages over ordinary hypotheses and empirical generalizations. Because they follow from theories, they tell why as well as how a phenomenon occurs, and so provide more complete explanations. Furthermore, although the plausibility of an hypothesis or an empirical generalization rests solely upon the evidence adduced in its support, a law or lawlike statement is also supported by the evidence for whatever additional hypotheses have been derived from the parent theory, and so has a firmer empirical anchorage. Finally, testing lawlike statements rather than isolated hypotheses contributes to the validation of theories because theories are tested by testing their ability to yield explanations for particular phenomena. And, in general, the more, and the more diverse, the phenomena that a theory can explain through the hypotheses that researchers derive from it, both the more valuable and the more valid it is held to be.

Here is a definition of a causal law (proposed by Stinchcombe [1968]) that is especially useful because it emphasizes an additional aspect of causal explanation: the importance of specifying the environment in which causation occurs. "A law is a statement or proposition in a theory which says that there exist environments (the better described the environments, the more complete the law) in which a change in the value of one variable is associated with a change in the value of another variable and can produce this change without any change in other variables in the environment" (p. 31).

Specifying the "environments" in which causation occurs (or fails to occur) serves to define a causal law's boundary conditions, the circumstances in which the law is expected to apply validly. Setting precise boundary conditions is important because no law has universal applications. For instance, Stinchcombe (1968) notes that even so elementary a "physical law" as "The shining of the sun causes the temperature to rise ... would not apply in a perfect vacuum, since temperature is not defined in such an environment" (pp. 31–32). And even more to the point, Durkheim (1897/1951) argued that reduced social integration did not lead to increased suicide in "altruistic" social environments (settings, such as the nineteenth-century European military, in which collective life has so much value that an individual's life has little). Rather, he suggested that in such environments reduced integration would decrease suicide. In support of this contention, Durkheim cited the finding that in nineteenth-century Europe the military (or altruistic) and the civilian (or egoistic) rates of suicide tended to vary inversely (the higher the civilian rate, the lower the military rate).

In constructing a causal explanation for a phenomenon, the researcher is concerned therefore not only with covariation, causal order, nonspuriousness, and interpretation but also with specification of the conditions under which a cause has its effect and the contrasting conditions under which that effect may be moderated or perhaps even reversed. And indeed, as Hirschi and Selvin (1967) suggest, "The most common outcome of introducing a third variable into a two-variable relation is neither the persistence of the original relation, as in demonstrating lack of spuriousness, nor the vanishing of the relation, as in demonstrating spuriousness or showing a link between two variables; instead, the analyst finds that the effects of the independent variable differ from one value of the new variable to another" (p. 47).

## Modes of Causal Analysis

Social researchers employ three principal modes of causal analysis: naturalistic observation, experimentation, and multivariate analysis of survey and archival data. There are variants of each type, but the characteristic procedures of each are described in the following sections.

### Naturalistic Observation

Naturalistic observation involves stationing researchers in natural social settings where either examples of the phenomenon to be explained are known to occur or where examples of its supposed cause occur. In the former type of study, the purpose is to observe firsthand the causal process that produces the phenomenon in particular instances and, from that data, to form a more general explanatory causal hypothesis. (In this fashion, Glaser and Strauss [1967] suggest that "general relations are often discovered in vivo; that is, the fieldworker literally sees them occur" [p. 40].) In the latter type of study, the purpose is to test a preformed hypothesis by determining if in the particular instances observed the supposed cause actually has the predicted effect.

Once an hypothesis has received some direct observational support, it is investigated further by means of a series of comparisons between situations selected to check for possible sources of spuriousness, to discover intervening causal links, and to specify the limits of the hypothesis' applicability. In making these comparisons, special attention is usually given to finding and studying "deviant" cases (instances in which $X$ and $Y$ fail to covary as the hypothesis predicts). Deviant and conforming cases are then compared to refine the analysis until a lawlike statement (a causal hypothesis, a description of its boundary conditions, and a theoretical interpretation) about the natural occurrence of the phenomenon in question can be made.

## Experimentation

Experimentation, in contrast to naturalistic observation, always begins with a hypothesis—ideally one derived from a theory. Guided by an understanding of its boundary conditions (the environment in which it is expected to hold true), the experimenter then contrives a situation in which the hypothesis can be tested by deliberately manipulating the occurrence of the supposed cause and then measuring the effects. The causal factor, operationalized as an experimental treatment, is systematically applied to one group of subjects (the treatment group) and withheld from a comparable group (the control group). Comparability is achieved either by matching subjects or by randomly assigning them to the treatment and control groups. (Randomization ensures comparability not by making the groups identical but by preventing systematic differences between them.)

The influence of third variables that may affect the hypothesized causal relationship is handled in one or two general ways, depending upon whether the particular variable is relevant or irrelevant to the theory from which the hypothesis was derived. Theoretically relevant variables are studied by systematically varying their values along with the treatment and determining the effects of the treatment under the different conditions. (For instance, if the theory predicts that the independent variable represented by the treatment has different effects for civilians than for military personnel, then the hypothesis would be separately tested for each group.) In this way, experimenters test alternative theoretical interpretations. The influence of theoretically irrelevant variables, however, is either eliminated through randomization (which in principle dissipates any systematic effects of subjects' background characteristics), blocked out (as by using soundproof rooms), or by holding them constant (as by studying only college sophomores and treating all subjects identically except for the treatment variations). In this way, experimenters rule out the influence of various possible sources of spuriousness, making it possible to attribute whatever differences they find to the experimental treatment. (Although as Cook and Campbell [1979] suggest, there always remains the possibility that differences between treatment and control subjects may be attributable to uncontrolled for method-related factors, such as the perceived arbitrariness of random assignment to one experimental group rather than to another.)

## Multivariate Analysis

Multivariate analysis is a procedure for making causal inferences from data about unobserved past events over which the researcher had no control. It substitutes statistical correlations between survey or archival measures of variables for firsthand observation of social processes, comparison of statistically created subgroups within a sample for fieldwork's comparison of different natural settings, and statistical control over third variables for experimental control. The experimental manipulation of the independent variables is approximated by comparing natural variations. And causation is inferred from correlations that persist when third variables representing possible sources of spuriousness are held constant.

Causal order, which the fieldworker observes directly and the experimenter creates by manipulating the independent variable, is ascertained either by dating observations, by studying only variables that could not possibly vary in any other order (for instance, place of birth, gender, race, etc., antedate nearly all other sociological variables), or—more rarely—by collecting data for the same respondents over time.

Multivariate analysis may be employed either to generate lawlike statements or to test them. Thus, the so-called *elaboration schema* (one type of multivariate analysis) outlines the logic for analyzing correlations between variables, introducing third variables statistically to test for spuriousness, to interpret a relationship, and to specify the conditions under which it occurs. The result is a causal generalization linked to a theory by the identification of intervening variables and provided with a set of boundary conditions by the specifying variables discovered in the analysis.

On the other hand, *causal modeling*—another form of multivariate analysis—translates a theory into a set of interrelated causal hypotheses. In total, these hypotheses attempt to describe the causal process through which a phenomenon is produced. By using simultaneous equations, these models take account of the possible sources of spuriousness and assess both the direct and indirect effects of independent and intervening variables on the phenomenon being studied.

## Assessing the Validity of Causal Research

Research to generate and test causal hypotheses is usually judged in terms of two standards: internal and external validity. *Internal validity* refers to confidence that $X$ and $Y$, as measured in the research, either are or are not causally related for the particular sample of persons, the social setting, and the time covered by the study. The level of internal validity attained depends upon the certainty with which the investigators establish the presence (or absence) of covariation, the clarity with which they distinguish the variables' temporal order, and the thoroughness with which they check for possible sources of spuriousness. Thus, low internal validity refers not to a false hypothesis but rather to ambiguity as to truth or falsity or the inability to make a clear causal inference from the data.

*External validity* refers to confidence in generalizing a causal relationship found in one study to other studies employing different measures of the same variables and involving different samples and populations, different social settings, and different time periods. The level of external validity attained thus depends upon the validity of the measures employed and the representativeness of the sample, research site, and time period studied—and also upon the thoroughness with which the research investigates the hypothesis with various measures and for various types of persons, settings, and times. Low external validity refers, therefore, to the inability to generalize a causal inference confidently, not necessarily to a false inference.

To assess the validity of research aimed at making and testing lawlike statements (not just simple causal hypotheses) we must introduce a third type of validity, one referring to success at achieving empirically grounded rather than merely conjectural interpretations of causal relationships. *Interpretive validity* may be defined as confidence in attributing a causal relationship between two variables to the operation of one intervening causal process rather than another. The level of interpretive validity attained depends upon the thoroughness with which the study investigates the influence of various intervening variables suggested by alternative interpretations of the relationship in question. Low interpretive validity refers, therefore, to the inability to do more than speculate as to "why" (rather than "how," "for whom," "where," and "when") one phenomenon causes another.

As we have said, neither low internal validity, external validity, nor interpretive validity necessarily indicates a false hypothesis. Rather, these conditions indicate different types of ambiguity, or uncertainty, as to the meaning of research findings. However, because research of low internal, external, and interpretive validity is ambiguous, it does little to refute allegations that its ideas are false. This is obviously true of low internal validity, but it is equally true of external and interpretive validity. Thus, an ungeneralizable causal inference is not only relatively useless but also of doubtful accuracy. And although, as we saw earlier, some analysts regard tests for intervening variables' influence as "icing on the cake" (necessary only to investigate the finer points of theory), failure to identify and establish the influence of intermediate causal links may lead skeptics to question the validity of the basic two-variable causal relationship.

For example, despite the impressive array of both experimental and nonexperimental evidence implying a causal relationship between smoking and cancer, many people (most notably, but not exclusively, people associated with the tobacco industry) continued to question that relationship on the grounds that the intervening disease mechanism by which smoking makes body cells cancerous was discovered in 1996.

## Research Styles' Generic Strengths and Weaknesses

The ideal research method for generating and testing causal explanations would include the following characteristics. First, to maximize internal validity, the method would incorporate the experimental techniques of deliberately manipulating possible causes, controlling extraneous variables, and randomly assigning subjects to treatment and control situations. Second, to facilitate realistic theoretical interpretation, the method would allow the researcher to observe directly the sequence of events through which the phenomenon to be explained naturally occurs, as field-workers sometimes can. Third, to promote external validity, the method would provide data for all of the various types of persons, social settings, and times pertinent to the hypothesis, as survey researchers attempt to do for persons by sampling populations. And finally, to improve measurement validity and test generalizability across measures (another aspect of external validity), the method would provide for totally unobtrusive observation and nonreactive measurement of changes and variations in the values of the variables in all of their possible empirical manifestations. Unfortunately, none of our research methods has all of these attributes. Instead, each approximates this "ideal method" in one or more respects but falls short in other respects.

Fieldwork, employing naturalistic observation, is strong for discovering causal hypotheses *in situ* and for constructing theories about natural causal sequences. Also, it has considerable strength for testing and refining hypotheses that assert either necessary or sufficient causes for phenomena, since hypotheses of this type may be disconfirmed by even one verified case in which the predicted effect occurs in the absence of the causal factor supposed to be either necessary or sufficient to produce it. However, naturalistic observation is usually confined to a relatively small number of cases for reasons of economy, avoids experimental manipulation and control deliberately, and, by definition, requires that an observer be present at the scene of events. These characteristics of the technique are potential sources of error. Small samples provide only a weak basis for inferring greater than chance covariation and so make it difficult to distinguish coincidence from probable causation. Small samples also interfere with the application of statistical controls to data. And in the absence of experimental controls, many possible sources of spuriousness, as well as alternative theoretical interpretations, must go unchecked. Finally, both small samples and the presence of an observer raise questions about the generalizability (or external validity) of the findings. Thus, on the one hand, it may be asked how well those few cases represent the variety of the larger social world; and, on the other, if the effect observed might not be attributable to observation itself, and so be ungeneralizable to unresearched situations.

Experimentation is a strong method for testing causal hypotheses of all sorts (those asserting probable and contributing causes as well as those asserting necessary or sufficient causes). Its manipulation and control of variables, plus random assignment of subjects to experimental and control conditions, provide high internal validity and good opportunities to test alternative theoretical interpretations. However, the limited range of persons, settings, and times for whom and in which experiments may be conducted, plus the reactivity and artificiality of many experimental procedures, all raise questions about the external validity of experimental results.

Survey research, employing multivariate analysis, provides a balance of moderately high internal and external validity, owing to the survey researcher's ability to control statistically for the influence of third variables in samples drawn to represent populations in all their variety. Moreover, survey data may be employed either to discover or to test hypotheses and theories. However, survey research shares with experimentation and fieldwork the disadvantage of employing reactive modes of measurement, which raises questions about the generalizability of its findings to natural or unresearched manifestations of the phenomena in question. Also, although survey research often employs randomly drawn samples of respondents to attain generalizability to populations, it does not randomly expose respondents to causal factors as experiments do. Rather, survey research studies the effects of natural exposure, which in many instances may be highly selective. This possibility raises a serious issue of internal validity: Are survey-based correlations genuine or spurious in relation to the operation of some nonrandom process of selection such as self-selection or special treatment, as in our earlier example of the spurious relationship between midwifery and healthy births?

The strength of nonreactive research lies in its ability to form and test hypotheses either with data obtained unobtrusively or with naturally occurring data. Unobtrusive data collection consists of undercover observation, disguised experiments, or (more rarely) concealed surveys, which may reduce the chance of subjects reacting to observation and measurement. However, concealment limits access to information, thereby reducing possibilities for controlling third variables. The use of naturally occurring data largely eliminates the possibility of reactions to data collection. But such data are rarely complete and often inaccurate owing to natural social biases (for instance, the structured variability with which societies keep records of even such basic facts as birth and death for persons of high and low social status) and indeed are generally used less to reduce bias than to study past or distant events that can only be studied indirectly. Studies of this sort most often use multivariate analysis.

In sum, fieldwork's strength is that its hypotheses and theories describe natural sequences of events as seen on-the-spot through the eyes of a detached observer. And this is important because while all social research strives for realism to some degree, none does so as directly as fieldwork. Survey researchers study the world through the eyes of their respondents and try to reconstruct natural causal sequences from that information. Experimenters seek a more direct view, but what they see is an artificially created microcosm in which causal processes may differ from those that operate in the world outside the lab. And analysts of naturally occurring data try to reconstruct natural causal processes with data that are real but also potentially reflect all the many and varied biases of the everyday social life that generated the data. However, each of these other research styles sacrifices direct observation of natural social causation for a purpose difficult to achieve through fieldwork. The purpose of the experiment is to attain a high level of internal validity. The purpose of survey research is to achieve high external validity in the sense of accurate generalizability of causal relationships from samples to populations. And the purpose of nonreactive research is to achieve external validity of another sort: generalizability to situations in which no overt observation has been conducted or is perhaps possible.

## Multimethod Assessments of Internal and External Validity

As the preceding discussion suggests, each style of social research characteristically involves some trade-off between internal and external validity. Most notably, experiments exchange ease of generalization to natural social settings and populations, and freedom from possible reactive measurement bias, for greater precision at causal inference; whereas nonexperimental studies exchange the experimental method's advantages for causal inference in order to study causation either in natural social environments (as in fieldwork), in samples accurately representing populations (as in survey research), or with measures derived from naturally occurring data (as in nonreactive research). A study employing rigorous experimental controls but carried out exclusively with students might, therefore, be presumed to have relatively low external validity but relatively high internal validity in comparison with a general population survey in which only a few statistical controls had been applied.

However, the fact of the matter is that a priori judgments of this sort may often be wrong because our assessments of research methods' characteristic strengths and weaknesses refer to potential rather than to necessary sources of error. Thus, the findings of the two studies in the preceding example might in fact be equally accurate if it happens that students are really no different from the population at large with respect to the hypothesis being investigated, and also if the uncontrolled variables in the survey happen to have negligible influence. The problem, of course, is how to determine whether or not a potential source of error is operative in the particular case.

The multimethod approach to this problem is to assess internal and external validity empirically (rather than relying upon a priori assessments) by comparing the results of different tests of hypotheses, each test conducted with a method chosen for its ability to cross-check the other. In this way, one can determine whether or not a potential source of error is actually important. For instance, experimental and nonexperimental studies may be combined to check the internal validity of the one and the external validity of the other. (And more generally, of course, any two methods that differ in their characteristic internal and external validity may be employed for this purpose, although the power of the assessment varies with the methods' characteristic strengths.)

Multimethod tests of a hypothesis may yield any of four results: both may confirm the hypothesis, both may disconfirm, or one may confirm while the other disconfirms. Let us assume that Test I employs a method (such as a survey) presumed to have relatively high external validity but relatively low internal validity; whereas Test II employs a method (for instance, experimentation) with the converse pattern of strengths and

| Test II. An Experiment | | Test I. A Survey (A priori judgment: High external but relatively low internal validity) | |
|---|---|---|---|
| (A priori judgment: High internal but | (+) | (+) | (−) |
| | | 1. Convergence | 2. Divergence |
| relatively low external validity) | (−) | 3. Divergence | 4. Convergence |
| (+) = Confirmation of hypothesis | | | |
| (−) = Disconfirmation of hypothesis | | | |

**Figure 7.1**     A Multimethod Assessment of Internal and External Validity

weaknesses—that is, high internal validity but relatively low external validity. (Of course, in practice one does not rely solely on general assessments of methods to determine their strength and weaknesses in particular instances. The judgment is also based on assessment of the skill and thoroughness with which each method was employed.) Figure 7.1 outlines the dimensions of this illustrative test and the possible outcomes.

The purpose of this multimethod test is to determine the accuracy of the a priori judgments of each method with respect to the particular hypothesis being investigated. The point is that although a method may be generically weak in some respect, it may nonetheless yield correct findings in the individual case because the diagnosis of characteristic strengths and weakness refers only to the relative probability of certain types of errors with different methods. The multimethod approach pits methods against one another that have different probabilities of making the same error. Thus, in Figure 7.1, outcomes 1 and 4 justify heightened confidence in the findings of each method because the findings converge despite the methods' differences. However, outcomes 2 and 3 empirically substantiate a priori doubts about the internal validity of Test II and the external validity of Test I.

Heath (1984) provides an example of this sort of multimethod research in a study of the impact of newspaper crime reports on fear of crime. She first conducted a telephone survey of 326 randomly selected readers of newspapers with different styles of crime reporting to determine their fears of crime in various situations. The results of the survey supported her hypotheses, which she had derived from social psychological theory. However, despite the fact that she was able to examine and discount statistically the influence of a number of third variables that might have been confounded with the independent variable, she was concerned about the internal validity of this phase of her study.

> Although quasiexperimental research done in field settings generally has greater external validity than laboratory experiments, the fear that lurks in every quasiexperimentalist's heart is that some unaccounted for variable is producing spurious effects. To allay this fear, a laboratory experiment was conducted in which the same conceptual variables were examined under controlled conditions. (p. 271)

The experiment, in contrast to the survey, allowed Heath to assign subjects randomly to read different materials designed to represent different values of the independent variable and to pretest her subjects concerning their perceptions of crime in order to test the adequacy of the randomization procedure. However, to gain these advantages, the experiment was conducted with 80 undergraduates and fictional crime scenarios. Heath's experimental results substantiated her survey's findings by demonstrating that her hypotheses could withstand this more causally precise test, whereas her earlier survey findings established that the experimentally confirmed hypotheses could be validly generalized to actual newspaper readers as well as to college students reading fictitious accounts of crimes.

In addition to testing theoretically derived hypotheses, Heath wanted also to make empirically and theoretically grounded policy recommendations for press coverage of crime. For this reason, the configuration of methods promising high external and high internal validity, respectively, was especially important in her study. In research intended to be applied to a particular social context, external validity with respect to that context (or target population) is obviously a prime consideration. As Cook and Campbell (1979, pp. 82–85) imply, this may create a dilemma in single-method research between randomly sampling the target population to assure generalizability versus randomly assigning subjects to assure internal validity. However, as Heath's (1984) study demonstrates, a multimethod design may resolve this apparent dilemma. (We consider the contribution of multimethod studies to applied social research more generally in Chapter 8.)

## Multitest Validity

We have just discussed the internal and external validity of causal research. These concepts refer, respectively, to confidence that a causal relationship has been found in a particular study and to confidence in generalizing that relationship beyond the original measures, samples of persons, settings, and times studied. And we have also discussed the multimethod approach to assessing internal and external validity empirically. As we demonstrated, this involves comparing tests of hypotheses conducted with different methods, each chosen for its ability to cross-check the others' findings. The purpose of such comparisons is to determine how in specific instances our various research methods' characteristic strengths and weaknesses for causal analysis actually influence findings. Now we will consider a somewhat different issue: not whether a particular research finding, or set of findings, is internally and externally valid but whether the hypothesis to which those findings refer is true or false.

The validity of particular research findings, and the validity of the hypotheses to which they refer, are of course related issues because the strength of the evidence for or against a causal hypothesis depends heavily upon the internal and external validity of the studies that produced that evidence. However, in deciding whether to accept or reject an hypothesis, as opposed to a particular finding about it, there is an additional consideration that we will call *multitest validity*. Multitest validity is confidence in a hypothesis based upon multiple empirical confirmations (or disconfirmations). It refers to the fact that, other things being equal (such as the validity of individual test results), we usually favor hypotheses that have been repeatedly tested and confirmed over those for which the evidence is sparse or mixed.

The rationale for multiple testing and for attributing greater validity to hypotheses that pass multiple tests is twofold: (1) the elimination of rival hypotheses, and (2) the accumulation of more representative evidence. First, as Stinchcombe (1968, pp. 18–20) suggests, the more numerous and varied the tests of an hypothesis, the less likely it is that any rival hypothesis can plausibly account for those same findings. And second, as Wallace (1971) writes: "Each test of a hypothesis is a sample drawn from the universe of possible tests, and as with any sample, the question of its representativeness arises. The manner in which this question is handled typically involves *repeated* tests of the same hypothesis— differently . . . operationalized at different times and places, sometimes by different researchers—such that the evidence for or against the deduced conceptual hypothesis 'accumulates,' becomes 'persuasive,' and finally is 'overwhelming'" (p. 83).

## Replications Versus Extensions

Multiple tests of hypotheses may first be roughly classified as either exact or modified replications. An exact replication, as the term implies, is a repetition of an earlier study designed to be as nearly identical as possible to the original. From the multimethod perspective, the most relevant dimensions of similarity and difference are (1) the research style employed, which determines the mode of causal analysis and techniques of data collection; and (2) the operationalization of the hypothesis being tested. The chief modes of testing and data collection are fieldwork employing naturalistic observation; surveys employing multivariate analysis; experimentation; and nonreactive research involving either unobtrusive observation, experiments and surveys, or multivariate analysis of naturally occurring data. The operationalization of the hypothesis refers to the particular operational definitions and measures of the variables and also to the selection of particular populations and samples of persons, social settings, and times in which to test the hypothesis. A modified replication is an extension of the original research employing either a different research style, a different operationalization of the hypothesis, or both.

The foregoing distinctions imply a finer classification comprising four types of multiple tests: exact replications plus three types of extensions. These three types of extensions are same-method studies operationalizing the hypotheses differently (Type I), multimethod studies operationalizing the hypothesis similarly (Type II), and multimethod studies operationalizing the hypothesis differently (Type III). Figure 7.2 presents this typology.

Considered in terms of the rationale for multiple testing (elimination of rival hypotheses and more representative evidence), each type of multiple test tests something different. First, replications and the three types of extension address different sorts of rival hypotheses. Replication tests reliability to rule out the possibility that the original finding was merely a fluke. Same-method extensions (Type I) test the hypothesis that the earlier finding was attributable to the idiosyncrasies of a particular set of operational definitions and measures or unique features of the initial population, sample, or test environment. Type II multimethod extensions address the rival hypothesis that the original finding was an artifact of the particular style of research employed. And Type III multimethod extensions address both of these possibilities simultaneously and also test the additional possibility that any one test result represents an interaction between research style and the operationalization of the hypothesis.

Second, each type of multiple test taps a different dimension of the universe of all possible tests. Replications sample the test factors that vary when the researcher tries to hold all factors constant from one study to another. Same-method extensions (Type I) sample the possible operationalizations. Type II multimethod extensions sample the tests possible with different research styles. And Type III multimethod extensions sample both research styles and operationalizations. This last type may seem to be overly complicated. But as we will see, its complexity has some advantages.

For example, Correll (2004) investigated the problem of if and how gender stereotypes of task abilities affect "the emerging career-relevant aspirations" of young men and women. She hypothesized that such stereotypes have an effect on aspirations through their influence on individuals' self assessments of ability, irrespective of their actual abilities. She researched this hypothesis first with a multivariate analysis of data from a probability sample of students presumed to be familiar with cultural stereotypes. The other variables in the hypothesis were operationalized in terms of self-assessed math and verbal ability; enrollment in a high school calculus class; and preferences for a college major in math, engineering, or science. Math ability was measured by grades and test scores. The results of this study supported her hypothesis but left doubts in her mind: "we must assume that the students in the sample were aware of the cultural beliefs about gender, mathematical abilities, and verbal abilities, and this awareness caused the observed gender differences in self-assessments of competence. Since we could not isolate and manipulate students' exposure to gender beliefs associated with these abilities, we could not rule out competing explanations for the findings" (p. 96). She was especially concerned about "the possibility that mathematical self-assessments tap an additional component of 'real' mathematical ability not captured by the math grades and test scores that served as controls of mathematical ability" (p. 96). She reasoned that it might be that the grades and test scores are imperfect so that men's higher self-assessments might reflect their greater actual ability in math rather than cultural beliefs.

| Research Style (Mode of Testing and Data Collection) | | |
|---|---|---|
| Operationalization of the Hypothesis | Same in Each Text | Different in Each Test |
| Same in Each Text | Exact Replication | Multimethod Extension (Type II) |
| Different in Each Test | Same-Method Extension (Type I) | Multimethod Extension (Type III) |

**Figure 7.2**    Types of Multiple Tests

To address these questions, Correll (2004) conducted further research that both operationalized and tested her hypothesis differently. She designed an experiment that we will describe very briefly. It involved controlling for ability by administering to subjects the "contrast sensitivity test"( a frequently used experimental instrument that actually has no right or wrong answers) and assigning all subjects identical scores, telling subjects prior to the test either that males performed better, or that there was no gender difference in performance, and asking subjects after the test to make self-assessments of their abilities and to say how likely they would be to undertake activities requiring high ability on the measured task. The experimental findings generally corroborated the findings of the earlier conducted survey, despite the differences in both operationalization and mode of testing. Moreover, Correll (2004) concluded that the experiment provided "a strong test of the causal argument" and that when combined with the survey findings "suggests that the causal process operates similarly in a 'real world' setting" (p.110).

## Convergence and Divergence

Assuming only two tests (of any type), the following are the major possible outcomes from multiple tests of hypotheses. First, both tests may either confirm or disconfirm the hypothesis (convergence). Second, one test may more strongly confirm the hypothesis than the other (convergence with residual divergence). Third, one test may confirm while the other disconfirms (divergence). Figure 7.3 summarizes these possibilities.

In general, the more numerous and varied the tests of an hypothesis, and the more closely their results converge, the more confidence one may

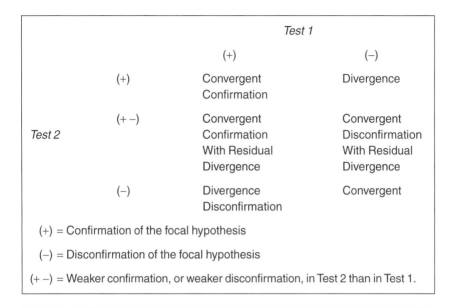

|  | | Test 1 | |
| --- | --- | --- | --- |
|  | | (+) | (−) |
|  | (+) | Convergent Confirmation | Divergence |
| Test 2 | (+ −) | Convergent Confirmation With Residual Divergence | Convergent Disconfirmation With Residual Divergence |
|  | (−) | Divergence Disconfirmation | Convergent |

(+) = Confirmation of the focal hypothesis

(−) = Disconfirmation of the focal hypothesis

(+ −) = Weaker confirmation, or weaker disconfirmation, in Test 2 than in Test 1.

**Figure 7.3**      Possible Outcomes of Multiple Tests

have in both the validity of each test and the truth (or falsity) of the hypothesis to which they all refer. Conversely, the fewer and more similar the tests, and the more their results diverge, the more skeptical one must be of the hypothesis, the individual tests, or both. In other words, the force of multiple tests in deciding whether to accept or reject an hypothesis depends not only upon their number but also upon their diversity and convergence.

Consider first the need for diversity. The results of any single test are highly problematic for a variety of reasons, ranging from doubts about reliability to suspicions of more systematic bias. However, similar multiple tests only partially solve this problem because each test is likely to be prone to many of the same sorts of nonrandom error. Assuming that only reliable research produces consistent results, all multiple tests test reliability. But the more similar the tests, the more they test only for reliability, ignoring the possibility of systematic biases that threaten validity.

As we said earlier, tests have two aspects: a method of testing and data collection, and an operationalization of the hypothesis. Each aspect may systematically bias it for or against a hypothesis. For instance, with respect to method, a field study's small sample of observations may bias it against the acceptance of any but necessary and sufficient (or at least very strong and general) causal hypotheses; while large survey samples may be biased toward detecting relatively weak probable and contributing causes. And experiments may be biased toward accepting hypotheses that work only under artificial conditions; while many nonreactive studies may be biased toward hypotheses that hold true only given the operation of the socially selective processes that produce and sift naturally occurring sociological data. Similarly, with respect to the second aspect of testing, measures and operational definitions of variables differ in their validity and so (as we saw in Chapter 6) in their abilities to represent accurately the variables named in the hypothesis. And (as we saw in Chapter 5) different populations, samples, settings, and times provide quite different contexts for testing hypotheses. This is one reason why precise statements of boundary conditions are essential to causal laws.

The greater chance of shared biases in similar tests of hypotheses means that convergence between such tests might be attributable to those biases rather than to the strength of the hypothesis. This possibility of spurious convergence, and the ambiguity in interpreting convergence that it creates, is clearly greatest in exact replications, but it is also present in same-method extensions. Convergence in the Type I situation (same-method extensions) may indicate high generalizability across different operational conditions (i.e., measures, persons, settings, times) or instead it may reflect the overriding influence of the studies' common mode of testing and data collection.

Danzger's (1975) work illustrates this interpretive problem and how the use of a second method (in this case, interviews with informants) may help to solve it. Danzger reanalyzed the results of two independently conducted studies of racial conflict. Both studies statistically analyzed conflict data obtained from newspapers' reports, but each operationalized the dependent variable of conflict very differently, studying different times and different types of conflict. However, their conclusions substantially converged despite these differences. The problem is that when converging tests of hypotheses differ in important operational respects but employ the same source of data (in this example, newspapers), then generalizability and shared methodological bias may be equally plausible interpretations.

To solve the problem of spurious convergence in this case, Danzger (1975) both consulted prior research on the press and interviewed journalists who had reported on civil rights and racial conflict. Danzger then tested the hypotheses that he derived from this phase against the news data. In this way, he determined that findings from conflict research based upon news stories might in fact be artifacts of the news gathering and publication process; in particular that correlations between cities and conflict appeared to be an artifact of the location of major press service offices. However, he also discovered that this source of contamination seemed to be eliminated if one studied only those cities for which some conflict had been previously reported. Having discovered this, he then retested the original hypothesis against the corrected data and found that although a major hypothesis continued to receive support, some others needed to be reexamined.

Danzger's (1975) questioning and probing of possible biases in news reporting of events has heavily influenced later research. It has prompted greater caution in the use of such data and further probes (e.g., Snyder & Kelly, 1977; Jenkins & Perrow, 1977; Jenkins & Eckert, 1986; Olzak, 1989; McCarthy, McPhail & Smith, 1996; Mueller, 1997; Oliver & Myers, 1999; Oliver & Maney, 2000; Smith, McCarthy, McPhail, & Augustyn, 2001; McAdam & Su, 2002). As a result, factors such as the intensity and context of events, the sensitivity of the media, multiple news sources, and cross-checks of news reports with police and other official data sources are routinely considered.

Multimethod tests solve the foregoing problem because they employ different methods. With these types of tests (Types II and III in Figure 7.2), the question is how closely do the tests converge; or if they diverge, how to interpret that divergence? Multimethod researchers have mostly stressed the importance of convergence. As a result, divergence may appear to be only a form of negative evidence that challenges the validity of either the methods employed, the operationalizations of the hypothesis, or the hypothesis itself. And sometimes this is the case, as when exact replications fail. However, it must be emphasized that in contrast to convergent disconfirmation, divergence (and especially residual divergence among converging tests) does not necessarily imply invalidity.

Especially with multiple tests that employ very different operationalizations, divergence may instead merely indicate a need, and provide an opportunity, to specify more closely the exact conditions under which the hypothesis is expected to hold true. Furthermore, residual divergence among converging tests may actually indicate improved validity. For instance, it may be that one of the methods is stronger than the other with respect to reliability or control over extraneous variables, for example, and that it was indeed employed for just that reason. In that case, convergence with residual divergence may demonstrate that greater reliability or control was achieved in later tests.

Also, as Lever (1981) points out, residual divergence can in some instances be interpreted substantively and perhaps in the same theoretical framework from which the hypothesis derives. For example, in a multimethod study conducted to test the hypothesis that boys' and girls' play activities differ in ways that reinforce conventional sex-role socialization, Lever found that although data from all the methods employed (interviews, questionnaires, diaries of private play activities, and observation of public play) supported her hypotheses, some did so more strongly than others. She concluded that this residual divergence might be explained in part by the tendency of some methods to elicit more role-stereotypic responses from respondents, but also by the fact that gender differences tend to be more pronounced in some social settings than others and that her different methods had tapped a variety of settings.

Similarly, Leonard (1995), studying children's negotiations with adults both through mothers' reports of everyday interactions at home and through a quasi-experiment using a puppet role-playing task, found that although her two methods' results largely agreed, there were some differences. How, she asked, are such discrepant findings in multimethod research to be interpreted? She suggests three possibilities: first, that one method is in fact superior to the other; second, that the discrepancies represent errors associated with each method; and third, that each method provides a different but possibly valid perspective on the substance of the research problem. She opts in this case for the third possibility: "The differences between the two methods used in the present study are not seen as error of measurement but rather as opportunities to view the topic in new ways" (p. 26). She then proceeds to interpret the research discrepancies in substantive theoretical terms by hypothesizing as to how the two different research settings and procedures may have altered the children's sense of active agency in their negotiations with adults.

We have been discussing *multitest validity*. This is an essential concept for evaluating hypotheses in the light of multiple test results. In our discussion, we have considered several different types of multiple tests, especially replications versus same-method and multimethod extensions. We have also considered how the interpretation of converging and diverging test results varies depending upon the types of tests employed.

Our discussion has obviously raised a number of complex issues that will require much additional analysis. But our general conclusion at this point is that multitest validation of hypotheses requires multimethod tests. Multimethod tests avoid the possibility of spurious convergence between findings owing to monomethod bias. And in the event of divergence, these tests may lead to important specifications of the hypotheses being tested and to improvements in the methods of testing.

# Eight

## A Postscript on Postmodernism

The central argument of this book has been couched within a traditional modernist framework. That is to say, we have accepted most of the assumptions of the positivist empirical "modernist" paradigm of science in general, and the social sciences in particular, about the types of issues methodology should address. For example, we have treated seriously issues such as measurement validity and measurement error, issues of sampling for purposes of generalization, and questions of causation in testing hypotheses. These are all classical questions about the scientific attempt to find the truth about the objective world—out there. But we have addressed these questions from a pragmatic postpositivist point of view. Here we will consider from that same viewpoint three issues—narrative, rhetoric, and social construction—raised by postmodern critiques of social research. We will ask what the consideration of each of these issues may add to the process of doing research and how a multimethod approach may be, and has been, employed to explore these newer dimensions of inquiry. And finally, we will consider the possible influence and significance for social research of some postmodern technological developments. For after all, the postmodern turn is not just a cultural revision of how scientists think but includes a technological component of developing new tools to help them do what they do.

# The Postmodern Critique

Within the past few decades, the positivist or modernist methods of the social sciences have come under increasing criticism and outright attack on a number of grounds. Many of these criticisms center upon some variant of the charge that the social sciences are engaged in a "naive empiricism." Core assumptions of the positivist tradition (e.g., an uncritical acceptance of assumptions about the positing of an external objective world of social phenomena, the validity of quantitative measurement of those phenomena, and the capacity to make empirical generalizations and formulate theoretical propositions of increasing abstraction) are now called into question. The critiques themselves have taken a number of forms, and we will touch upon only three of the more significant of these: the ideas of narrative, rhetoric, and the social construction of scientific facts.

These critiques are often summarized as a "deconstructionist" or a "postmodern" questioning of science. Since the label of the critique is itself somewhat self-reflexively, open to a number of different meanings and interpretations, we prefer to follow the lead of Donald Campbell and refer to it as a "postpositivist" critique. The multimethod perspective does not fight the general thrust of the critique but rather welcomes it and attempts to subsume it within the central argument of multimethod research. This central argument, that there is no one best singular way to the truth and that a variety of different methods should be considered in its pursuit, both antedates and resonates with many of the postpositivist critiques. In this light, multimethod research calls for a "soft" postmodern revision of more extreme versions of positivistic, scientistic modernity; and yet, at the same time, it is a postpositivist critique that still retains modernity's ultimate goal of a meaningful pursuit of scientific truth.

The postpositivist critique is often connected with a challenge to science rooted in humanistic disciplines such as aesthetic and literary criticism. As such it represents the older dichotomy of C. P. Snow's "two cultures" (1971) and is but a contemporary example of the conflict between scientific and humanistic disciplines with their distinct claims to objectified knowledge and interpretive knowledge, respectively. It is no accident that sociology and related social sciences should be sensitive to the arguments of both cultures, positioned as they are between them, and should correspondingly search for a reconciliation or synthesis.

One such attempt at synthesis is the claim of "consilience"—the unity of all knowledge across all disciplines—made most recently in the work of E. O. Wilson (1998). This term, first proposed by William Whewell in the nineteenth century as a term for the increased validity attached to theoretical explanations that were able to explain seemingly disparate observations from different fields, was originally restricted in its application to "truth" within the domain of science. Wilson attempts to extend this across the humanities and scientific divide and even into the moral realm, arguing for a reductionist and deterministic unity to all knowledge. Stephen Jay Gould (2003) challenges this meaning of consilience by pointing to the twin ideas of emergence and contingency. The former suggests that different "truths" and theories are emergent at different scales of reality and in different domains such that the philosopher's ethics cannot be reduced to the physicist's elements; and furthermore, that chance rules the universe such that classical scientific predictions of ever more complex systems of reality fail due to the innate probabilistic path dependency of history that cannot be replicated.

In pursuing multimethod research, we propose a slightly different synthesis—one rooted more in the amalgamation of methods to knowledge rather than the substantive unity of the knowledge itself. In short, epistemological questions about "how" one knows, and the appreciation of multiple ways of knowing, are at the core of multimethod research, not a reified, abstract unity of "what" one knows. In this sense, multimethod research is agnostic in its critique of all methods and simultaneously catholic in its call for the use of many different methods.

As Stephen Jay Gould (2003) observes, quoting Vladimir Nabokov, there is a unity in the idea of precision of observation and recording in both the sciences and the humanities: "The tactile delights of precise delineation, the silent paradise of the *camera lucida*, and the precision of poetry in taxonomic description represent the artistic side of the thrill which accumulation of new knowledge, absolutely useless to the layman, gives its first begetter. . . . There is no science without fancy, and no art without facts" (p. 167).

The merger of methods in multimethod research can and does go beyond classical conceptions of science and unites the humanities and the sciences in a postpositive perspective. The three postpositive approaches we propose—narrative, rhetoric, and social construction—are also noted by Gould (2003) as the contribution of the humanities to scientific ways of knowing. As he writes:

> I have here extolled the superior understanding of the humanities in three areas (1) acknowledging and analyzing the social influences and cognitive biases within and behind all creative work, including empirical studies;

(2) emphasizing the importance of stylistic and rhetorical concerns in the presentation and acceptance of any good argument; and (3) developing certain modes of knowing [historical contingency or narrative] that science needs but, for contingent reasons of its own history, never emphasized or even downgraded. (p. 138)

## Narrative

The first critique of classical positivism is what may be called the narrative framing of social phenomena. In part stemming from a hyper historicism, this perspective argues in a somewhat ideographic manner that the relatively static, synchronic, or cross-sectional nature of most social science research may generate internally consistent theories (e.g., theories comprised of logically interrelated testable hypotheses) that still leave one begging for more in the way of explanation of the phenomena under investigation. In its most simplistic formulation, the narrative critique is a call to take time seriously.

A narrative approach argues for the need to elucidate a concatenated set of temporal factors that may have small, distinct, and separate origins that over time come together or coalesce to create the conditions that produce the phenomenon being studied. The narrative approach stresses such ideas as "contingency," "path dependency," and "sequence" that speak to a potential multiplicity of outcomes rather than a mechanical determinism often contained in positivist explanations. It is a call for sociologists to stop overgeneralizing about reified phenomena that have been wrenched from their spatio-temporal context.

The most recent positivist attempt to capture "time" in some manner is through such techniques as "event history analysis" that (in spite of its name) attempts to analyze "events" as autonomous "units" existing apart from their embeddedness in a rich and complex historical context. The narrative critique would call for a more discursive and nuanced verbal rendering of events, while the event history analysis would stress the sophisticated quantitative statistical controls that render history and time as but a variable, not an intrinsic property, of the very idea of "explanation" itself. Narrative is, in short, not variable-based linear regression but linear unfolding of concatenated reciprocal paths.

All good narratives have a beginning, a middle, an end, and (more often than not) a moral—a lesson to be learned, an insight to be gained—sometimes a surprise prompted by a discovery. The novelist and critic David Lodge (1996) observes that "Narrative is concerned with *process*, that is say with change in a given state of affairs; or it converts problems and contradictions in human experience into process in order to understand or cope with them. Narrative obtains and holds the interest of its audience by raising questions in their minds about the process it describes and delaying answers to these questions. When a question is answered in a way that is both unexpected and plausible, we have the effect known since Aristotle as *peripeteia* or reversal" (p. 182).

One variant of narrative is biography, or in today's parlance "life history," which may be construed as constructing a life narrative. And, to paraphrase C. Wright Mills's classic definition, "sociology is the intersection of biography and history"—the mutual playing out of two different scales of narrative time (individual and collective). Methodologically, life histories may be considered a form of in-depth interviewing or (if the subjects write out their own life histories) a form of archival document. Life histories have become significant at the intersection of history and sociology as "social history" has emerged as a distinct subdiscipline. Social history is the study of the lives of ordinary folk in different historical periods, not simply a concern with kings, generals, and other rulers and elites. Early sociologists brought such life histories to the fore such as the early Chicago School's studies of The Jackroller, The Wayward Girl, and The Hobo (Cressey, 1953; Thomas, & Znaniecki, 1918/1958; Anderson, 1923/1961). As James Bennett has noted, often these "biographies" were a complex methodology that were produced as an amalgam of a number of different life histories. As to their veracity, the claim could be maintained that "nothing in this has been made up" (1981).

Life histories speak to a further critique of positivism with its search for more or less determinist theories. This critique concerns the role of "agency," or the ability of the individual to rise above his or her social and historical condition and by exercising will to alter the course of their own life, the course of events, and ultimately the course of history. The idea of agency is a deeply rooted philosophical assumption in modern Western thought that directly confronts the assumptions of a predictive science of society focused on the behavior of objectified subjects. The narrative conception of explanation seems to challenge the positivist scientific assumption of generalizable laws, but the multimethod perspective acknowledges that the very meaning or idea of what constitutes an "explanation" is itself method-specific. Different methods of research applied to the same phenomenon may produce confirmatory agreement or disconfirmation. But a third alternative is the possibility of distinct types of explanation rooted in distinct methods. For example, a number of physicists using a classical causal perspective argue that recent findings from "chaos theory" and fractal geometry—which can represent in a simple, elegant, and probabilistic way the form and shape of mountains, clouds, and branching trees—are not engaged in explanation but "merely" description. In short, these different analytical methods have different conceptions of what constitutes "explanation."

This raises the possibility that multimethod research can contribute not just to theoretical synthesis but also to a grander synthesis of different conceptions of science itself. In the debate between scientists adhering to a "causal logic" of scientific explanation versus those advancing chaos theory, the former characterize the latter as engaging in mere description with insufficient specification of causal mechanisms, while the latter suggest that what we have are two different types of "questions" and two different types of "explanation." In short, by adding their new methods of probabilistic and contingent "narrative" to the multimethod arsenal, chaos theorists are attempting to broaden the conception of what constitutes valid science. This need for narrative methods, in order to capture an historically contingent versus an overly deterministic and reductionist view of life, has been expressed most forcefully by the biologist Stuart Kauffman (2000) of the Santa Fe Institute in his discussion of "emergence" as a counterconcept to "determinism." He writes: "And 'emergence and story?' What manner of foolishness is this? Story? Surely story is not the stuff of science. I'm not so sure. Story is the natural way we autonomous agents talk about our raw getting on with it, mucking through, making a living. If story is not the stuff of science yet is about how we get on with making our ever-changing livings, then science, not story, must change. Our making our ever-changing livings is part of the unfolding of the physical universe" (p. 119).

## Rhetoric

The art of rhetoric, according to Aristotle, consists of three key modes of speech acts: forensic (legal/dialectic), political (deliberative), and epideitic (ceremonial). Forensic or dialectical rhetoric (as seen in legal and scientific discourses) is concerned with persuading others of the truth of one's assertions. Sir Francis Bacon's development of the logic of modern science in the sixteenth century can be seen as a reaction to the degenerate place of rhetoric as "mere rhetoric." For as he says, he took the questions that the scholastic rhetoricians of the Middle Ages posed to one another and turned and posed them to nature itself. The scholastic dialogue was now a scientific dialogue between empirical researcher and the natural world. Nonetheless, the reporting of the research was still a rhetorical exercise in which scientists had to convince peers and others of the truth of their assertions. The scientific method was, in this sense, a "tool," a set of rules, such that if they were used properly, others would more likely be convinced that they had produced valid results (Hunter, 1990a).

The rhetorical view of science critiques this naive positivism for masking or rendering the rhetorical elements invisible. Scientists use the passive voice, for example, so as to render the individual scientist transparent and to highlight the central role of the method itself: not "I found . . ." but "It was found that . . ." The rhetorical critique calls for a greater consciousness of what is being done in scientific research and, above all, more truth and accuracy in reporting what it is that scientists actually do in their research.

The format of the modern scientific report in its standardized form, a genre of writing which some attribute to Newton himself, contributes to this unconscious, unreflective masking of numerous decisions, compromises, and outright serendipity that are part and parcel of the messy conduct of most scientific investigations. Most research is, in fact, pragmatically eclectic.

This rhetorical critique has been applied to a number of the social sciences, such as Donald McCloskey's *The Rhetoric of Economics* (1985); and Richard Harvey Brown's *A Poetic for Sociology* (1977) and his *Sociology as Text* (1987). The questions become the following: How does this rhetorical quality directly affect the use of different research methods? And, more specifically for our concerns, what might it contribute to a multimethod approach? We suggest that rhetoric's major contribution lies in seeing the process of research not only as a question of the search for truth in some objectified, abstracted, positivistic sense but also as a concern with the variety of tools that might be employed to better convince other reasonable people of the truth of one's assertions. Different audiences, with different substantive interests and, above all, different methodological predilections, are more likely to be convinced if research findings are the result of their specific preferred styles. The outcome is both a broader audience of support and a deeper, more staunch commitment and intense agreement with one's assertions. From a rhetorician's view, the more arguments (methods), the better.

That such an approach is consistent with the cutting edge of modern science is evidenced by the following remarks of the theoretical physicist and cosmologist Brian Greene (2004):

Just as you may seek a second opinion to corroborate a medical diagnosis, physicists, too, seek second opinions when they come upon data or theories that point toward puzzling results. Of these second opinions, the most convincing are those that reach the same conclusions from a point of view that differs sharply from the original analysis. When the arrows of explanation converge on one spot from different angles, there is a good chance they they're pointing at the scientific bull's-eye. (pp. 296–297)

## Social Construction

To view science as a social process and the institutions of science as but one more institutional sphere ripe for sociological investigation is a further extension of the narrative and rhetorical critiques of the positivistic, modernist conception of science. In its extreme, the postmodern social constructionist view asserts that all truth is but a "social agreement," and stresses less the empirical and positivist notion of truth that lies in the "agreement" between hypotheses (theory) and data from a real objectified world (research)—Bacon's classic "dialogue." Even the seemingly unequivocal and mundane question of what is a "fact" is held up to detailed scrutiny and seen to be the outcome of a complex social process, wherein sometimes ambiguous and contradictory research results are subjected to debate and deliberation (Latour & Woolgar, 1979). Facts, the basic building blocks of an empirical science, are the product of social negotiation and all that this implies. Differences in power, prestige, and positions in social networks, not simply the truth as defined by unambiguous and reliable measurement, are highlighted as determining the acceptance of a given fact.

The implications of this for the multimethod strategy are first, once again, the heightened awareness that allows one to be sensitive to how it is that the social processes involved in one's research (from the largest structural features of inequality to the most quotidian nuance of approbation) may be influencing the nature of the research results. Second, this awareness can lead to a proactive research strategy that through the use of different styles of research may mitigate, though never obliterate, the social embeddedness of the research process. Where face-to-face contact may result in biased measurement, for example, archives far removed from direct interpersonal contact with subjects may counter these biases. Arguments with peers about the purity of one's research techniques should be tempered with a healthy skepticism about the inevitable threats to validity that may have been unanticipated when initially developing one's research design. Consciously using more than one method allows one to (1) answer threats to validity, internally, within the research process itself; and (2) to broaden the dialogues with others who are involved in the constructing of scientific facts. Again, Gould (2003) offers this as the primary benefit in his judgment "that scientists could gain from their colleagues in the humanities: exposing the myth of objectivity by a positive acknowledgement (not cynical and despairing shrug for inevitable loss) of the mental quirks and social influences upon all factual study of the natural world—for honest recognition can only breed self-awareness and greater practical sophistication about the mental processes that scientists must use to reach their accurate conclusions" (p. 132).

## Some Research Examples

The preceding discussion of postmodern social research has emphasized three concerns: narrative, rhetoric, and the social construction of scientific facts. Let us now consider some contemporary research examples in which the multimethod approach has been employed to address these concerns as they impinge upon survey research, often more conventionally depicted as naively positivistic.

The first example, a study conducted by Dykema and Schaeffer (2000), asks "how the patterning of experiences in the lives of respondents leads to errors in understanding survey questions and in recalling the experiences they ask about" (p. 619). The narrative (our term here, not theirs) variables that they consider are: "complexity (how frequent, regular, and similar the payments are), clarity (how distinct the payments are from like events), and the intensity of affect about exchanging child support" (p. 619). They hypothesize that reports "should be less accurate when events are complex, indistinct from like events, and emotionally neutral" (p. 619). In sum, the recall of significant events is dependent upon the nature of their embeddedness in a meaningful narrative that orders and routinizes the flux of everyday life. They test their hypotheses by comparing the results of two telephone surveys of divorced parents asking for self-reports of child support payments with actual court records of child support payments. They conclude that survey "instruments that take the patterning of events into account may substantially increase the accuracy of reports" (p. 628).

The second example, a study conducted by Krysan (1999), considers some surprising survey findings dealing with attitudes toward racial equality. The findings are that in surveys over time the United States population appears to be becoming more liberal on the issue of residential integration but not on the issue of equal employment opportunities. She hypothesizes that this may, in fact, be due to differences between survey researchers' and survey respondents' understandings of the questions being asked. To explore her hypothesis, she conducted individual qualitative interviews with 14 respondents from a large-scale survey in Detroit concerning their earlier questionnaire responses to items about open housing and fair employment. Her findings suggest to her that differences in understanding might well explain the surprising findings, and they lead her to recommend more regular follow-ups to surveys of this qualitative sort.

She concludes that "Our survey answers will mean very little to us if we do not understand what they mean to respondents" (p. 217). This is clearly, at least in part, a rhetorical problem: how to open research to competing rhetorics, including the rhetoric of the research subjects that may be very different from that of the researcher, as the following exchange suggests:

*Respondent:*   What do you mean by fair treatment in jobs?

*Interviewer:*   Whatever it means to you.

*Respondent:*   Oh, come on! (p. 217)

In a third example, Gioia and Thomas (1996) have recently used a multimethod strategy to explore an interesting organizational issue of concern to most academics: the strategy of academic administrators in pursuing a move up in academic rankings. Specifically, they explore how administrators symbolically perceive or define certain issues as either (1) routine and maintenance oriented, not affecting prestige ranking, or (2) strategic and likely to affect such rankings. They combined an initial qualitative case study of a single university with a quantitative regression analysis based on a sample of more than 300 universities. They show how "identity" and "image" are distinct, with the former referring to self-perception, and the latter to others' perceptions—and that the two show distinct patterns of differential attention on the part of administrators as they label different types of issues as either routine or strategic. The qualitative case study lays out a detailed narrative of how administrators think about, classify, and act upon different types of issues, while the quantitative analysis supports and generalizes these findings to a larger universe. In short, this explicitly multimethod study epitomizes the best of subjective and objective insights. The researchers nicely show the way in which the social construction of "issues" and the "identity" question of symbolic interaction can be explored using the strengths of both qualitative in-depth case studies and survey research, and the value that both have for understanding the hard-nosed reality of organizational change and decision making.

The final example comprises a series of studies bearing upon the apparently high—and widely publicized—rate of church attendance in the USA compared to similar nations. The first of these studies is Hadaway, Marler, and Chaves's (1993) controversial research entitled "What the Polls Don't Show: A Closer Look at U.S. Church Attendance." National polls conducted over the past 30 years or so had generally reported that 40 percent or more of people in the United States attend church weekly. This estimate of attendance had been widely accepted, both in academic publications and the media. The editor of the *American Sociological Review*, in which the article appeared, aptly labeled Hadaway et al.'s work a study of "the social construction of stylized facts." The research problem implied by this phrase is to what extent may accepted "facts " about social life reflect the style of inquiry and reporting by which these "facts" have become known rather than the social reality that they purport to represent? Hadaway et al. addressed this problem with a study of Protestants and Catholics in one Ohio county using a variety of data sources, including surveys, church records, actual head counts, and counts of cars in church parking lots. Their findings suggested that the actual rate of church attendance was far less than that suggested by the earlier polls, perhaps as much as fifty percent less.

Their results are both challenged and supported by later research reported in a symposium later published in the *American Sociological Review* (1998). Various aspects of Hadaway et al.'s multimethod study are severely criticized. But Smith (1998) in reviewing church attendance mea- sures and redesigned national surveys based upon subsequent survey experiments, concluded that, in fact, church attendance in the United States has been overestimated, although to a lesser extent than Hadaway et al.'s (1993) study suggests. And Presser and Stinson (1998) conclude that "respondents in conventional surveys overreport their religious attendance. Apparently, misreporting-error is caused mainly by social desirability pressures associated with interviewer-administration. The error can be minimized through either self-administration or asking about time-usage" (p. 145).

Interestingly, Presser and Stillson (1998) also find that although Americans have often been portrayed as being strongly and consistently religious, "misreporting has increased in the last 30 years, thus distorting trends in religious attendance. Although reports to interviewer-administered direct items have shown little change in attendance over time, measures less subject to misreporting (time-use items and self-administered items) reveal a continuous decline in attendance since the mid-1960s, providing support for the hypothesis that America has become more secularized" (p. 145).

Research that is prone to social desirability effects (e.g., overreporting socially approved behavior) is clearly vulnerable to the criticism that it is an artifact of social construction rather than a discovery of the "facts." However, as the preceding example illustrates, multimethod research can be very helpful in sorting out such issues. Indeed, Marier and Hadaway (1999) did further pursue the issue in this case in a multimethod study of an established evangelical congregation in the deep South. Their findings confirm their earlier study discussed previously but also probes more deeply into the causes of misreporting. They find that "Most of the misre-porting was by church members who considered themselves to be among the most active members of the congregation. . . . Misreporting apparently is not caused by memory lapses but instead results from active church members reporting behavior that is consistent with their perceptions of themselves as active churchgoers. They suggest that this self affirmation may even be more important than 'trying to appear religious to an inter-viewer" (p. 5). Clearly the social construction perspective is amenable to multimethod exploration and elaboration.

## The Technology of Method

Postmodern critiques of empirical inquiry, accompanied by a prolifera-tion and growing interest in qualitative research styles (Denzin & Lincoln, 1994, 2000), plus the continuing development of sophisticated quantita-tive research techniques, virtually ensure that sociology in the foreseeable future will be at least as methodologically diverse and contentious as it has been in the past. In an important way, this continuing methodological diversity and contentiousness is a healthy sign. Skepticism is, of course, an essential aspect of scientific inquiry, and contending methodologies obviously represent important critical perspectives on one another and on social reality. Equally important, however, is the fact that newer emerging methodologies may also offer solutions not yet conceived for existing methodological problems and present surprising opportunities to increase the depth and scope of social inquiry.

To think of social science methods as "tools," as the "technology" of science, has a venerable legacy. John Madge (1953/1965) even titled his book on methods from the 1950s *The Tools of Social Science: An Analytical Description of Social Science Technique*. Viewing methods as tools and technique highlights several important characteristics that are pertinent to a multimethod approach. First there is the pragmatic question: Do they "work?" Does the technology, the tool, allow you to perform the job, and in this case get the type of data you need to perform the appropriate analysis to answer your question? One can, of course (as we have pointed out throughout this book) critique different methods based on their epistemological assumptions, but the pragmatic critique is one that is more concrete and likely to spin off a host of detailed and grounded questions of the following sort: Can you use it ethically under those circumstances? Can you carry that off given the limited time or resources at your disposal? Can you readily shift directions and emphasis if need be during the course of the research? If you cannot get the data you want, how else can you get it, or what other data can you get? Madge (1953/1965) gives a succinct justification of this overall pragmatic approach: "The truth that is powerful in the world is the truth that is sufficiently exact to get things done" (p. 335). At greater length, he adds: "We can see around us a multitude of practical problems that call for action, and a multitude of people torn by their imperfect understanding of the situation in which they have to act. What they need are not absolute truths and watertight theories but the skills to guide themselves toward realistic and sensible decisions. In this tormented world, the clarifications of which our social science is capable should surely be thrown productively into the scales" (p. 339).

Just as a good carpenter, plumber, or other craftsman has different tools in the toolbox, so too social scientists need different tools to do their jobs of gathering and analyzing data. Commonly noted is the idea that different questions and different jobs require different methods or tools. But, the most important aspect of the toolbox metaphor from a multimethod perspective is that answering any given question routinely requires more than one method or tool, though this fact often goes unrecognized or unnoted. Researchers tend to focus their own thinking and public write-up of research on their primary method, only parenthetically noting (if at all) the way in which other methods or tools have been used to deal with this or that aspect of the research. It is the use of multiple tools in a single piece of research that lies at the heart of the multimethod thesis. That is why the workman carries not a single tool but the whole toolbox to the job, knowing that more than one tool is likely to be needed. And again, John Madge (1953/1965) explicitly foreshadows this multimethod thesis: "In practice we shall learn that no single technique is adequate for the grasp of a situation of any depth and complexity, and in time we shall learn that these methods can most effectively and most economically be combined in a more less regular sequence" (p. 3).

A second key question is "Where do the tools come from?" As in any technology, tools become increasingly modified by their users over time. Refinements over time in the social sciences might include, for example, developments in questionnaire construction, in sampling procedures, in recording and retrieving observations, in manipulating experimental variables, and the like. Such refinements are made by real-world practitioners as they go about the business of doing their research in given settings—making slight adjustments here and fine-tuning there—as needed by the real-world contingencies of the moment. Just as there are accumulations of substantive scientific knowledge on given topics, there is also an accumulation of practical wisdom in the technology of conducting scientific research. Such innovations and adjustments are most often the result of applying some little technique or skill that one has learned elsewhere in order to solve the immediate problem at hand. Familiarity with other methods–the outcome of a multimethod sensitivity—increases the likelihood of these little methodological innovations and developments.

The introduction of definably new methods of research may come from changes outside the discipline and often are the result of truly new technologies—both material and social. The use of video cameras in experimental small groups and focus groups research, or for systematic observation of street behavior, is a contemporary case in point (Sampson & Raudenbush, 1999). The continuing refinement and miniaturization of integrated micro sensors-processors-communicators; that is, "motes" (*Scientific American*, 2004) that can be affixed to units in field settings to record networks of relationships hold great potential for creative social scientists, as does the ability to use GPS tracking.

Moving beyond material technology to the realm of social technology modern survey research, for example, is a product of innovations in the technology of social organization of the "survey research center" with its staff of analysts and a professionally trained field staff of interviewers. These are exemplified academically by Michigan's Survey Research Center, Columbia's Bureau of Applied Social Research, and Chicago's National Opinion Research Center; as well as the more commercial centers such as the Harris and Roper polling organizations. The mobilization of resources on a grand scale of social organization for social research purposes involving a variety of methods was clearly a product of the Allied effort during World War II (see Stouffer et al., 1949).

More recently, the melding of material technology and social technology in a creative new method is the use of the Internet, both as a survey instrument (Witte, 2004) and as a database for archival research (Wellman & Haythornthwaite, 2002). James Witte (2004), a pioneer in the use of Internet surveys, points out in his article titled "The Case for Multimethod Research" the need to reconsider the calculus of costs and benefits of research provided by the Internet. Questions of sampling and sample size, questionnaire construction, data-collection efficiency, and the validation of generalizations all may require a rethinking of the comparative advantages of different sampling strategies given the new technology of the Internet. One observation and a related question arise from the efficiency of these new methods in creating large quantities of both qualitative and quantitative data. For example, Witte's Internet survey generated a sample of over 20,000 respondents, and Sampson's systematic social observation using drive-by video recordings generated 28,316 face blocks of observation. Many of these new techniques increase the efficiency of the traditional four major categories of methods we have outlined in this book—experimental, field observation, survey, and nobtrusive/archival—but are not necessarily new methods per se. For example, Neustadtl, Robinson, and Kestnbaum (2002), in a discussion of "Doing Social Science Research Online," focus on the Internet as a tool for conducting research and use the traditional categories or styles: "survey," "experimental," "qualitative/observational," "archival," and they add one additional "new" category—"social networks."

The question that arises is when and how do new technologies, with their large and efficient data collection, shift from being simply the same methods writ large to becoming new methods in and of themselves? That is, when does a quantitative increase become so large that it results in a qualitative shift and the creation of a distinct new method? The history of methodological specialization and differentiation into our four current dominant styles of research outlined in earlier chapters suggests that the new methods have evolved out of one another to answer specific questions in a more rigorous fashion that the other methods were relatively inadequate at answering. New methods or styles are, therefore, likely to evolve out of existing methods in a continuing process of refinement and specialization, but the new methods will, in turn, continue to reflect and be related to their methodological parentage. And some of these new methods reflect combinations of the four dominant styles in a true multimethod synthesis; for example "historical sociology" as a distinct method as proposed by Skocpol (1984) and Stinchcombe (1978), or Charles Ragin's (2000) "fuzzy logic" that combines some of the logic of larger sample survey research with comparative logic rooted in the "case study" method of field research.

In general, the four major methods we have outlined in this book reflect a union of specific types of data collection and specific types of data analysis that together serve to define the specific styles. Yet combinations of diverse types of data collection and data analysis also reflect a multimethod perspective. One such example is the sophisticated sampling and statistical analysis of observational data in what Sampson and Raudenbush (1999) refer to as "systematic social observation." This is a far cry from the ethnographer's detailed field notes of a single case or setting, and is also a distinct form of data compared to the survey researcher's analysis of interview data from a large sample of respondents.

We conclude with the observation that new technologies may point simultaneously to methodological innovation and specialization, and also to the unity underlying diverse research styles and a more ready appreciation of a multimethod strategy. For example, with respect to the new technology of the Internet, Williams, Rice and Rogers (1988) state that "Although we consider possible research methods for new media as mainly extensions of existing methods, we propose that the new media researcher should consider alternative methods, or even multiple methods, and to attempt a triangulation of methods" (p. 15).

The point here is not to engage in social science fiction and prophecy when it comes to the future technology of social science research methods, nor to conclude with some trite pabulum about the need for openness to innovation. Rather, the point is that prior socialization into, appreciation of, and training in a multimethod perspective will facilitate the experimental exploration and evaluation of new technologies of social science methods in the light of well-established existing methods. Furthermore, new technologies may actually facilitate the simultaneous use of qualitative and quantitative methods as demonstrated with respect to the Internet.

The tools, the methods, and the technology are means to substantive truths, not ends in and of themselves. One becomes wedded to a technology if one has a vested interest in it, within the social sciences for example, to the degree that one has invested time and resources and career in developing certain methodological skills, one has a commitment to the method and may search for different substantive arenas in which to apply it. The old adage is "give a child a hammer and the world is for hammering." Such crossovers are not to be discouraged and may even be innovative and fruitful if, for example, a certain subject area has long been dominated by an existing literature based on its own traditional methods. Such methodological crossovers can lead to positive multimethod development if both the innovative and too-often brash monomethod invader and the too-often defensive establishment methodologies each recognize their own limitations and the unique positive contributions of the other. Again, it takes a multimethod sensitivity to appreciate both the insights of the new and the wisdom of the old.

# Nine

## Making Research Public

### The Social Context of Multimethod Research

S ocial science research is not only *about* society, it is also produced *in* society. *What* we study and *how* we study it are phenomena that can be separated analytically, but they are nevertheless part and parcel of the same social world. Questions about the interweaving of science and society have become a subject of study of the social sciences themselves. How knowledge is produced, how the content of knowledge is shaped by how it is produced, and how knowledge affects various individuals and groups in society are some of the central questions raised by this perspective.

Here we will consider questions of this sort as they pertain to multimethod research and also how multimethod research may ease some dilemmas that their consideration suggests. First, we will look at the internal politics of social science research, focusing briefly upon the structure of the disciplines and then upon the publication of research. Finally, we will consider the external political impact of social science research on public policymakers' and others' definitions of social problems and on the evaluation of social programs designed to deal with those problems, and we will examine ethical issues concerning the conduct of social science inquiry.

## Internal Politics

The adages "knowledge is power" and (its reverse) "power creates knowledge" may be aptly applied to the development of the social sciences. Different methodological as well as theoretical "styles" have competed for acceptance and for the disciplines' scarce resources, which include not only research funds and faculty positions but also the brightest students and publication space in journals. This competition might be described metaphorically as a struggle in which the best ideas, being the most powerful, survive. However, the history of American social science is as much a social history of competition between "theory groups," "methodological clusters," and "schools" as it is an intellectual history of competing ideas (Mullins, 1973).

In this social competition, location within prestige networks of scholars and institutions appears to be central in establishing the acceptance and dominance of different styles of work. Hierarchies of theoretical and methodological dominance were first established regionally in major universities. However, the great expansion of the academy in the 1960s and early 1970s led to what some have called a "democratization of prestige," as faculty and graduate students from leading universities dispersed throughout the nation to take positions in new or growing institutions. As a result, the styles of work that once characterized a few elite universities now cross-cut institutions. Today, networks of social scientists working in the various styles extend throughout the country with representatives of each network coexisting, if not always cooperating, within the same universities.

This structural development has fostered a greater awareness of the methodological diversity of the social sciences than previously existed. Social science departments may still be labeled and known best by the dominant theoretical and methodological styles of their "stars," but most also expect of their students at least passing familiarity with other styles as well. Most departments, therefore, now have faculty who have been trained in and who teach and do research in each style. Because of this, the structural preconditions for collaborative as well as individually conducted multimethod research are now met far more fully than in the past.

In this arena of competing perspectives, multimethod researchers have a vested interest in bridging differences and bringing about common understanding. They may play an almost ambassadorial role similar to that sometimes played by persons who are subjected to cross-pressures in other politicized situations. Structurally, they are positioned between social worlds, and, although they may experience internal conflict, they serve to mitigate conflict within the system as a whole. Although conflict mitigation is not a goal of science, nor necessarily an end in itself, in this instance it may ease the process of inquiry and encourage the achievement of a more general understanding of social reality.

The competition for scarce resources is closely connected to the competition of ideas. The elaborate and varied reward structures of science ensure that new ideas will be developed and disseminated by making scientists' career advancement dependent not only upon their productivity but also upon their originality. To achieve distinction for oneself and one's ideas requires distinguishing one's work from others'.

The need to make one's work distinct in order to achieve distinction has two seemingly contradictory implications for multimethod research. First, there is the push toward increasing differentiation and specialization, which would seem to be detrimental. As researchers become more differentiated in defining problems and selecting methods for pursuing them, they are likely to be less able to interact with one another and to understand one another's work, let alone engage in multimethod research as individuals. In addition, because of competition, collaborative research is probably least likely to occur among those who are most similar and working parallel to one another's problems and methods. Second, however, increasing differentiation has created a greater need for coordination of research efforts and results. Many social scientists are now keenly aware of this need and are attempting to meet it by a variety of means, including new theoretical syntheses and meta-analyses of particular bodies of research. Multimethod research offers the additional option of building an important measure of unification into the primary research process itself.

Yet another implication of the pressure for distinctive research is a heightened search for innovative approaches to research problems. In this context, the multimethod approach has the advantage that it may generate more innovations not only because it is a relatively fresh approach but also because it is open to ideas and information from more sources. Furthermore, the internal politics and competitive reward structures that link egos to ideas encourage researchers not only to find ingenious solutions to existing research problems but also to break old molds and recombine the pieces into new perspectives. Multimethod tactics such as triangulated measurement, multimethod testing of hypotheses, multiple sampling, and building theories with diverse data may help solve problems in established research areas and encourage more innovative theorizing, such as the metaphorical application of ideas from one area to another (see Chapter 3), which defines new research areas or, in Kaplan's (1964) terms, effects the growth of knowledge by extension (p. 305).

## The Publication of Research

Research is of little, or at least greatly diminished, significance if its results remain unpublished or are otherwise (as by secrecy or censorship) removed from the open give-and-take of scientific inquiry. The sharing of research results among scientists is critical for the external social control of the two basic scientific criteria of reliability and validity. Moreover, debates and even controversies are the very process by which problems, methods, analyses, and theories become sharpened and refined. The public clash of ideas is essential to the collective scientific process. Furthermore, publication is equally essential to scientific cooperation, for obviously researchers can build upon one another's work only if they know what others have done.

Science provides a variety of incentives to researchers to complete this final step of writing it up and getting it out. These incentives range from the satisfaction of seeing one's name in print and the prestige of contributing to science, to the rule of publish or perish. Publication requires special incentives because it can be very demanding. Not the least of these demands is the frustration of having one's work rejected and then having to rethink, rewrite, and resubmit that work.

Here is a successful but obviously exasperated psychologist's description of the publication process in professional journals.

In recognition of the scientific nature of the psychological enterprise, the new trend is toward simply listing the number of methodological flaws and conceptual alternatives that can be imputed to a given study. . . . The author is then required to deal with the 10–14 pages of methodological, statistical, and conceptual criticism and must cut the length of the article by one third. . . . This initiates what is usually the first of several challenging exchanges between the editor and author. Along the way, authors of less superior manuscripts tend progressively to drop out, leaving only the finest manuscripts for publication. These manuscripts, of course, have been greatly improved by dealing at length with all possible methodological and conceptual criticisms and by largely abandoning the theoretical considerations that give rise to the study. (Nisbett, 1978, pp. 519–520)

It is hoped that most submissions for publication are neither as aggravating nor as stifling as the foregoing implies. But nonetheless author Nisbett's (1978) comments illustrate an important point. Scientific publication involves exposing one's work to criticism by colleagues whose viewpoints, priorities, and even criteria of excellence may differ from one's own. His comments also suggest the importance, in evaluating completed research, of avoiding an attitude of unrestrained skepticism—one that critically invokes *all possible* methodological flaws and conceptual alternatives—and, instead, taking a more closely reasoned approach or, as we suggested in Chapter 2, a healthy skepticism.

Freese and Rokeach (1979) have suggested the following guidelines for responsible criticism of single studies. They argue that for an alternative interpretation of a researcher's findings to be valid grounds for rejecting those findings, one or more of the following conditions must be met:

(1) a statistical artifact be identified; (2) a faulty research design be identified; (3) a theoretically relevant uncontrolled variable be identified which should have been controlled (a) given the specific problem of an investigation and the role of investigation within a larger research program, or (b) given an independent body of theory and data which establish that the phenomenon or process under investigation is contaminated by the setting in which it is investigated. (p. 200)

Freese and Rokeach (1979) stress further that "Assessing the significance of contaminating factors, however, must be tempered by the overall results of the research program in which the supposedly contaminated investigation is situated" (p. 200). Looked at from this point of view, statistically sound, well-designed multimethod research programs have the advantage in answering criticisms that among the research conducted or planned will be studies that address issues of contamination that might well be unaddressable in a single-method investigation. However, this is not just a matter of silencing critics (among whom the harshest may be the investigators themselves). We may reduce the area of uncertainty surrounding any given investigation by enlarging the methodological context of research, and in particular committing ourselves to research programs that include studies employing an appropriately selected variety of methods.

At several points, we have suggested a metaphor in addition to that of the "evolutionary struggle" of ideas competing and the "fittest" surviving; namely, the world of art, in which aesthetic criteria are raised and debated, and different styles vie for acceptance in terms of those criteria. Combining the "evolutionary" and the "aesthetic" perspectives allows us to understand better the role of publication in the scientific process. Publication is the social scientist's equivalent to the artist's showing, a statement that lays claim to the scarce resources required for public display. The central question "Is it any good?" (not simply "Do you like it?") acknowledges that in both worlds judgments to expend these scarce resources are based on a larger social and cultural world, not simply personal preference. One often hears among critics that a piece of work is technically competent, but trivial. In science, as in art, technical mastery is a necessary—but not always a sufficient—basis for acceptance. Struggle as they will, critics and reviewers find it difficult to recommend for publication work that is faultless but in their view uneventful; sound but not insightful.

In recent years, the number of journals publishing social science research has increased dramatically. This increase reflects the growth and differentiation within the social sciences as new substantive, theoretical, and methodological subdisciplines have emerged. For example, journals of substantive specialties exist for education, health, urban affairs, and the family; theoretical differences are reflected in different journals for theory; and there are method-specific journals for quantitative, mathematical research, field research, and evaluation research.

Given this differentiation and specialization, the inclusion of multiple methods in a single research report presents both a promise and a problem for social science. The promise is the potential to bridge this increasing specialization and to pass the first hurdle of exhibiting different styles of research to those more oriented to a single method. Assuming, of course, that the multimethod research is done well according to the differing criteria of each method, it can demonstrate the utility of alternative approaches to problems for those initially more convinced by one of the other methods. The practitioner of multimethod research, however, may encounter the problem of reviewers and critics who question the rationale for including the results of two or more methods in a single research report. A common suggestion for revision is to de-emphasize or leave out entirely that method toward which the reviewers are least inclined and to strengthen the method they most favor. In short, the author of multimethod research may run the risk of alienating rather than appealing to advocates of particular styles of research. The least-desirable response to this problem would be to propose yet another journal specifically geared to publishing MULTIMETHOD RESEARCH! A better response is to submit one's work to the many journals that already publish (although perhaps in separate articles) research that relies on a number of different methods.

Publication is demanding of readers as well as of authors, and social science publications vary greatly in their accessibility and general appeal. For many researchers, this situation creates little difficulty because in fact the targeted audience is a relatively small circle of colleagues in a subdiscipline, who may be virtually the only competent and immediately concerned readers. However, beyond such scientifically important but restricted audiences, there are often other readers who either might be usefully addressed or—in some important instances—must be addressed for one's work to have the maximum desired impact. For example, much research on social problems is aimed not only at immediate colleagues but also at policymakers, the media, and the public.

These broader audiences may be better addressed by different modes of presentation and may be more receptive to and appreciative of some styles of research than others. For example, research involving sophisticated quantitative analysis is undoubtedly more difficult than qualitative research to present in total to either a general intellectual or lay audience. But while simplifications and summaries of technically difficult work may catch the general reader, they generally fail to satisfy the writer's professional colleagues, who may regard them as mere popularizations and so not to be taken seriously.

Multimethod research offers a possible resolution to this dilemma. In research that must reach both a professional and a more general audience, some methods might be employed for their appeal to the methodologically sophisticated, while others (equally rigorous but less esoteric) might be used for their accessibility to a wider group. Methods may differ in their appeal and ease of access to various audiences without necessarily differing either in their scientific rigor or appropriateness in particular investigations. Rigor and appropriateness depend after all upon the researcher's skill and sound judgment, not upon the reader's sophistication. Moreover, while simplified summaries of more difficult quantitative research may be unacceptable as serious scientific work when presented in isolation, they may be quite acceptable when presented in conjunction with the detailed report of a qualitative or simpler quantitative phase of a research program involving both kinds of studies.

# External Politics

Debates over the appropriate role of social science knowledge in society have continued to rage since its inception. Whether it can be or should be "value-free" knowledge for knowledge's sake or "value-focused" knowledge for "goodness'" sake is the important central issue. Regardless of one's position on this issue, the fact is that social science has influenced the larger social world, sometimes in ways that neither the scientists nor the public have anticipated or desired.

## Defining Problems

Throughout this book we have emphasized the significance of research methods for addressing problems within social theory. This perspective may be considered "pure science," research driven by the questions and problems internal to the discipline itself. The application of scientific knowledge to the problems and affairs of society requires a somewhat broader perspective, one that sees science itself operating within, not above, the social landscape. Questions and issues that emerge from society—in short, "social problems"—also generate social research. Social science knowledge is often called upon to answer questions about important concerns such as the impact of school desegregation upon student achievement or of subsidized housing programs upon the improvement in housing quality for the poor. These are social problems to be researched by applied science, not the theoretical problems of a pure science. However, the distinctions between "pure" and "applied" science are themselves "ideal types" that often blur in actual research projects. A single piece of research may simultaneously be addressing *both* social science problems identified in the discipline and social problems defined by society. In most human endeavors, mixed motives and multiple consequences are embodied in any concrete action, and so it is with social research.

One of the most striking ways in which social problems have become central in guiding the course of social science research is in the funding of that research by both public and private agencies. Research funds are usually allocated in the service of particular policy arenas, policy arenas that are seen to be linked to existing and emerging social problems. Social scientists themselves often play an important role in the definition of the problems and in setting research agendas to generate knowledge leading to their amelioration. At this point the cutting edge of social science methods and theories can be brought to bear in defining social problems in such a way that they are also raised as relevant social science problems. Strategies for tackling the problems also often implicitly contain theoretical and methodological predilections. In defining problems, designing programs, and evaluating effects, the various methods of social research often come under scrutiny by publics outside of the discipline itself and may generate political issues within the larger society. (For example, the "dark figure of crime" that was revealed in comparing victimization surveys with official statistics raised issues not only about the extent of crime but also about the efficacy of police in dealing with it.)

In the popularization of a rational, scientific approach to society's problems, the conception of science itself has often been distorted both as to what constitutes appropriate scientific procedures and what represents valid scientific results. A prevailing scientism overly stresses the ideal of experimental methods and a correlated desire for quantification. The old adage of the British empiricist Lord Kelvin has taken firm hold on the minds of policymakers searching for legitimation and rationalization of programs, "If you cannot measure, your knowledge is meager and unsatisfactory." Measurement has come to mean quantification.

However, social scientists know that the validity of numbers is only as good as the procedures and methods used to generate them and that the contemporary response to Lord Kelvin is that "bad numbers drive out good judgment." Similarly, college admissions officers are well aware that SAT scores are but one type of information that must be interpreted cautiously and in the light of other qualitative data (letters of recommendation, for example) in evaluating the quality of college applicants. As a result of the partial and selective understanding of the limits of individual social science methods, social science research is often castigated in the public forum of political debate as "playing with statistics," or wasting public funds on trivia (the Golden Fleece Award of Senator Proxmire), or going through mystifying machinations to discover what everybody already knows.

It is a truism that how questions are asked may determine the form of their answers. Similarly, how social problems are defined affects the form of programs designed to deal with them. For example, if crime is defined as a problem because its perpetrators escape the criminal justice system, then programs may be designed to increase apprehension, to speed trials, and to require certain punishment for convicted criminals. However, if crime is instead defined as a problem for its victims, then programs may be designed to reduce victimization through Block Watch or Whistlestop programs, through "target hardening" with burglar alarms and locks, through self-defense training, or through psychological and economic aid for victims. How various individuals and groups selectively define the problem will influence which of the many possible programs are finally selected to address it.

Different methods of social research may also influence the definition of problems. Particular methods selectively identify the units of analysis and the central variables that may be measured in studies of particular social problems. Scientists and policymakers looking for data and analyses that will aid them in defining a problem are likely to cast the problem in terms of the units and variables of existing research. For example, early research on crime focused on the captive perpetrators variously trying to account for and ameliorate criminal behavior through psychological testing and identifying social characteristics of offenders. More recently, surveys of victims (Ennis, 1967) have defined the crime problem in terms of different units and variables, as have participant observation of police in action (Black, 1970) and of residents' collective responses to crime (Hunter & Maxfield, 1980). Multimethod approaches to the definition of social problems, therefore, are beneficial for policymakers as a way to increase the number of possible definitions of a problem and, consequently, to suggest a wider range of programs from which they may select. Increasing such options has important political and economic advantages in addition to the heightened possibility of ameliorating the problem.

Research methods also vary in their usefulness for studying different aspects of social problems. More quantitative analyses relying either upon survey or upon census and archival materials are often most useful in understanding the extent and scope of specific problems. Such methods are, thus, particularly useful for defining the parameters within which various potential solutions may be debated. Field research and case studies of particular populations and settings are, on the other hand, extremely useful in defining the social process by which problems emerge and for suggesting strategic points of programmatic intervention to deal with particular problems.

Scientistic beliefs about the role of science in public policy can be corrected in part by a conscious positive affirmation of the varying strengths and weaknesses of different methods in the social scientist's research repertoire. Furthermore, the incorporation of multiple methods in the same piece of research (given careful presentation and appropriate qualifications) will give a more realistic and balanced view of the role of social sciences in such policy debates. At question, once again, is the appropriate role of social science in society. To the extent that social scientists place ideology above their craft, they will be pitted against one another as spokespersons for different ideological positions, rather than working together as reasonable researchers aiding the policy process through their commitment to the goals of science itself. The balance provided by multimethod research can aid in presenting society's policymakers with more valid and reliable conclusions as well as encouraging a more sophisticated understanding of social research.

## Evaluating Results

One of the most important ways in which social science research is currently used in policy arenas is in evaluating the effectiveness of different programs. Evaluation research is the "new" tool linking policymakers and social scientists, but, though the label is new, this type of research is not (for example, studies done in World War II that evaluated the effectiveness of Allied propaganda were precursors). However, as accountability in government spending has increased, evaluation research has assumed increasing importance. Accountability, previously based on the watchfulness of competing political interests or the media, has been supplemented by the presumed objective rationality of social science research. Most evaluation researchers, however, are quick to acknowledge that theirs is not an exact science and that biases and value judgments often impinge on the process.

Moreover, the increasing acceptance of our "experimental society," as Campbell (1969) has noted, must be coupled with the realization that (a) not all experiments work, and (b) newly implemented programs are often far departures from the rigorous scientific experiment. These departures have forced evaluation researchers to explore a variety of alternative research methods ranging from the older classic ethnographies of participant observers to new and sophisticated quantitative techniques such as "interrupted time series with switching replications."

As Weiss (1972) notes:

Evaluators use the whole gamut of research methods to collect information—
interviews, questionnaires, tests of knowledge and skill, attitude inventories,
observation, content analysis of documents, records, examination of physical
evidence. Ingenious evaluators can find fitting ways of exploring a wide
range of effects. The kind of data-collection scheme to be used depends on
the type of information needed to answer the specific questions that the evaluation poses. (pp. 8–9)

One of the major attractions of multimethod evaluation research is its
compatibility with a real world action approach. Dealing with specific
programs in concrete settings and being concerned with bureaucratic
needs of decision making as they must, evaluators are especially aware of
time and resource constraints and of the need to provide usable analyses
from readily available data. These constraints and needs are often less
pressing (but ultimately still present) for more theoretically oriented academic researchers, who can therefore afford to be more doctrinaire about
methods and ontological assumptions. Perhaps for this reason, evaluation
researchers have been in the forefront of multimethod research.

To know if something has had an effect is the central problem
addressed by both the experimental style of research and by evaluation
research. One would think, therefore, that a natural affinity would exist
between the two. However, evaluation research is mostly conducted outside the laboratory where "true," or ideal, experiments are often either
ethically or practically impossible. Furthermore, evaluation research has
broadened its scope beyond simple demonstration of "effects" to include
a series of sequentially staged research questions. According to Rossi,
Freeman, and Wright (1979) these include (1) program planning questions, (2) program monitoring questions, (3) impact assessment questions,
and (4) economic efficiency questions. And nonexperimental methods are
often more apt for answering these questions.

Evaluation researchers do not retreat from the field because of the
imperfections of experimental design in the real world; instead, they
frame their research questions to fit more appropriate methods and available data as necessary. Knowing that more objective answers are needed
to inform public policy, they have drawn widely from the social scientist's
bag of methods in an attempt to provide systematic procedures for arriving at those answers. Increasingly, evaluation researchers have recognized
the joint strengths and liabilities of different types of methods and have

begun to call for multimethod research. For example, Cook and Reichart (1979) have strongly urged using combinations of qualitative and quantitative methods. Much as we have argued in this book with respect to theoretically oriented research, they argue that evaluation research has multiple purposes, which different methods may best serve and that when applied to the same purpose, different methods may offer unique insights and cross-checks of one another's results. Greene, Caracelli and Graham (1989) and Rallis and Rossman (2003) have studied and discussed at length the variety of uses to which multiple methods—in particular the mixing of qualitative and quantitative techniques—have been put in evaluation studies.

In summary, multimethod research is a practical and practiced reality in the world of policy analysis and policy research. Research conducted under conditions of time and resource constraints and geared toward action programs in an experimental society, where decision makers need analyses to weigh alternatives objectively, requires the social science community to provide the best that it can offer.

## Considering Research Ethics

The way scientists work and the goals they hope to achieve are guided by the norms and values of scientific inquiry. However, scientific norms and values do not stand over and above, or apart from, the prevailing norms and values of the larger society. As the example of German genetics in the Nazi era makes clear, there may be considerable tension between the ideal of science and the reality of scientists engaged in specific studies socially rooted in particular places and times. This tension between the ideal and the reality of science has been used by critics both within and outside the scientific community to argue respectively for either (a) the need to protect and defend the autonomy of science within a rationally oriented society; or (b) the need to be wary of scientific claims to knowledge because the relativism of these claims demonstrates the presence of veiled ideological positions and possibly questionable epistemological assumptions and premises.

These controversies (such as the current disputes over evolutionary theory) most often concern the end products or goals of science—the substantive, theoretical conclusions derived from empirical research. More recently, however, similar issues have been raised on another level in critiques of the practices by which scientists conduct their inquiries. Norms governing how scientists conduct research are now being scrutinized through a set of norms and values that lie outside of the more limited rules of science and that question the ethics of scientific practices. These ethical issues are generally relevant for the life sciences (which, broadly conceived, are concerned with the study of all living organisms) and are particularly pertinent for the human sciences (which are concerned with studying human organisms). A scientist bombarding water molecules with radiation to measure ionization of deuterium atoms does not confront these ethical issues, unless the water is contained in the cells of a cancer patient who is a research subject in a radiation therapy experiment.

The universal rights of scientists to investigate are now being challenged and weighed against the rights of others in society who may be the subjects of that research. Among these competing rights are the right to privacy, the right to be informed, the right to be free from coerced participation, and the right for protection from willful physical, psychological, and social harm by others. Allegations of medical and scientific misconduct in research on the treatment of syphilis patients (Reverby, 2000) and on the effects of radiation on human subjects (Faden, 1996) have raised images of Drs. Frankenstein and Strangelove. Social scientists have also been caught up in the fear and criticism of unfeeling and unfettered scientists. A number of studies have assumed a dubious place of distinction in the social science debates on ethics. These include Milgram's study (1974) of people's compliance to an authority figure's request to inflict pain on another human being; Humphries's study (1970) of homosexual encounters in public washrooms followed up by seemingly unrelated interviews in the men's homes; and Project Camelot (Horowitz, 1974), a government-supported research effort by a group of social scientists attempting to understand rebellions in Third World nations with an eye toward their suppression.

The major outcome of these revelations has been the passage of governmental legislation and agency regulations covering the use of human subjects in scientific research. Institutional review boards of peers have been mandated at universities to oversee proposed research and assess its ethical propriety. The central criteria used in these reviews are risk/benefit assessments and assurance of informed, voluntary consent of subjects asked to participate in research. Although clearly essential in some areas, these heightened ethical standards nonetheless might stifle certain methodological approaches to some research topics. As Cassell (1978) points out, the criteria and requirements for ethical scientific investigations were drawn primarily with a model method and a targeted population in mind—the experiments of medical researchers. As a result, social researchers relying on fieldwork, surveys, or archival data may be evaluated by inappropriate criteria.

Appropriately assessing the benefits to be derived from research, as against the risks that may be incurred, unavoidably requires value judgments in assigning relative weights to specific benefits and risks. For example, how many units of potential benefit to the alleviation of the pains of poverty are to be weighed against the relative risk of an individual's loss of anonymity in a survey interview? Not only do such judgments require comparing pears and peaches, they also require a hypothetical projection of worst-case scenarios, a procedure whose logic parallels that of evaluation research and impact assessment. Without adequate data from prior research to construct models of *probable*—not simply *possible*—consequences, differing judgments reflecting different values must ultimately fall back upon the strength, prestige, or power of different factions of the scientific community to provide legitimating support for claims of specific benefits and risks. In such debates, the social sciences, when compared with medical, biological, and other natural sciences, are likely to fare poorly. That social research continues to be permitted under such risk/benefit evaluations is probably attributable more to the fact that its risks are nebulous than to the fact that its benefits are well-specified. Actually, peremptory exclusion of most social science research from the governmentally mandated human subjects review process has been considered. This is not to encourage social scientists to conduct unethical research but rather to reduce the risk of inappropriate assessments and constraint in potentially sensitive areas of social investigation.

Multimethod research may help researchers to resolve some of these issues in a practical way while also being scientifically rigorous and ethically resolute. Multimethod research allows one to switch methods if ethical questions are raised, by either the researcher or by others, about one of the methods. This may require shifting units of analysis, redefining a universe or sample to be studied, and altering slightly the nature of the initial problems, questions, or propositions that were to be investigated. For example, if one cannot gain access to a site for participant observation except by being deceptive about one's intentions, then one may explore the use of informant interviewing. Similarly, if it is difficult to get survey data pertaining to a sensitive topic, then one may search for published sources about that topic or engage in observation of public behavior that inferentially may be linked to the sensitive topic. By using multimethod designs, ethical issues may be faced directly as such and seen as a challenge to more creative research. Few researchers would be blamed by their colleagues for shifting from a "best-fit" research design to a creative alternative because the latter posed fewer ethical problems. Furthermore, by combining two or more ethically appropriate methods, one may heighten the validity of research to a level approaching that of a single best-fit method.

Moreover, the multimethod approach can be used and may be necessary to evaluate steps taken to improve ethical practices. For example, what effects does informed consent have on survey research results? To answer that question, as Singer (1978) demonstrated, requires more than a conventional survey. It requires a survey conducted in the framework of an experimental design to test the effects of systematically manipulating and varying the nature of informed consent during various stages of data collection.

Finally, we must address an ethical problem posed by multimethod research. This problem stems from the ability of multimethod research to identify and combine a variety of discrete data points from different methods, thereby linking information about individuals and groups that could not be linked if the methods were used separately. This is the same kind of threat to the invasion of privacy that is being posed by attempts to combine the files on individuals that now exist separately in the computers of different public and private agencies. This aspect of multimethod research contributed to the ethical issues raised by Humphries's (1970) research. If he had used either of his two methods (observation or survey) alone, the ethical issues would not have been raised so sharply. This ethical dilemma is also a practical design problem for multimethod research in that it impinges upon some of the important issues discussed in Chapter 4: When and to what degree should different methods be kept separate to avoid contaminating biases or brought together to heighten triangulation on individual units of observation and analysis? There are no easy or total solutions to the ethical problems of social research. However, the multimethod approach can provide ethically concerned researchers with a few new options, as well as some new concerns.

## Multimethod Research in Relation to Society

We conclude this discussion of the social context of multimethod research by considering how the multimethod perspective may promote social science's central contributions to the societies in which (and about which) it is conducted. As the contemporary "crisis" of multiple visions of social research and theory implies, it is difficult to attribute to social science a single mission. Moreover, social science has historically been ambivalent about its role in society. This ambivalence is reflected today in continuing debates over whether social science is essentially a humanistic or a scientific enterprise (Gouldner, 1970).

Humanistic social science is rooted in the ideas of social and cultural relativism, which explain differences in human behavior by reference to societies' varying structures and processes rather than by reference to basic differences in human nature. These ideas encourage an attitude toward social life that might be called skeptical tolerance. This is skepticism about any and all claims to superiority, virtue, or righteousness that demean or deny others' basic humanity, but a tolerance for human differences that rests upon a firm social scientific understanding of the social basis for those differences.

The multimethod perspective on research emphasizes a similar skeptical tolerance with respect to the pursuit of knowledge; skepticism of any and all claims to have discovered the truth, but a tolerance of all reasonable methods of pursuit. If we successfully maintain this attitude in the ways we individually and collectively study societies, then we may also more effectively communicate social science's important humanistic message. This may be accomplished not only by the example of our own tolerance of differences within our disciplines but more importantly by the concern and skill that we demonstrate in ensuring that the content of our work reflects fairly on all persons and groups.

The employment of different types of research methods is essential not only to determine the scientific validity of our research in a formal sense but also to determine and eliminate any substantive social biases that might be introduced by the overuse of a single type of method. Particular types of research methods are not in all cases inherently biased for or against particular types of persons or groups. However, as research on the connection between social class and crime illustrates (see Chapter 3), there is little doubt that in particular instances the use of a particular method may bias our work. Such biases may be discovered and corrected more easily if a method of a different type is applied to the same situation.

The scientific side of social science, which stems from the Enlightenment's attempts at rational and empirical understanding of all natural phenomena, implies a parallel attitude of empirical skepticism. This attitude challenges claims to knowledge by questioning their empirical basis. *What* you say you know is questioned by asking, *how* do you know that? The skeptic's questions, which have run throughout this book, and the insistence that each style of research must address them all are expressions of this attitude.

The multimethod perspective on research stresses that there are a variety of ways of arriving at knowledge but that all entail chances of error, although fortunately not always the same errors. This viewpoint is quite tolerant of these different methods because it sees multiple approaches as a scientific necessity and understands methods' fallibility to be a given of scientific inquiry. However, it is also very skeptical about either overrelying upon any one approach or offhandedly rejecting alternative approaches. And it is downright intolerant of ambiguities that result simply from either overreliance upon a single type of method or the failure to consider alternatives. If this multimethod perspective can be communicated widely, then a more sophisticated and reasoned reading of scientific knowledge about human societies may come to prevail.

Much has been made in recent decades of the assertion that social science is a perspective requiring a particular imagination. Too often we think of this as referring only to our theoretical viewpoints and knowledge. However, the social scientific perspective is displayed as much in how one studies society as in how one thinks about it and what one knows. The theories and findings of social science have diffused widely into other fields and into the institutions of the larger society. Equally important has been the diffusion of social science's research methods. One result of this diffusion is that there are now many new practitioners and consumers of social research.

For these newcomers, an understanding of the multimethod perspective may help to demystify social research and to guard against tendencies toward naive scientism in the use of social science methods and in the interpretation of social science data. Social scientists have become accustomed to, and adept at interpreting, methodologically diverse and often contradictory research findings. Routinely faced with diversity and contradiction, they have also become keenly aware that one can hardly ever take any set of data at face value. It has been learned through experience that the so-called duck test of knowledge (if it walks like a duck, quacks like a duck, etc., then it's a duck) is all too rarely applicable. The fact of the matter is that research findings are determined both by the reality we seek to comprehend and by the patterns of thought and behavior involved in the conduct of inquiry itself. And because different methods of inquiry involve different patterns of thought and behavior, they may generate very different patterns of research results. This can be discouraging and frustrating to beginners with high hopes. However, a great benefit of the multimethod perspective is that it teaches both humility and confidence. One must openly admit to the chance of error and misinterpretation, but one can also assert that there is a chance of truth because there are multi-method procedures for increasing the probability that one has in fact touched the truth.

# References

Anderson, N. (1923/1961). *The hobo: The sociology of the homeless man.* Chicago: University of Chicago Press.

Archer, D., & Gartner, R. (1976, December). Violent acts and violent times: A comparative approach to postwar homicide rates. *American Sociological Review, 41,* 937–963.

Arnold, D. (1970). Dimensional sampling: An approach for studying a small number of cases. *American Sociologist, 5,* 147–149.

Aronson, E., & Carlsmith, J. M. (1968). Experimentation in social psychology. In G. Lindzey & E. Aronson (Eds.), *The handbook of social psychology* (2nd ed.) (pp. 1–79). Reading, MA: Addison-Wesley.

Babbie, E. (1979). *The practice of social research.* Belmont, CA: Wadsworth.

Bailey, K. D. (1978). *Methods of social research.* New York: The Free Press.

Barnes, H. E., & Becker, H. (1938). *Social thought from lore to science, II: Sociological trends throughout the world.* Boston: D.C. Heath.

Becker, H. S. (1963). *Outsiders.* New York: Free Press.

Becker, H. S., & Geer, B. (1957). Participant observation and interviewing. *Human Organization, 16,* 28–32.

Bennett, J. (1981). *Oral history and delinquency: The rhetoric of criminology.* Chicago: University of Chicago Press.

Bernstein, I. N., Kelly, W. R., & Doyle, P. A. (1977). Societal reaction to deviants: The case of criminal defendants. *American Sociological Review, 42,* 743–755.

Black, D. (1970). Production of crime rates. *American Sociological Review, 34,* 733–748.

Blalock, H. M. (1964). *Causal inferences in non-experimental research.* Chapel Hill: University of North Carolina Press.

Blalock, H. M. (1967). *Theory construction.* Englewood Cliffs, NJ: Prentice Hall.

Blalock, H. M. (1978). Ordering diversity *Society, 15* (3), 20 22.

Blalock, Hubert M. (1979). Measurement and conceptualization problems. *American Sociological Review, 44,* 881–894.

Blau, P. M. (1960). Structural effects. *American Sociological Review, 25,* 178–193.

Bloch, M. (1953). *The historian's craft.* New York: Vintage Books.

Bollen, K. A, & Paxton, P. (1998). Detection and determinants of bias in subjective measures. *American Sociological Review 63*, 465–478.

Brannon, R., Cyphers, G., Hesse, C., Hesselbart, S., Keane, R., Schuman, H., Viccaro, T., & Wright, D. (1973). Attitude and action: A field experiment joined to a general population survey. *American Sociological Review, 38*, 625–636.

Brewer, J. (1971). Flow of communications, expert qualifications, and organizational authority structures. *American Sociological Review, 36*, 475–485.

Brewer, J., & Hunter, A. (1989). *Multimethod research: A synthesis of styles.* Newbury Park, CA: Sage Publications, Inc.

Brown, R. (1963). *Explanation in social science.* Chicago: Aldine.

Brown, R. H. (1977). *A poetic for sociology.* Cambridge: Cambridge University Press.

Brown, R. H. (1987). *Sociology as text: Essays on rhetoric, reason, and reality.* Chicago: University of Chicago Press.

Burgess, E. W. (1927/1974). Statistics and case studies as methods of sociological research. Reprinted in D. J. Bogue (Ed.), *The basic writings of Ernest W. Burgess* (pp. 367–373). Chicago: Community and Family Study Center, University of Chicago.

Butler, S., & Snizek, W. E. (1976). The waitress-diner relationship: A multimethod study of subordinate influence. *Sociology of Work and Occupations, 3*, 209–222.

Camic, C., & Xie, Y. (1994). The Statistical turn in the American social sciences. *American Sociological Review, 59*, 773–805.

Campbell, D. T. (1957). Factors relevant to the validity of experiments in social settings. *Psychological Bulletin, 54*, 294–312.

Campbell, D. T. (1969). Reforms as experiments. *American Psychologist, 24*, 409–429.

Campbell, D. T. (1986). Science's social system of validity-enhancing collective belief change and the problems of the social sciences. In D. W. Fiske and R. A. Shweder, (Eds.), *Metatheory in Social Science* (pp. 108–135). Chicago: University of Chicago Press

Campbell, D. T., & Fiske, D.W. (1959). Convergent and discriminate validation by the multitrait-multimethod matrix. *Psychological Bulletin, 54*, 297–312.

Campbell, D. T., & Stanley, J. (1963). *Experimental and quasi-experimental designs for research.* Chicago: Rand McNally.

Cassell, J. (1978). Risk and benefit to subjects to fieldwork. *The American Sociologist, 13*, 134–143.

Cicourel, A. (1962). *Method and measurement in sociology.* New York: Free Press.

Clark, T. (Ed.). (1968). *Community structure and decision making: Comparative analyses.* San Francisco: Chandler.

Clark, T. N., Kornblum, W., Bloom, H., & Tobias, S. (1968). Discipline, method, community structure, and decision-making: The role and limitations of the sociology of knowledge. *American Sociologist, 3*, 214–217.

Cook, T. D., & Campbell, D. T. (1979). *Quasi-experimentation.* Chicago: Rand McNally.

Cook, T. D., & Reichart, C. S. (Eds.). (1979). *Qualitative and quantitative methods in evaluation research.* Beverly Hills, CA: Sage.

Correll, S. J. (2004). Constraints into preferences: Gender, status, and career aspirations. *American Sociological Review, 69,* 93–113.

Cortese, A. J. (1995). The rise, hegemony, and decline of the Chicago School of Sociology, 1892–1945. *Social Science Journal, 32,* 235.

Crane, S. (1972). *The complete poems of Stephen Crane.* Ithaca, NY: Cornell University Press.

Cressey, D. R. (1953) *Other people's money: A study in the social psychology of embezzlement.* Glencoe, IL: Free Press.

Culler, D. E., & Mulder, H. (2004). Smart sensors to network the world. *Scientific American, 290*(6), 85–93.

Dahl, R. (1961). *Who governs?* New Haven, CT: Yale University Press.

Danzger, H. M. (1975). Validating conflict data. *American Sociological Review, 40,* 553–569.

Davis, J. A., Spaeth, J. L., & Huson, C. (1961). A technique for analyzing the effects of group composition. *American Sociological Review, 26,* 215–225.

Denzin, N. K. (1978). *The research act* (2nd ed.). New York: McGraw-Hill.

Denzin, N. K., & Lincoln, Y. S. (Eds.). (1994). *Handbook of qualitative research.* Thousand Oaks, CA: Sage.

Denzin, N. K., & Lincoln, Y. S. (Eds). (2000). *Handbook of qualitative research* (2nd ed.). Thousand Oaks, CA: Sage.

Deutscher, I. (1966). Words and deeds: social science and social policy. *Social Problems, 14,* 233–254.

Dunaway, R. G., Cullen, F. T., Burton, V., Jr., Evans, T. D. (2000). The myth of social class and crime revisited: An examination of class and adult criminality. *Criminology, 38,* 589–632.

Duncan, G. J., & Raudenbush, S. (2001). Neighborhoods and adolescent development: How can we determine the links? In A. Booth & A. C. Crouter (Eds.), *Does it take a village? Community effects on children, adolescents, and families* (pp. 105–136). State College, PA: Pennsylvania State University Press.

Durkheim, E. (1897/1951). *Suicide.* New York: Free Press.

Dykema, J., & Schaeffer, N. C. (2000). Events, instruments and error reporting. *American Sociological Review, 65,* 619–629.

Dyson, F. (1979). *Disturbing the universe.* New York: Harper & Row.

Ennis, P. (1967). *Criminal victimization in the United States: A report of a national survey.* Chicago: National Opinion Research Center.

Erikson, K. (1976) *Everything in its path.* New York: Simon & Schuster.

Faden, R. (1996). The Advisory Committee on Human Radiation Experiments: Reflection on a presidential commission (Trusting science: Nuremburg and the human radiation experiments). *The Hastings Center Report, 26*(5), 5–30.

Fischer, Claude S. (1982). *To dwell among friends.* Chicago: University of Chicago Press.

Fiske, D. W., & Shweder, R. A. (1986). Introduction: Uneasy social science. In D. W. Fiske & R. A. Shweder (Eds.), *Metatheory in social science* (pp. 1–18). Chicago: University of Chicago Press.

Freese, L. (1972). Cumulative sociological knowledge. *American Sociological Review, 37*, 472–482.

Freese, L., & Rokeach, M. (1979). On the use of alternative interpretations in contemporary social psychology. *Social Psychology Quarterly, 42*, 195–201.

Gioia, D. A., & Thomas, J. B. (1996). Identity, image, and issue interpretation: Sensemaking during strategic change in academia. *Administrative Science Quarterly, 41*, 370–403.

Glaser, B. G., & Strauss, A. (1967). *The discovery of grounded theory.* Chicago: Aldine.

Gould, S. J. (1989). *Wonderful life.* New York: W. W. Norton.

Gould, S. J. (2003). *The hedgehog, the fox and the magister's pox.* New York: Harmony Books.

Gouldner, A. W. (1970). *The coming crisis of Western sociology.* New York: Basic Books.

Greene, B. (2004). *Fabric of the cosmos: Space, time, and the texture of reality.* New York: Knopf.

Greene, J. C., Caracelli, V. J., & Graham, W. F. (1989). Toward a conceptual framework for mixed-method evaluation designs. *Educational Evaluation and Policy Analysis, 3*, 255–274.

Greenwood, E. (1945). *Experimental sociology.* New York: King's Crown Press.

Haas, D. F. (1982). Survey sampling and the logic of inference in sociology. *The American Sociologist, 17*, 103–111.

Hadaway, C. K., Marler, P. L., & Chaves, M. (1993). What the polls don't show: A closer look at U.S. church attendance. *American Sociological Review, 58*, 741–752. (Gerald Marwell, Editor's Comment, in the same issue, pp. iii–iv)

Hagood, M. (1939). *Mothers of the south: Portraiture of the white tenant farm woman.* Chapel Hill, NC: University of North Carolina Press.

Hammond, J. L. (1973). Error in ecological correlations. *American Sociological Review, 38*, 764–777.

Heath, L. (1984). Impact of newspaper crime reports on fear of crime: Multimethodological investigation. *Journal of Personality and Social Psychology, 47*, 263–276.

Heirich, M. (1977). Change of heart: A test of some widely held theories about religious conversion. *American Journal of Sociology, 83*, 653–680.

Hindelang, M. J., Hirschi, T., & Weis, J. G. (1979). Correlates of delinquency. *American Sociological Review, 44*, 995–1014.

Hirschi, T., & Selvin, H. C. (1967). *Delinquency research.* New York: Free Press.

Horowitz, I. L. (Ed.). (1974). *The rise and fall of project Camelot: Studies in the relationship between social science and practical politics* (Rev. ed.). Cambridge: MIT Press.

Hovland, C. I. (1959). Reconciling conflicting results derived from experimental and survey studies of attitude change. *American Psychologist, 14*, 8–17.

Huber, J. (1973). The bias of emergent theory. *American Sociological Review, 38,* 274–284.

Hughes, E. C. (1960). Introduction: The place of field work in social science. In B. H. Junker, *Field work: An introduction to the social sciences.* Chicago: University of Chicago Press.

Humphries, L. (1970). Tearoom trade: Impersonal sex in public places. *Trans-Action, 7* (January), 11–25.

Hunter, A. D. (1974). *Symbolic communities.* Chicago: University of Chicago Press.

Hunter, A. D. (1975). Loss of community: An empirical test through replication. *American Sociological Review, 40,* 537–552.

Hunter, A. D. (1990a.). Introduction: Rhetoric in research, networks of knowledge. In A. D. Hunter (Ed.), *The rhetoric of social research: Understood and believed* (pp. 1–22). New Brunswick, NJ: Rutgers University Press.

Hunter, A. D. (1990b.). Setting the scene, sampling, and synecdoche. In A. D. Hunter (Ed.), *The rhetoric of social research: Understood and believed* (pp. 111–128). New Brunswick, NJ: Rutgers University Press.

Hunter, A. D., & Fritz, R. (1985). Class, status, and power structures of community elites: A comparative case study. *Social Science Quarterly, 66,* 3.

Hunter, A. D., & Maxfield, M. (1980). *Methodological overview of the reactions to crime project.* Evanston, IL: Center for Urban Affairs and Policy Research, Northwestern University.

Hunter, F. (1953). *Community power structure.* Chapel Hill, NC: North Carolina University Press.

Hyman, H. H. (1955). *Survey design and analysis.* New York: Free Press.

Jahoda, M. (1992). Reflections on Marienthal and after. *Journal of Occupational and Organizational Psychology, 65,* 355–359.

Jahoda, M., Lazarsfeld, P. F., & Zeisel, H. (1971). *Marienthal: The sociography of an unemployed community.* Chicago: Aldine.

Jenkins, J. C., & Eckert, C. M. (1986). Channeling black insurgency. *American Sociological Review, 52,* 812–829.

Jenkins, J. C., & Perrow, C. (1977). Insurgency of the powerless: Farm worker movements (1946–1972). *American Sociological Review, 42,* 249–267.

Jick, T. D. (1979). Mixing qualitative and quantitative methods: Triangulation in action. *Administrative Science Quarterly, 24,* 602–611.

Jones, C. (1992) Was there a Hawthorne effect? *American Journal of Sociology, 98*(3), 451–68.

Jones, S. (Ed.). (1999). *Doing Internet research.* Thousand Oaks, CA: Sage.

Kadushin, C. (1966). The friends and supporters of psychotherapy. On social circles in urban life. *American Sociological Review, 31,* 786–802.

Kaplan, A. (1964). *The conduct of inquiry.* San Francisco: Chandler.

Kasarda, J. (1974). The structural implications of social system size. *American Sociological Review, 39,* 19–28.

Kauffman, S. (2000). *Investigations*. New York: Oxford University Press.

Krysan, M. (1999). Qualifying a quantifying analysis on racial equality. *Social Psychological Quarterly, 62*, 211–218.

Kuhn, T. S. (1970). *The structure of scientific revolutions*. Chicago: University of Chicago Press.

Latour, B., & Woolgar, S. (1979). *Laboratory life: the social construction of scientific facts*. Beverly Hills: Sage.

Lazarsfeld, P. F., Jahoda, M., & Zeisel, H. (1933). *Die Arbeitslosen von Marienthal*. Leipzig: Hirzel.

Leik, R. (1972). *Methods, logic, and research of sociology*. Indianapolis: Bobbs-Merrill.

Leonard, R. (1995). The interpretation of discrepancies in multimethod research: A comparison of children's negotiations in two research contexts. *Early Development and Parenting, 4*, 21–28.

Lever, J. (1981). Multiple methods of data collection: A note on divergence. *Urban Life, 10* (July), 199–213.

Levine, J. P. (1976, November). The potential for crime overreporting in criminal victimization surveys. *Criminology, 14*, 307–330.

Lindzey, G., & Aronson, E. (1968). *The handbook of social psychology* (2nd ed.). Reading, MA: Addison-Wesley.

Lipset, S. (1964). The biography of a research project: Union democracy. In P. E. Hammond (Ed.), *Sociologists at work* (pp. 96–120). New York: Basic Books.

Lipset, S., Trow, M. A., & Coleman, J. S. (1956). *Union democracy*. Glencoe, IL: The Free Press.

Lodge, D. (1996). *The practice of writing*. New York: Penguin.

Lundberg, G. A. (1942). *Social research* (2nd ed.). New York: Greenwood.

Lynd, R. S. & Lynd, H. M. (1929). *Middletown*. New York: Harcourt, Brace.

Madge, J. (1953/1965). *The tools of social research: An analytic description of social science technique*. New York: Longmans, Green (reprinted by Doubleday Anchor, Garden City, NY).

Marier, P. L., & Hadaway, C. K. (1999). Testing the attendance gap in a conservative church. *Sociology of Religion. 6*, 175–182.

McAdam, D., & Su, Y. (2002). The war at home: Antiwar protests and congressional voting, 1965 to 1973. *American Sociological Review 67*, 696–721.

McCarthy, J. D., McPhail, C., & Smith, J. (1996). Images of protest: Media bias in the coverage of Washington, D.C. demonstrations. *American Sociological Review 61*, 478–499.

McCloskey, D. M. (1985). *The rhetoric of economics*. Madison, WI: University of Wisconsin Press.

Mead, G. H. (1934). *Mind, self, and society*. Chicago: University of Chicago Press.

Melbin, M. (1978). Night as frontier. *American Sociological Review, 43*, 3–22.

Merton, R. K. (1957). *Social theory and social structure*. Glencoe, IL: Free Press.

Merton, R. K., Broom, L., & Cottrell, L. S. (Eds.). (1959). *Sociology today*. New York: Basic Books.

Milgram, S. (1974). *Obedience to authority*. New York: Harper & Row.

Mills, C. W. (1959). *The sociological imagination*. New York: Oxford University Press.

Mueller, C. (1997). International press coverage of East German protest events, 1989. *American Sociological Review, 62*, 820–832.

Mullins, N. J. (1973). *Theory and theory groups in contemporary American sociology*. New York: Harper & Row.

Myers, D. J., & Caniglia, B. S. (2004). All the rioting that's fit to print: Selection effects in national newspaper coverage of civil disorders, 1968–1969. *American Sociological Review, 69*, 519–543.

Neustadtl, A., Robinson, J. P., & Kestnbaum, M. (2002). Doing social science research online. In B. Wellman & C. Haythornthwaite (Eds.), *The Internet in everyday life* (pp. 186–211). Oxford: Blackwell.

Newman, O. (1972). *Defensible space*. New York: Macmillan.

Nisbett, R. E. (1978). A guide for reviewers: Editorial hardball in the '70s. *American Psychologist, 33*, 519–520.

Northrop, F. S. C. (1966). *The logic of the sciences and the humanities*. Cleveland: World Publishing Company.

Oliver, P. E., & Maney, G. M. (2000). Political processes and local newspaper coverage of protest events: From selection bias to triadic interactions. *American Journal of Sociology, 106*, 463–505.

Oliver, P. E., & Myers, D. J. (1999). How events enter the public sphere: Conflict, location, and sponsorship in local newspaper coverage of public events. *American Journal of Sociology, 105*, 38–87.

Olzak, S. (1989). Analysis of events in the study of collective action. *Annual Review of Sociology 15*, 119–141.

Park, R., & Burgess, E. W. (1924). *Introduction to the science of sociology* (2nd ed). Chicago: University of Chicago Press.

Pennings, J. (1973). Measures of organizational structure. *American Journal of Sociology, 79*, 668–704.

Perrucci, R., & Pilisuk, M. (1970). Leaders and ruling elites: The interorganizational bases of community power. *American Sociological Review, 35*, 1040–1057.

Phillips, B. S. (1971). *Social research: Strategy and tactics*. New York: Macmillan.

Platt, J. (1983). The development of the "participant observation" method in sociology: Origin, myth and history. *Journal of the History of the Behavioral Sciences, 19*, 379–393.

Platt, J. (1996). *A history of sociological research methods in America 1920–1960*. Cambridge: Cambridge University Press.

Presser, S., & Stinson, L. (1998). Data collection mode and social desirability bias in self-reports. *American Sociological Review, 63*, 137–145.

Ragin, C. (2000). *Fuzzy-set social science*. Chicago: University of Chicago Press.

Rallis, S., & Rossman, G. B. (2003). Mixed methods in evaluation contexts. In Tashakkori, A., & Teddlie, C. (Eds.), *Handbook of mixed methods in social and behavioral research* (pp. 491–512). Thousand Oaks, CA: Sage.

Rand, M. R., & Rennison, C. M. (2002). True crime stories? Accounting for differences in our national indicators. *Chance, 15*, 47–51.

Reinharz, S. (1992). *Feminist methods in social research.* New York: Oxford University Press.

Reverby, S. M. (Ed.). (2000). *Tuskegee's truths: Rethinking the Tuskegee syphilis study.* Chapel Hill: University of North Carolina Press.

Ritzer, G. (1980). *Sociology: A multiple paradigm science* (Rev. ed.). Boston: Allyn & Bacon.

Roethlisberger, F. J., & Dickson, W. J. (1939). *Management and the worker.* Cambridge, MA: Harvard University Press.

Rossi, P., Freeman, H. E., & Wright, S. R. (1979). *Evaluation: A systematic approach.* Beverly Hills, CA: Sage.

Sampson, R. J., & Raudenbush, S. W. (1999). Systematic social observation of public spaces: A new look at disorder in urban neighborhoods. *American Journal of Sociology, 105*(3), 603–651.

Sandole, Dennis J. D. (1999). Capturing the complexity of conflict. London: Pinter.

Schatzman, L., & Strauss, A. (1973). *Field research.* Englewood Cliffs, NJ: Prentice Hall.

Selltiz, C., Jahoda, M., Deutsch, M., & Cook, S. (1959). *Research methods in social relations.* New York: Holt.

Selltiz, C., Wrightsman, L. S., & Cook, S. W. (1976). *Research methods in social relations* (3rd ed.). New York: Holt.

Sieber, S. D. (1973). Integrating field work and survey methods. *American Journal of Sociology, 78*, 1335–1359.

Singer, E. (1978). Informed consent: Consequences for response rate and response quality in social surveys. *American Sociological Review, 43*, 144–162.

Skocpol, T. (Ed). (1984). *Vision and method in historical sociology.* New York: Cambridge University Press.

Skogan, W. G. (1977). Dimensions of the dark figure of unreported crime. *Crime and Delinquency, 23* (January), 41–50.

Smith, J., McCarthy, J. D., McPhail, C., & Augustyn, B. (2001). From protest to agenda building: Description bias in media coverage of protest events in Washington, D.C. *Social Forces, 79*, 1397–1424.

Smith, T. W. (1998). A review of church attendance measures. *American Sociological Review, 63*, 131–136.

Snow, C. P. (1971). *Public affairs.* New York: Scribner.

Snyder, D., & Kelly, W. R. (1977). Conflict intensity, media sensitivity, and the validity of newspaper data. *American Sociological Review 42*, 105–123.

Spencer, H. (1898). *The principles of sociology.* New York: Appleton.

Stinchcombe, A. L. (1964). *Rebellion in a high school.* Chicago: Quadrangle.

Stinchcombe, A. L. (1968). *Constructing social theories.* New York: Harcourt.

Stinchcombe, A. L. (1978). *Theoretical methods in social history.* New York: Academic Press.

Stouffer, S. A. (1940). Intervening opportunities: A theory relating mobility and distance. *American Sociological Review, 5,* 845–867.

Stouffer, S. A., Suchman, E. A., DeVinney, L. C., Star, S. A., Williams, R. M., Jr. (1949). *The American soldier: Adjustment during army life (Vol. 1).* Princeton, NJ: Princeton University Press.

Strauss, A., & Corbin, J. (1998). *Basics of qualitative research: Techniques and procedures for developing grounded theory* (2nd ed.). Thousand Oaks, CA: Sage.

Tashakkori, A., & Teddlie, C. (Eds.). (2003). *Handbook of mixed methods in social and behavioral research.* Thousand Oaks, CA: Sage.

Thomas, W. I., & Znaniecki, F. (1918/1958). *The Polish peasant in Europe and America.* New York: Dover.

Thurow, L. C. (1996). *The future of capitalism.* New York: Morrow.

Tittle, C. R., Villemez, W. J., & Smith, D. A. (1978). The myth of social class and criminality. *American Sociological Review, 43,* 643–656.

Trow, M. (1957). Comment of participant observation and interviewing: A comparison. *Human Organization, 16,* 33–35.

Turk, J. I., & Bell, N. W. (1972). Measuring power in families. *Journal of Marriage and the Family, 34* (5), 215–222.

Turner, S. P., & Turner, J. H. (1990). *The impossible science: An institutional analysis of American sociology.* Newbury Park, CA: Sage.

U.S. Department of Justice. (2003). *The nation's two crime measures.* Author: Fact Sheet NCJ 122705.

Wallace, W. (1971). *The logic of science in sociology.* Chicago: Aldine.

Walton, J. (1966). Discipline, method, and community power. *American Sociological Review, 31,* 684–689.

Warner, W. L., & Lunt, P. S. (1941). *The social life of a modern community.* Yankee City Series, Volume 1. New Haven, CT: Yale University Press.

Webb, E. J., Campbell, D. T., Schwartz, R. D., & Sechrest, L. (1966). *Unobtrusive measures: Nonreactive research in the social sciences.* Chicago: Rand McNally.

Webb, E. J., Campbell, D. T., Schwartz, R. D., & Sechrest, L. (2000). *Unobtrusive measures* (Revised ed.). Thousand Oaks, CA: Sage.

Weber, M. (1949). The methodology of the social sciences. New York: Free Press.

Weiss, C. H. (1972). *Evaluation research.* Englewood Cliffs, NJ: Prentice Hall.

Wellman, B., & Haythornthwaite, C. (Eds.). (2002). *The Internet in everyday life.* Oxford: Blackwell.

Wellman, B., & Leighton, B. (1979). Networks, neighborhoods, and community: Approaches to the study of community. *Urban Affairs Quarterly, 14,* 363–390.

Whyte, W. F. (1955). *Street corner society.* Chicago: University of Chicago Press.

Willer, D., & Webster, M., Jr. (1970). Theoretical concepts and observables. *American Sociological Review, 35,* 748–757.

Williams, F., Rice, R. E., & Rogers, E. M. (1988). *Research methods and the new media.* New York: Free Press.

Wilson, E. O. (1998). *Consilience: The unity of knowledge.* New York: Knopf.

Witte, J. (2004). The case for multimethod research: Large sample design and the study of life online. In P. N. Howard & S. Jones (Eds.), *Society online: The Internet in context* (pp. xv–xxxiv). Thousand Oaks, CA: Sage.

Wrong, D. H. (1978). Encouraging diversity. *Society, 15*(3), 27–29.

Zelditch, M. (1962). Some methodological problems of field studies. *American Journal of Sociology, 67,* 566–576.

# Index

# About the Authors

**John Brewer** is Professor of Sociology Emeritus at Trinity College in Hartford, Connecticut. Previously, he taught at the University of California, Los Angeles, York University in Toronto, Canada, and Wesleyan University in Middletown, Connecticut and has held a visiting appointment at the University of Connecticut School of Law. He received BA, MA, and PhD degrees from the University of Chicago, where he was a Woodrow Wilson Fellow. He has studied formal organizations, written about problems in organizational research and theory, and served in the elected position of Secretary to the American Sociological Association's Section on Organizations and Occupations. His current interests include collegial administration, organizations and the law, the sociology of art and architecture, and strategies—such as multimethod research—for encouraging and assessing the growth of social science knowledge.

**Albert Hunter** is Professor of Sociology at Northwestern University. Previous faculty positions include the University of Chicago, Wesleyan University, and the University of Rochester. He has had visiting appointments at Yale University, the London School of Economics, the University of Paris, and the University of Edinburgh. He received his BA degree from Cornell University and his MA and PhD degrees from the University of Chicago. His primary area of research is on urban communities, and he is the author of *Symbolic Communities: The Persistence and Change of Chicago's Local Communities* (1974). He has also served as the elected chair of the Urban and Community Section of the American Sociological Association and editor of the journal *Urban Affairs Review*. He also does work on research methods including the coauthored book, *Multimethod Research: A Synthesis of Styles* (with John Brewer, SAGE, 1989) and the book *The Rhetoric of Social Research: Understood and Believed* (1990). He is currently at work on a number of multimethod community case studies including a comparative study of four Chicago suburbs, a comparative study of three neighborhoods' responses to gangs, a case study of an elite suburb, and a coauthored book with Carl Milofsky relating civil society and community titled *Pragmatic Liberalism*. He also continues to explore the relationship between poetic and scientific claims to truth.